VISUAL QUICKSTART GUIDE

DIRECTOR 4

FOR MACINTOSH

ANDRE PERSIDSKY
HELMUT KOBLER

Peachpit Press

Visual QuickStart Guide
Director 4 for Macintosh
Andre Persidsky and Helmut Kobler

Peachpit Press
2414 Sixth Street
Berkeley, CA 94710
510/548-4393
510/548-5991 (fax)

ISBN 1-56609-138-1

9 8 7 6 5 4 3 2 1

♲ Printed on Recycled Paper

Printed and bound in the United States of America

Thank you.

Cyclone Studios of Redwood City for their supportive work environment.

William Karneges at *Pax Publishing* for his invaluable and non-deleterious advice.

Roslyn Bullas and *Peachpit Press*.

Onward Designs Company of San Francisco.

Zoria Persidsky for copy editing.

Table of Contents

Chapter 1: **Basics**

Introduction... 1
The Director screen and main windows................... 2
Menus...4
Hardware requirements..9
Keyboard shortcuts..9
Start Director..10
New...10
Open.. 10
Save a Movie...11
Save and Compact...11
Revert...11
The Help window...12
Movie Info...13
Preferences..15

Chapter 2: **How Director Works**

The Cast window..17
Create Cast members in the Paint window..............18
The Stage..19
Animation...19
Frames.. 20
The Score window..20
Cast Members in the Score...21
Control Panel... 21
Movie example.. 22

Chapter 3: **Cast Window**

The Cast window..23
Place button...24
Previous & Next arrows... 24
Cast window buttons..25

Import cast members..26

Import using Link to File...27

Import a cast member palette...................................28

Cast Info...28

Purge Priority...29

Duplicate cast members..30

Delete cast members...30

Delete unused cast members...................................31

Repositioning cast members....................................32

Name a cast member 33

Find a cast member by name...................................34

Find a cast member by color palette........................35

Sort cast members..36

Chapter 4: **Score**

The Score window...37

Frames...38

Playback head...38

Score Channels...39

Cells..40

Sprites..40

Place cast members on the Stage............................41

Drag cast members to the Score..............................43

Assign Lingo Scripts to the Score............................44

Score notation..45

Foreground/background priorities...........................48

Move cells within the Score.....................................49

Insert new frames in the Score................................50

Cut cells from the Score..51

Delete cells..52

Add a marker to the Score......................................52

Find and annotate markers......................................53

Color cells in the Score...54

Ink Effects in the Score...55

Anti-aliasing...58

Apply trails to sprites...59

Make sprites moveable during playback..................60

Make text sprites editable during playback.............. 61
Stretch and squeeze sprites......................................62

Chapter 5:   **Control Panel**
Control Panel buttons...63
Frame Counter...65
Tempo Display...65
Actual tempo vs. set tempo...................................... 66
Actual mode button..67
Lock playback speed...67
Stage background color chip......................................68

Chapter 6:   **Paint Window**
The Paint window.. 69
Cast members in the Paint window...........................70
Multiple easels.. 71
Lasso and Selection rectangle tools..........................72
Selection rectangle options..73
Lasso tool.. 74
Lasso options.. 75
Hand tool.. 75
Text tool..76
Paint bucket.. 76
Paint brush.. 76
Air brush... 76
Pencil..76
Shape tools..77
Eraser tool.. 77
Line tool.. 78
Arc tool 78
Registration points...78
Set a new registration point......................................79
Align registration points.. 80
Eyedropper tool...80
Ink effects in the Paint window.................................81
Line width selector.. 84
Set foreground color..85

Background color.. 86
Gradient destination color..86
Set color depth of cast members....................................... 87
Pattern selector.. 88
Edit or create a pattern..89
Store custom patterns in the Scrapbook.................. 90
Create a gradient... 91
Gradient settings 92
Show/Hide rulers..95
Zoom in...95
Create a Tile...96
Choose a Paint brush shape..................................... 98
Edit a Paint brush shape.. 99
Store custom brush shapes in the Scrapbook...........100
Adjust Air brush spray pattern................................. 101
Choose an Air brush shape..102
Rotate left, right.. 103
Free Rotate... 103
Flip horizontal, vertical..104
Distort..104
Invert colors...105
Trace edges...105
Fill..106
Lighten...106
Smooth.. 106
Switch Color..106
Auto Distort..106
Ink Masks...107

Chapter 7:   **Tools Window**

Text tool... 109
Line tool... 109
Shape tools...110
Button tools...111
Foreground and background color chips.................. 111
Text window color.. 112
Pattern chip..112
Line width selector... 112

Chapter 8: **Color in Director**

Color palette.. 113
Set a default palette......................................114
Set the current palette in the Score........................... 115
Set palette transition over a single frame.................116
Set palette transition over frames........................... 117
Import palettes into Director.....................................118
Remap cast members to different palettes................119
Remap entire cast to a new palette.......................... 120
Create an optimal palette.. 121
Eyedropper tool.. 126
HSB and RGB color models....................................127
Edit a color in the Palette window.......................... 128
Color Picker.. 129
Copy and paste colors in a palette.......................... 130
Blend colors within a palette................................... 131
Reverse order of palette colors................................133
Sort colors in a palette... 134
Color cycling.. 135

Chapter 9: **Auto Animate**

Auto Animate command.. 139
Animating a banner... 140
Set animation speed for banners............................... 141
Animating a bar chart..142
Set text styles for bar charts.................................... 143
Set animation speed for bar charts.......................... 144
Animating a bullet chart... 145
Set text styles for bullet charts................................ 146
Set animation speed for bullet charts......................147
Animating credits..148
Set text styles for credits animation........................ 149
Zoom text..150
Set zoom text style and speed.................................. 151
Animating text effects...152
Set text effects style and speed................................153

Preview an auto animation...........................154
Position an auto animation.........................155

Chapter 10:   Animation Techniques

Step recording................................ 157
Cast to time...................................160
Space to time..................................162
Paste relative...................................163
In-between animation.................................164
Accelerate.....................................166
Stretch sprites with In-between...................166
In-between animations that curve..............168
Circular In-between..170
Real-time recording.....................................170
Film loops.. 173
Multichannel film loops............................... 174
Real-time record with a film loop............... 175
In-between with a film loop........................176

Chapter 11:   Creating Text in Director

Text cast members...177
Create bitmap text...178
QuickDraw text... 180
Create QuickDraw text on the Stage...........181
Apply Ink effects to QuickDraw Text......... 182
Edit QuickDraw text on the Stage...............183
Create QuickDraw text in Text windows....184
Edit QuickDraw text in Text windows........185

Chapter 12:   Sound

Sound channels... 187
Importing sound..188
MIDI.. 189
Record a sound in Director.........................190
Sound production outside Director............. 191
Place sounds in the Score...........................192

Extend sounds in the Score to play completely....... 193

Repeat sounds in the same channel......................... 194

Sound loops.. 195

Chapter 13: **Setting Scene Transitions**

Set a transition... 197

Chapter 14: **Tempo**

Tempo channel... 199

Set a new tempo in the Score...................................200

Set a pause in the movie's tempo............................201

Actual playback speed... 202

Locking playback speed..202

Lock playback speed of selected frames..................203

Chapter 15: **Interactivity and Lingo**

Lingo Scripts...205

Create a button... 206

Scripts... 206

Open a Cast member script window.........................207

Open a Score script window..................................... 207

Assign scripts to sprites and frames..........................208

Create an interactive cast member............................209

Frame scripts... 210

Pause a movie with a frame script............................211

Sprite scripts...212

The Go To Statement.. 213

Branching.. 215

Scripts that quit a movie...216

Lingo menu... 216

Chapter 16: **Create a Projector**

Create a projector.. 217

Projector options... 218

Appendix A: **Glossary**... 221

Appendix B: **Keyboard Shortcuts**.............................225

Index..229

Table of Contents

BASICS 1

Introduction

Macromedia's Director is a powerful and extensive multimedia development tool. Use it to create animation, interactive movies, marketing presentations, technical simulations, and even full scale commercial productions such as entertainment titles for CD-ROM. The multimedia possibilities that you can synthesize with Director's powerful features are truly endless.

This book teaches the fundamentals of using Director, and covers the latest version 4.0 features. You will learn all the steps involved in creating a **movie**—the term used to describe any multimedia piece created in Director. You will learn how to create and assemble cast members in the Cast window. How to orchestrate the cast members in your movie using the Score window. How to use the Paint and Tools windows to create and edit cast members. You will learn how to control movie playback, set scene transitions, alter color palettes, and add interactive controls to your movies. You will also learn about the tools and techniques that Director supports for creating animation.

In the *Visual QuickStart Guide* format, this book provides step-by-step instructios, and numerous screen shots as well as tips. Where necessary, concise explanations are given. The emphasis is to get the reader up and running as quickly as possible through practical examples.

Chapter 2 provides an overview of the steps involved in creating a simple Director movie. Once you have mastered the basic techniques, the multimedia presentations you can create are limitless!

The Director screen and main windows

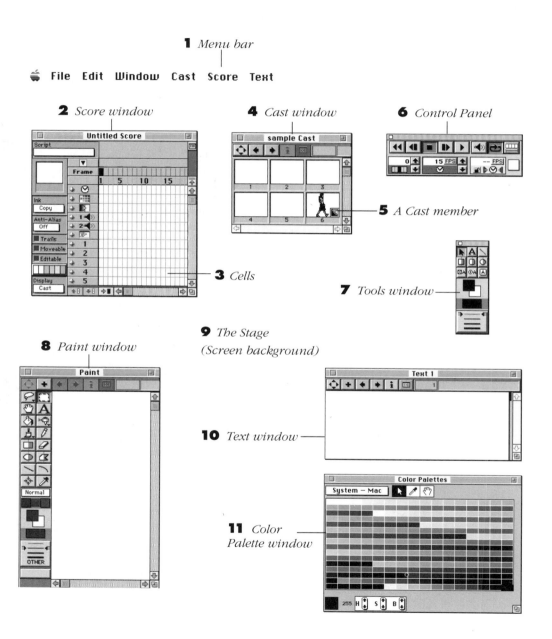

1 *Menu bar*

 File   Edit   Window   Cast   Score   Text

2 *Score window*

4 *Cast window*

6 *Control Panel*

5 *A Cast member*

3 *Cells*

7 *Tools window*

9 *The Stage
(Screen background)*

8 *Paint window*

10 *Text window*

11 *Color
Palette window*

The Director Screen and Main Windows

Key to the Director screen and windows

1 *Menu bar*

There are seven standard menu choices available in Director's menu bar—Apple, File, Edit, Window, Cast, Score, and Text menus. There are four additional menu choices that become available when certain windows are made active. These are Palette, Paint, Effects, and Lingo menus.

2 *Score window*

The Score window is the center of Director. This is where all the components of your movie are organized and stored on a frame by frame basis. This includes information such as the positions of each of your sprites during each frame, sounds effects, color palette transitions, tempo changes, scene transitions—in short, all details pertaining to your movie.

3 *Cells*

The Score is composed of cells, the storage units that hold all the information about your movie. Columns of cells are organized into frames, while rows of cells make up the Score channels.

4 *Cast window*

The Cast window is the storage place that holds all the cast members you plan to use in your movies. The Cast window allows you to organize your cast members, group them together by their cast member type, and even delete those cast members that aren't being used in your movie.

5 *A Cast member*

A cast member is just that, a member of the cast that can be placed into various segments of your movie. There are many different cast member types—they are not all just graphic images of characters. Sounds, color palettes, text blocks, buttons, bitmap images, and shapes are examples of cast member types.

6 *Control Panel*

The Control Panel provides you with VCR-type control over your movie. You can rewind, play, fast forward, stop, and pause your movie from the Control Panel, as well as set the tempo of the playback head.

7 *Tools window*

The Tools window allows you to create QuickDraw shapes, QuickDraw text, and buttons on Director's Stage.

8 *Paint window*

The Paint window is Director's built-in paint program that allows you to edit and create cast members. The Paint window offers a menu of effects such as rotate and distort that can be applied to your images.

9 *The Stage*

The Stage is the background on which your movie plays.

10 *Text window*

The Text window is used to create and edit blocks of text that are placed into your movies.

11 *Color Palette window*

The color palette displays the current set of colors used to draw your cast members on the Stage.

The Director Screen and Main Windows

Menus

About menus.

Director has seven standard menus in its menu bar—Apple, File, Edit, Window, Cast, Score, and Text menus. Four additional menus (Palette, Paint, Effects, Lingo) become available when their related windows are opened.

The Apple menu

The Apple menu offers three Director commands. The first summarizes Director's memory usage, and the last two are the Director help commands.

The File menu

The File menu selections such as Save, Open, Import, Preferences, and Create Projectors apply to your Director movie as a whole.

About Director...	
Help...	
Help Pointer	⌘?

File	
New	⌘N
Open...	⌘O
Close Window	⌘W
Save	⌘S
Save and Compact	
Save As...	
Revert	
Import...	⌘J
Export...	
Update Movies...	
Create Projector...	
Movie Info...	⌘U
Preferences...	
Page Setup...	
Print...	
Quit	⌘Q

The Edit menu

The Edit menu provides standard cut and paste commands that are applied to various windows in Director. The Edit commands vary according to which Director window is currently active. Below, the Score window is the active window since the Edit commands apply to cells. The bottom two sections of the Edit menu deal with Control Panel functions such as Rewind and Loop.

The Window menu

Choosing a selection in the Window menu either opens or closes the corresponding window. Open windows have checkmarks beside their names, and the name of the currently active window is underlined.

Edit	
Undo Cast	⌘Z
Cut Cells	⌘X
Copy Cells	⌘C
Paste Text	⌘V
Clear Cells	
Select All	⌘A
Play	⌘P
Stop	⌘.
Rewind	⌘R
Step Backward	
Step Forward	
Disable Sounds	⌘~
✓Loop	⌘L
Selected Frames Only	⌘\
Disable Lingo	
Lock Frame Durations	

Window	
✓<u>Stage</u>	⌘1
Control Panel	⌘2
Cast	⌘3
Score	⌘4
Paint	⌘5
Text	⌘6
Tools	⌘7
Color Palettes	⌘8
Digital Video	⌘9
Script	⌘0
Message	⌘M
Tweak	
Markers	
Duplicate Window	

Menus

The Cast menu

The Cast menu commands, such as Cast Member Info, Find Cast Members, and Duplicate Cast Member, relate to managing your cast members.

The Score menu

The Score menu commands relate to editing the frames and cells in your Score and setting effects in the Effects channels. The In-between and Auto Animate commands are accessed from here as well.

Cast

Cast Member Info...	⌘I
Open Script	⌘'
Edit Cast Member	
Launch External Editor	⌘,
Record Sound...	
Paste as PICT	
Convert to Bitmap	
Transform Bitmap...	
Align Bitmaps	
Cast to Time	
Duplicate Cast Member	⌘D
Find Cast Members...	⌘;
Sort Cast Members...	
Cast Window Options...	

Score

Sprite Info...	⌘K
Delete Sprites	
Set Sprite Blend...	
Set Tempo...	
Set Palette...	
Set Transition...	
Set Sound...	
Insert Frame	⌘]
Delete Frame	⌘[
In-Between Linear	⌘B
In-Between Special...	
Space to Time...	
Paste Relative	
Reverse Sequence	
Switch Cast Members	⌘E
Auto Animate	▶
Score Window Options...	

The Text menu

The commands in the Text menu are used to set the font, size, style, and other attributes of text used throughout Director.

The Palette menu

The Palette menu selection becomes available in the menu bar when a Color Palette window is opened. Use these commands, such as Blend Colors and Reverse Colors, to modify the choice and order of colors available in a color palette.

Menus

Text	
Font	▶
Size	▶
Style	▶
Alignment	▶
Border	▶
Margin	▶
Box Shadow	▶
Text Shadow	▶
Find/Change...	⌘F
Find Again	⌘G
Change Again	⌘T
Find Selection	⌘H
Find Handler...	⌘:
Comment	⌘>
Uncomment	⌘<
Recompile Script	
Recompile All Scripts	

Palette
Duplicate Palette...
Reserve Colors...
Invert Selection
Set Color...
Blend Colors
Rotate Colors
Reverse Color Order
Sort Colors...
Select Used Colors...

Menus

The Paint menu

The Paint menu selection becomes available in the menu bar when the Paint window is opened. These commands such as Zoom In and Brush Shapes affect the Paint window display and tools.

The Effects menu

The Effects menu becomes available in the menu bar when an image is selected in the Paint window. These commands such as Invert Colors, Rotate Left, and Distort are used to transform your artwork selections.

Hardware requirements.

In order to create movies with Director, you need at least a 68030 Macintosh computer with a minimum 13-inch monitor (640x480 pixels), color definitely preferable. Anything less will result in unacceptable performance (except for the case of very simple movies with moderate tempo settings that can be made to run on slower computers without problems). Also a second large monitor will greatly enhance the production of movies.

The Lingo menu

The Lingo menu becomes available in the menu bar when a Script window is opened. An alphabetical listing of Lingo commands can be viewed and inserted into your scripts from this menu.

Lingo
Operators ▶
A B ▶
C ▶
D ▶
E ▶
F ▶
G H ▶
I K ▶
L ▶
M ▶
N O ▶
P ▶
Q R ▶
S ▶
T ▶
U V W X Z ▶

Keyboard shortcuts:

Most Director commands that can be chosen from the menus have a keyboard equivalent called a keyboard shortcut. To perform a keyboard shortcut, hold down one or more keys such as Command and Shift, and then press and release another key to execute the Director command.

(*See Appendix B for a list of keyboard shortcuts*)

To perform the Open command:

1. Hold down the Command key.

2. Press and release the "O" key.

3. Release the Command key.

Lingo Menu, Hardware, Keyboard Shortcuts

To start Director:

Open the Macromedia Director folder that was installed on your hard drive by double-clicking it. Then double-click the Director application icon **(Figure 1)**.

or

double-click a Director movie icon **(Figure 2)**.

✔ Tip

■ Chances are, your Macintosh will be running System 7 or greater. If so, you can create an alias for Director that allows you to launch the program easily from the Apple menu. Single-click the Director application icon and choose Make Alias from the File menu. Now drag the alias icon into the Apple Menu Items folder in your System Folder.

To create a new movie:

Director normally opens a new movie window when you start the program. If at any point you wish to start over from scratch, choose New from the File menu **(Figure 3)**. You assign a name to a movie when you save it—by choosing Save from the File menu.

To open an existing movie:

To open a movie, choose Open from the File menu **(Figure 4)**. In the Open dialog box, select the movie's name and click the Open button, or double-click the movie's name **(Figure 5)**. The dialog box displays only the names of Director movies created with the Macintosh version of Director, or movies with a ".DIR" extension that were created with the Microsoft Windows version of the program.

Director 4.0

Figure 1. Double-click the Director application icon to start Director.

sample

Figure 2. A movie icon.

Figure 3. Choose **New** from the **File** menu to open a new untitled movie.

Figure 4. Choose **Open** from the **File** menu to open an existing movie.

Figure 5. In the **Open** dialog box, select the movie's name from the file directory.

Start Director, New, Open

Figure 6. Choose **Save** from the **File** menu to save the current version of your movie.

Figure 7. Choose **Save and Compact** from the **File** menu to save an optimized version of your current movie.

Figure 8. Choose **Revert** from the **File** menu to open the last saved version of your current movie.

To save a movie:

Choose Save from the File menu to save the current version of your movie to disk, writing over the movie's previous saved version **(Figure 6)**. You should save often to preserve your most recent work in case Director crashes, or your Macintosh loses power.

When you save a movie for the first time, Director brings you to the Save As dialog box, where you can name your movie and choose the area of your hard disk the movie should be saved to.

To save and compact a movie:

Choose Save and Compact from the File menu to save an optimized version of your movie under its original file name **(Figure 7)**. This takes longer than the Save command since Director reorders the cast, reduces the movie to its minimum size, and eliminates any unused space that might have accumulated in the original file. Use this command to gain optimal playback performance on a slow CD-ROM or hard drive.

Revert

Choose the Revert command from the File menu to open the last saved version of your current movie **(Figure 8)**. This is useful if you have made some undesirable changes to your movie, and wish to quickly go back to the previous saved version.

Save a Movie, Save and Compact, Revert

The Help window

To open Director's Help window, choose Help from the Apple menu. Many dialog boxes in Director also feature Help buttons that open directly into the Help window. The Help window initially displays a list of all Director menus.

Click the **Previous** button to move to the Help window that was displayed previously.

Click **Notes** to open a dialog box into which you can enter notes regarding the current help topic. Director will append your note to the topic for future reference.

Search opens a window where you can type in a word or phrase to search for.

Click the **Topics** button to return back to the main listing of menu choices.

Click the name of the menu that contains the command you wish to get help on.

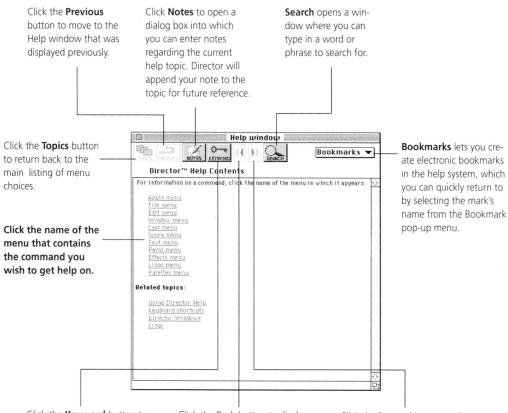

Bookmarks lets you create electronic bookmarks in the help system, which you can quickly return to by selecting the mark's name from the Bookmark pop-up menu.

Click the **Keyword** button to open the keyword window, where you can view every keyword in Director's Help system. Click a keyword in the list on the window's left, and the list on the right will display all the topics that are linked to that keyword. Click a topic to see its help information.

Click the Back button to display help information on the previous command in the currently selected menu.

Click the Forward button to display help information for the next command in the currently selected menu.

✔ Tip

■ Choose Help Pointer from the Apple menu to get context-sensitive help. The mouse pointer turns into a question mark shape, and when you choose a command or click a window, an appropriate help screen is displayed.

MOVIE INFO

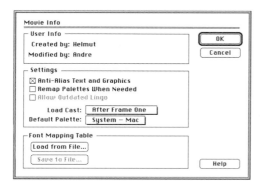

Figure 9. The **Movie Info** dialog box lets you set some general settings for your current movie.

Choose Movie Info from the File menu to set and review some general settings for your current movie in the Movie Info dialog box **(Figure 9)**.

User Info

Displays the creator and modifier as indicated during the installation of the Director application.

Anti-Alias Text and Graphics

Check this box if you wish anti-aliasing to be applied to your text and bitmap cast members. Anti-aliasing will only be applied to those cast members that have already had an anti-alias modifier applied to them from the Anti-alias pop-up menu in the Score. Anti-aliasing is a process to remove or reduce the rough jagged edges that can often appear on bitmap graphics and text cast members.

Remap Palettes When Needed

If this box is checked, cast members displayed on the Stage having a different color palette than the currently active palette will be remapped to a common palette that Director creates. This is a useful feature to enable when you have many cast members that use many different palettes.

Allow Outdated Lingo

Allows you to include Lingo commands used with previous versions of Director.

Movie Info

Load Cast

The Load Cast pop-up menu provides three ways of pre-loading cast members into memory **(Figure 10)**.

When Needed:

Cast members are loaded into memory only when they are required. This is sensible for interactive movies, but will slow down your animation.

After Frame One:

The first frame of your animation is displayed and any sounds in the first frame will start to play while the rest of the movie is loaded into memory. This is the best choice for large movies where an opening scene and sound is played while the rest of the movie is being loaded into memory. This is the default setting.

Before Frame One:

The entire movie is loaded into memory before it is played—an appropriate choice for small movies.

Default Palette

The Default Palette pop-up menu allows you to set the default color palette for your movie **(Figure 11)**.

Figure 10. The **Load Cast** pop-up menu.

| When Needed |
| ✓ After Frame One |
| Before Frame One |

| ✓ System – Mac |
| System – Win |
| Rainbow |
| Grayscale |
| Pastels |
| Vivid |
| NTSC |
| Metallic |
| VGA |

Figure 11. The **Default Palette** pop-up menu.

Movie Info

Preferences

Select the Preferences command from the File menu to modify and view some of Director's default settings in the Preferences dialog box.

Stage Size:
You can change the size of the Stage by choosing a monitor size from the pop-up menu, or by entering values into the Width and Height fields. This is useful when you wish to display movies on a smaller or larger monitor.

Stage Location:
Click the Centered radio button for the Stage to appear in the center of your monitor or enter values into the Left and Top fields to indicate by how many pixels the Stage should be off-set from the top left corner of the screen.

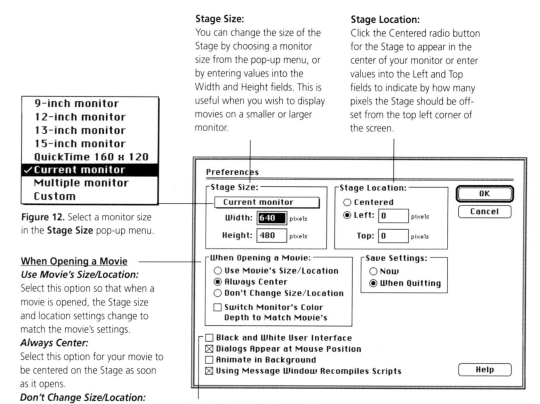

```
  9-inch monitor
 12-inch monitor
 13-inch monitor
 15-inch monitor
 QuickTime 160 x 120
✓Current monitor
 Multiple monitor
 Custom
```

Figure 12. Select a monitor size in the **Stage Size** pop-up menu.

Preferences

Stage Size:
Current monitor
Width: 640 pixels
Height: 480 pixels

Stage Location:
○ Centered
● Left: 0 pixels
Top: 0 pixels

OK
Cancel

When Opening a Movie:
○ Use Movie's Size/Location
● Always Center
○ Don't Change Size/Location
☐ Switch Monitor's Color Depth to Match Movie's

Save Settings:
○ Now
● When Quitting

☐ Black and White User Interface
☒ Dialogs Appear at Mouse Position
☐ Animate in Background
☒ Using Message Window Recompiles Scripts

Help

When Opening a Movie

Use Movie's Size/Location:
Select this option so that when a movie is opened, the Stage size and location settings change to match the movie's settings.

Always Center:
Select this option for your movie to be centered on the Stage as soon as it opens.

Don't Change Size/Location:
Choose this option for the Stage size and location to remain the same as the current movie.

Switch Monitor's Color Depth to Match Movie's:
When checked, Director changes the color depth of the monitor to match the color depth of the movie you open.

Black and White User Interface:
If checked, Director displays the user interface in black and white. This improves performance since Director doesn't need to update the colors in the user interface when the current color palette is switched.

Dialogs Appear at Mouse Position:
When checked, dialog boxes are displayed at the position of the mouse pointer. If this option is not selected, the dialog boxes will be centered on the monitor.

Animate in Background:
When checked, your movie will run in the background. This allows you to work with other applications in the Finder while your animation run on the Stage behind the application windows.

Using Message Window Recompiles Scripts:
This is checked by default. If not checked, your scripts should be manually recompiled using the Recompile All Scripts command under the Text menu before Lingo is entered in the Message window.

CREATING MOVIES

The steps involved in creating a Director movie mirror many of the ideas behind traditional Hollywood film production. You start by assembling a group of **cast members**, which in Director are the multimedia elements that comprise your movies, such as graphics, sound, text, buttons, QuickTime movies, and color palettes, among others.

You create a movie by assigning cast members to various parts of the **Score**. The Score is a detailed record that tells Director what your cast members should do on a frame-by-frame basis, very much like a script *(see page 20)*. These actions play out on Director's **Stage**, which is the background screen upon which your movie animations are viewed.

Cast Window

Your cast members are stored in Director's **Cast window**, which is a kind of multimedia database **(Figure 1)**. Cast members are numbered in the small windows they occupy, and their type is indicated by a small icon in the lower right corner. *(See the Cast Window chapter, page 23, for more details)*

To open the Cast window:

1. Choose Cast from the Window menu **(Figure 2)**.

✓ Tip

■ You can double-click a bitmap cast member in the Cast window to open it in the Paint window.

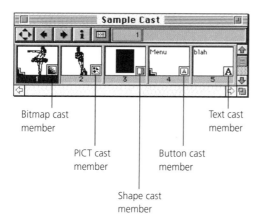

Figure 1. Cast members are stored in Director's **Cast** window. Each cast member occupies a small numbered window, and its type is indicated by a small icon in the lower right corner.

Figure 2. Choose **Cast** from the **Window** menu.

The Cast Window

Creating cast members

Director has its own set of in-house tools for producing cast members. These tools include the Paint window, Record Sound command, Text window, and the Tools window. For high end production, you may prefer to create your cast members using applications such as Photoshop or SoundEdit Pro, which offer more advanced tools. Director allows you to import such cast members *(see page 26)*. You can then use Director's tools to edit these imported cast members.

The **Paint window** in Director is actually quite extensive and can be used to create fairly elaborate graphical cast members **(Figure 3)**. The Paint window includes a variety of tools in its tool palette **(Figure 4)** such as the Air brush, Shape, and Text tools, and also offers a menu of special effect commands such as Rotate and Distort that can be applied to your cast members. *(See the Paint Window chapter on page 69 for more details)*

To create a cast member using the Paint window:

1. Choose New from the File menu **(Figure 5)**.

2. Choose Paint from the Window menu to open the Paint window **(Figure 6)**.

3. Click the shaded Ellipse tool in the tool palette (in this example we create a shaded ellipse cast member).

4. Select a foreground color for the ellipse by clicking and holding the Foreground color chip **(Figure 3)**. Choose a color from the pop-up color palette that appears.

5. Drag the mouse in the Paint window to size and draw your ellipse.

6. Click the check box in the upper left corner to close the Paint window. Your ellipse automatically becomes a cast member and is placed into the first available slot in the Cast window.

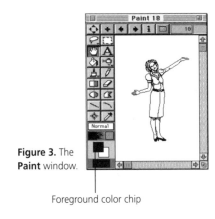

Figure 3. The **Paint** window.

Foreground color chip

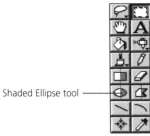

Shaded Ellipse tool

Figure 4. The **Paint** tool palette.

Figure 5. Choose **New** from the **File** menu to open a new untitled movie.

Figure 6. Choose **Paint** from the **Window** menu.

Window

Stage	⌘1
Control Panel	⌘2
Cast	⌘3
Score	⌘4
Paint	⌘5
Text	⌘6
Tools	⌘7
Color Palettes	⌘8
Digital Video	⌘9
Script	⌘0
Message	⌘M
Tweak	
Markers	
Duplicate Window	

Figure 7. Choose **Cast** from the **Window** menu.

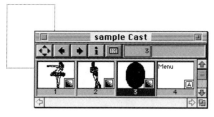

Figure 8. Drag one of the selected cast members to the Stage, shown here by the dotted outline.

Optional

7. Choose Cast from the Window menu. The Cast window appears and you should now see your ellipse in the first cast member position. Notice that the cast member type is a bitmap as indicated by the small icon.

Stage

Once you have assembled your cast members in the Cast window (either by creating them in Director or importing them), you will want to start building your movie. Director movies play out on what's known as the **Stage**—the background upon which all your graphical cast members are animated.

To place a cast member onto the Stage:

1. Choose Cast from the Window menu to open the Cast window **(Figure 7)**.

2. Drag a cast member (such as the ellipse created on the previous page) onto the Stage, that is, onto any area of the screen not occupied by an open window **(Figure 8)**. This action automatically records the cast member in a single frame of your movie at a specific point on the Stage.

Animation

Animation is created by positioning cast members on the Stage, and then slightly changing the positions of each of these cast members in the successive frames of your movie. When the frames are played back at a high speed, animation is achieved. Director provides a number of animation tools, such as the In-Between command and Real-time recording feature that greatly simplify the task of creating animation. With the **In-Between** command, you set up the key frames—the first and last frames of your animation sequence—and Director automatically fills

Stage, Animation

in all the "in-between" frames, sparing you from having to manually create each frame **(Figure 9)**. Director's Real-time recording feature lets you record the path of mouse movements and then substitute a cast member to follow this recorded path to produce animation. *(See the Animation Techniques chapter for more details)*

Figure 9. Director can automatically generate a series of frames that lie between two key frames using the In-Between feature.

Frames

A Director movie like any movie is broken down into a series of frames. **Frames** are snapshots of your movie that hold all the information about what's happening in a particular time segment. This information includes the positions of each of your cast members on the Stage, and what sound effects are being played at that instant.

Score

Director's Score window is a frame-by-frame record of your movie **(Figure 10)**. You use the Score to orchestrate all the components of your movie on a frame-by-frame basis. These components include all cast member types like sound effects and bitmaps, as well as effects such as color palette and scene transitions. All this information is stored in **cells**—the Score's storage units, organized similarly to that of a spreadsheet. Frames in the Score are organized into vertical columns of cells, and each frame is numbered at the top. You can scroll through the frames using the arrows at the bottom of the Score window. There is no limit to the number of frames your movies can have.

Each cell in a frame belongs to a **Score channel**, and contains specific types of information such as the position of a cast member on the Stage in that particular frame. Score channels are organized into rows of cells, and hold certain types of information, such as sounds, color palette transitions, and cast member positions **(Figure 11)**. There are 54 Score channels

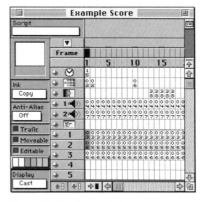

Figure 10. The **Score** window.

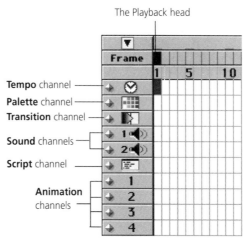

Figure 11. The Score channels run vertically along the left side of the **Score** window. Each channel forms a row of cells.

Window	
Stage	⌘1
Control Panel	⌘2
Cast	⌘3
Score	⌘4
Paint	⌘5
Text	⌘6
Tools	⌘7
Color Palettes	⌘8
Digital Video	⌘9
Script	⌘0
Message	⌘M
Tweak	
Markers	
Duplicate Window	

Figure 12. Choose **Score** from the **Window** menu.

Window	
Stage	⌘1
Control Panel	⌘2
Cast	⌘3
Score	⌘4
Paint	⌘5
Text	⌘6
Tools	⌘7
Color Palettes	⌘8
Digital Video	⌘9
Script	⌘0
Message	⌘M
Tweak	
Markers	
Duplicate Window	

Figure 13. Choose **Cast** from the **Window** menu.

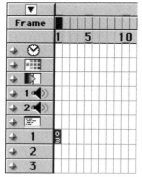

Figure 14. Drag a graphical cast member from the Cast window into the first animation channel in the first frame of the Score window.

Figure 15. The Control Panel.

in all, five of which are called effects channels (Tempo, Palette, Transition, Sound 1 & 2), one script channel, and 48 animation channels, which keep track of the positions of individual cast members on the Stage. *(See the Score chapter for more details)*

The Score has a **Playback head**, which indicates which frame of the movie is currently displayed on the Stage **(Figure 11)**. You can drag the Playback head to display different frames on the Stage.

To place a cast member into the Score:

You can enter a cast member into the Score by dragging it from the Cast window and placing it into a specific frame and cell. If the cast member is a graphical type (Bitmap, Shape, or PICT) it also appears positioned on the center of the Stage in the frame you place it in. You can change a cast member's position on the Stage by dragging it to a different area.

1. Choose Score from the Window menu to open the Score **(Figure 12)**.

2. Choose Cast from the Window menu to open the Cast window **(Figure 13)**.

3. In this example, drag a graphical cast member type from the Cast window into the first animation channel in the first frame of the Score **(Figure 14)**. You can use the ellipse cast member created on page 18. The cast member is recorded into the Score and also appears on the center of the Stage.

Control Panel

Director's Control Panel offers you VCR-type control over the playback of your movie. You can rewind, play, jump forward to any frame, and even change the tempo setting of your movie by using the Control Panel **(Figure 15)**.

Cast Members in the Score, Control Panel

A simple movie example:

The following steps create a simple movie animation. Follow the steps on page 18 to create the ellipse cast member first that's used in the following example:

1. Open the Cast and Score windows by choosing them from the Window menu.

2. Drag the ellipse cast member from the Cast window into frame 1, animation channel 1 in the Score **(Figure 16)**. The ellipse appears on the center of the Stage.

3. Drag the ellipse from the center of the Stage to the left-hand-side.

4. Drag the ellipse cast member again from the Cast window but now place it into frame 15, animation channel 1 in the Score **(Figure 17)**. The ellipse appears on the center of the Stage.

5. Drag this ellipse from the center of the Stage to the right-most-side.

6. In the Score, drag to select all the cells in animation channel 1 that lie between frames 1 and 15, including frames 1 and 15 **(Figure 18)**.

7. Choose In-Between Linear from the Score menu **(Figure 19)**. Director fills in all the empty frames between frames 1 and 15 with the ellipse cast member, but slightly shifting it to the right in each successive frame, creating an animation sequence.

8. Choose Control Panel from the Window menu to open the Control Panel **(Figure 20)**.

9. Click the rewind button to set the Playback head to frame 1.

10. Click Play to watch your movie. The ellipse moves across the Stage from left to right.

Figure 16. Drag the ellipse from the Cast window into frame 1 in animation channel 1.

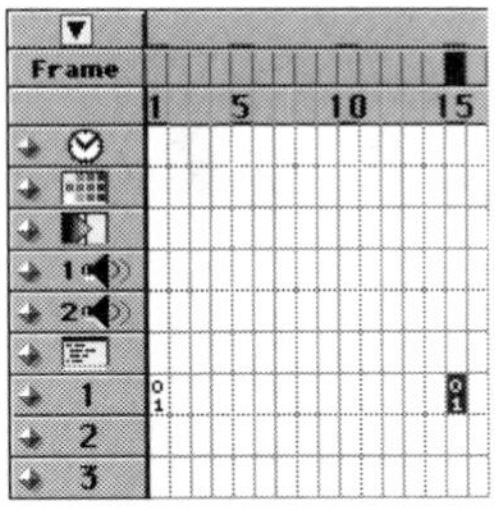

Figure 17. Drag the ellipse from the Cast window into frame 15 in animation channel 1.

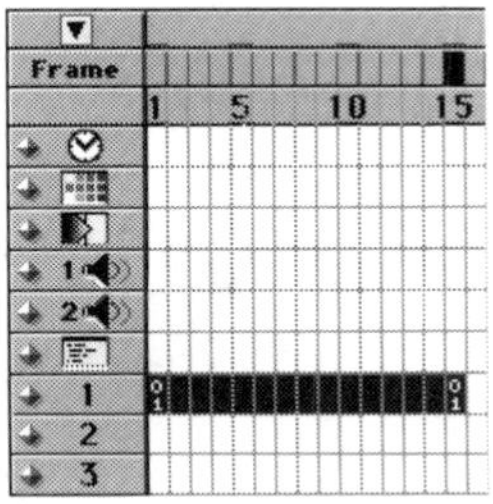

Figure 18. Select all the cells between frames 1 and 15 in animation channel 1.

Figure 19. Choose In-Between Linear from the Score menu.

Rewind button   Play button

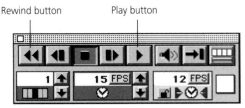

Figure 20. The Control Panel.

CAST WINDOW 3

Cast window.

The Cast window is used throughout this chapter. Choose Cast from the Window menu to open it **(Figure 1)** or press Command-3.

Window

Stage	⌘1
Control Panel	⌘2
Cast	⌘3
Score	⌘4
Paint	⌘5
Text	⌘6
Tools	⌘7
Color Palettes	⌘8
Digital Video	⌘9
Script	⌘0
Message	⌘M
Tweak	
Markers	
Duplicate Window	

Figure 1. Choose **Cast** from the **Window** menu.

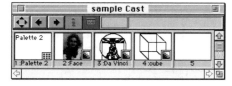

Figure 2. Cast window showing four cast members.

Director's **Cast window** acts as the viewing and storage area for all the cast members incorporated into your movie (remember that cast members include pictures, sounds, strings of text, color palettes, QuickTime movies, film loop animation or interactive scripts). When you're ready to incorporate a cast member into your movie, simply drag it from the Cast window onto Director's Stage or right into its Score window. *(See the Score chapter on page 41, for more about actually incorporating cast members into Director's Score)*

In order for a cast member to become available for your movie, it must first be placed in the Cast window **(Figure 2)**. If the cast member has already been created and saved by some other program (for instance, a background created in Fractal Painter or a sound effect mixed with SoundEdit Pro), the cast member must then be imported into the Cast window before it can be incorporated into your movie. However, if you're creating a cast member within Director itself (for instance, using Director's built-in painting tools, or its Record Sound feature), **the cast member is automatically added to the Cast window**.

The Cast window is divided into positions, and each position can contain a unique cast member that's available for use in your movie. You can have up to 32,000 cast members available at one time. Each cast member in the Cast window is represented by a thumbnail image, and identified by a number that's respective to the position it occupies. A descriptive name can be given to each cast member (for instance, "Sunset1", "GunFire1", or "mood Music"). Cast member graphics appear in

Cast Window

the Cast window as miniatures of themselves. All cast member types, such as sound effects, text, or color palettes, are distinguished by a small icon that appears in the lower-right corner of the cast member **(Figure 3)**.

THE CAST WINDOW

Place button

Use the Place button to drag selected cast members to new positions within the Cast window, even if the selected cast member is no longer visible in the Cast window. First click the cast member in the Cast window **(Figure 4)**. You may Shift-click to select more than one cast member at a time and move them together. Now scroll through the Cast window to the position to which you wish to move the selected cast member. Drag the Place button to the new position in the Cast window. Release the mouse button to move the selected cast member **(Figure 5)**.

Previous, Next Arrows

Click the Previous or Next arrow to select the previous or next cast member (in relation to whatever cast member is currently selected) in the Cast window **(Figure 4)**. The key combination Command-Shift-Left Arrow selects the previous cast member, and Command-Shift-Right Arrow moves to the next cast member.

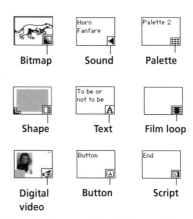

Figure 3. Cast member types are indicated by a small icon in the lower-right corner of each cast member.

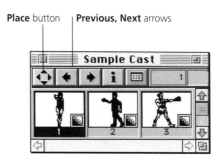

Figure 4. The **Place** button is used to move selected cast members to new positions in the **Cast** window. Click the cast member you wish to move, such as cast member 1 depicted here.

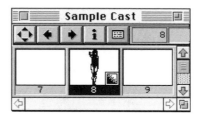

Figure 5. Drag the **Place** button to the new position in the **Cast** window. Release the mouse button to move the selected cast member.

Info button

Click the Info button to display the Cast Member Info dialog box for the cast member that is currently selected (you can also press Command-I). *(See page 28 for more about the Cast Member Info feature)*

Script button

Click the Script button to open the existing Script window for the currently selected cast member. If the cast member has no script, a new window is opened where you can type in a script from scratch. *(See page 206 for more about scripts)*

Cast member number

Displays the numerical position that the currently selected cast member occupies in the Cast window. Positions are numbered left to right, and row by row in the window.

Cast member name

Displays the name of the selected cast member assuming you have opted to assign one. *(See page 33 for more about Cast member names)*

Scroll bars

Use the scroll bars to move through the cast member positions in the Cast window.

Window sizer

Shrink or enlarge the Cast window by dragging the window sizer which appears in its lower-right corner.

Info button

Script button

Cast member number

Cast member name

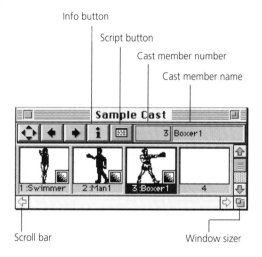

Scroll bar

Window sizer

Figure 6. The **Cast** window.

Cast Window Buttons

To import cast members into the Cast window:

If you want your Director movie to incorporate graphics or sounds that have already been created in some other application (for instance, a matte background created in Photoshop, or a set of sound effects compiled in SoundEdit Pro) you'll first have to import those elements into the Cast window.

You can import the following items into the Cast window: PICT, Macpaint, and PICS graphics (PICS is a format that contains several PICT pictures, which usually are frames of an animation sequence); Macintosh Scrapbook files, sounds saved in the SoundEdit, AIFF, AIFC, or 8-bit SND resource formats; Apple QuickTime movies; and other Director movies that can be incorporated within your current movie.

To import a cast member:

1. Choose Import from Director's File menu (or press Command-J on the keyboard) **(Figure 7).**

2. In the Import dialog box, use the Type pop-up menu to indicate what kind of cast member you'd like to import **(Figures 8-9).** Only files in this selected format are displayed in the dialog box.

3. Use the Folders pop-up menu to navigate through your hard drive's file folders, and open the folder that contains the cast member you wish to import.

4. Click the desired cast member file, and choose the Import button to bring the cast member into the Cast window. Choose Import All to import all cast members displayed in the current folder. All imported cast members will be placed in the first available position in Director's Cast window.

Figure 7. Choose **Import** from Director's **File** menu.

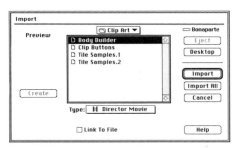

Figure 8. The **Import** dialog box.

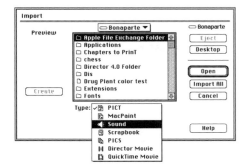

Figure 9. Use the **Type** pop-up menu to select a cast member type.

Using Link to File.

When you import a cast member file, Director actually copies the contents of that file, installs those contents in your current movie, and thus increases your movie's file size. You can avoid this by checking the Link to File checkbox before importing a cast member **(Figure 10)**. If you check Link to File, Director will note the location of the original file on your hard drive and then refer to the file when necessary. Not only does this approach keep your movie from bloating up in size, but also it means that if you ever change that linked cast member (for instance, if you use Photoshop to retouch an image file after it's been imported), Director will automatically reflect that change, and the updated cast member won't have to be imported again. The drawback to linking Director to its cast member files is that those files must always be on hand when you play your movie. If not, Director will ask you to locate any missing files before going on.

Note: When importing Scrapbook or PICS files, each image contained in those files will be imported as a separate cast member in the Cast window. Before actually importing the file, Director will determine how many cast members it contains, and will allow you to specify a selective range of the positions they should occupy in the Cast window **(Figure 11)**.

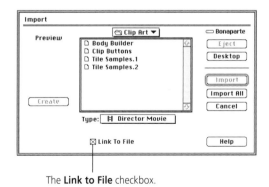

The **Link to File** checkbox.

Figure 10. Check the **Link to File** checkbox.

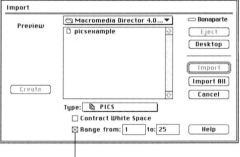

The **Range** checkbox.

Figure 11. You can specify a cast member range when importing **Scrapbook** or **PICS** files.

Import using Link to File

To import cast members with unique color palettes:

When you are importing a graphical cast member that has been saved using a color palette different from Director's currently active palette (*see the Color in Director chapter for information about palettes*), a dialog box appears asking whether you wish to remap the cast member to Director's current color palette or to install the cast member's original palette in the Cast window **(Figure 12)**. Remapping the cast member at this stage may be undesirable, because Director will try to paint it in the colors of its current palette, which could be significantly different from the colors that the cast member was originally designed with. By installing the cast member's palette into the Cast window, you can ensure that the cast member will maintain its original colors when its palette is active.

To get (and set) info on a cast member in the Cast window:

The Cast Member Info command provides a variety of information regarding each cast member in your movie. For instance, you can use the Cast Member Info command to find out how much memory a sound effect requires or what color palette is assigned to a cast member. Cast Member Info also allows you to control a variety of cast member settings; you can turn accompanying sound on or off in a film loop cast member or a linked movie. For a digital video cast member (which is a QuickTime movie), you can specify the frame rate at which the video plays. You can also use the Cast Member Info command to determine how Director will manage all your cast members within the memory limitations of your Macintosh.

Figure 12. When importing a cast member that has been saved with a color palette different from the active one, a dialog box appears that allows you to remap the colors of the cast member using the active palette or to install the original palette of the cast member in the **Cast** window.

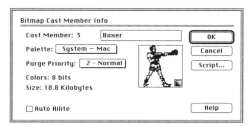

Figure 13. Cast Member Info dialog box for a bitmapped graphic.

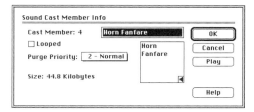

Figure 14. Cast Member Info dialog box for a sound.

Purge Priority.

Director allows you to set the following Purge Priority values in the Cast Member Info dialog box:

3 (Normal) Cast member is purged from memory as necessary.

2 (Next) Cast member is among the next group to be purged from memory

1 (Last) Cast member is among the last group to be purged from memory

0 (Never) Cast member is never purged from memory.

To get information on a cast member in your movie:

1. From the Cast window, select the cast member that you wish to see information on.

2. Choose Cast Member Info from the Cast menu or click the Info button in the Cast window.

3. The Cast Member Info dialog box appears. The dialog box differs depending on the type of cast member you've selected—for instance, a bitmap graphic, a sound effect, a color palette, or a QuickTime movie **(Figures 13–14)**. This dialog box offers key information about the selected cast member, and lets you specify a variety of settings that control the cast member's behavior.

4. Click OK to save any settings you may have made to the cast member.

Note: In most cases, the Info dialog box allows you to establish the **Purge value** for the selected cast member. Purge values are important to know about. If your Macintosh begins to run low on memory while playing your movie, Director tries to purge certain cast members from RAM to free more memory. If a purged cast member is required again, Director must load it back into memory from your hard disk, which can delay your movie's playback for a moment. For this reason you can manually set the Purge value for individual cast members, telling Director which cast members are least important to your movie and can be purged first in case memory is low, and which are really key and should not be purged at all.

Cast Member Info, Purge Priority

To duplicate a cast member in the Cast window:

Being able to duplicate a cast member in the Cast window is useful for a couple of reasons: First of all, if you wish to create a number of cast members that make up an animation sequence, you can base each distinctive frame on duplicates of one or more cast members, making minor changes to each duplicate. Also, if you wish to make modifications to a cast member's color palette it's a good idea to try out your ideas on a duplicate cast member. If you don't like the results, you can always go back to the original version.

1. From the Cast window, click the cast member that you wish to duplicate (**Figure 15**).

2. Choose Duplicate Cast Member from the Cast menu **(Figure 16)**. Director places a copy of the selected cast member in the next available position in the Cast window.

Note: You can also create a duplicate cast member by using Director's Copy and Paste commands, located under the Edit menu. Just select a cast member in the Cast window, choose Copy, click a new position in the Cast window, and choose Paste.

To delete a cast member from the Cast window:

1. From the Cast window, click the cast member you wish to delete. Shift-click to select a range of cast members or hold down Command and click to select multiple non-adjacent cast members.

2. Choose Clear Cast Members from Director's Edit menu to remove the cast member(s) **(Figure 17)**. Even if the cast member has already been assigned to the Score, it will no longer appear when you play your movie.

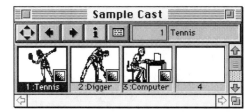

Figure 15. Click the cast member you wish to duplicate.

Figure 16. Choose **Duplicate Cast Member** from the **Cast** menu.

Figure 17. Choose **Clear Cast Members** from the **Edit** menu.

Figure 18. Choose **Find Cast Members** from the **Cast** menu.

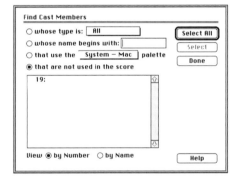

Figure 19. Click the fourth radio button in the **Find Cast Members** dialog box to find all cast members not used in the **Score**.

To delete all unused cast members:

If your Director movie is a large, involved production, you may find you've imported a number of cast members that you never ended up using and want to delete. Deleting unused cast members is a good practice, since it frees disk space and memory used by your movie.

1. Open the Cast window.

2. Choose Find Cast Members from Director's Cast menu **(Figure 18)**.

3. In the Find Cast Members dialog box, click the radio button labeled "that are not used in the score" **(Figure 19)**.

4. Click the Select All button and Director finds and selects all unused cast members in the Cast window.

5. Choose Clear Cast Members from the Edit menu.

Note: This process finds cast members that are not used in the Score of your movie. However, cast members may also be incorporated into your movie by way of Lingo scripts, in which case certain cast members would not necessarily appear in the Score. So before deleting all the cast members that Director finds, make sure that they are all indeed unused throughout your entire movie, not just its Score.

✔ Tip

■ Once you've deleted a series of cast members, save your movie by using the Save and Compact command under the File menu. If you simply use the standard Save command, Director will note that cast members have been deleted, but it will not free the storage space that they once occupied. Using Save and Compact, however, will do just that.

Delete Unused Cast Members

To reposition cast members in the Cast window:

In some cases it's necessary to place all related cast members together in the Cast window. For instance, suppose that you are building an animation sequence of a dog running. If you place the first frame of the animation in position 1 of the Cast window, you'll want to place the next frame in position 2, the next in position 3, and so on **(Figure 20)**. Placing related cast members together is not only efficient from an organizational standpoint but also required if you want to create a film loop or perform other animation-related tasks. *(See page 173 on creating film loops)*

Director makes it easy to reorder cast members within the Cast window by dragging them from one position to another.

1. From the Cast window, click to select the cast member you wish to reposition **(Figure 21)**. You can Shift-click to choose multiple adjacent cast members or hold the Command key to select multiple non–adjacent cast members.

2. Drag the selected cast member (or one cast member in a multiple selection) to a new position in the Cast window **(Figure 22)**.

3. Release the mouse button to actually place the cast members in their new location. They will be positioned sequentially from that point.

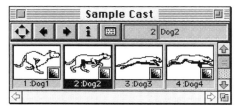

Figure 20. Related cast members, such as multiple frames in an animation, should be placed side by side in the **Cast** window.

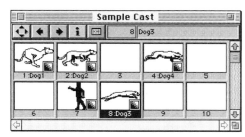

Figure 21. Click the cast member, such as the dog in position 8.

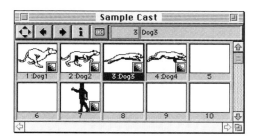

Figure 22. Drag the selected cast member to its new location and release the mouse button.

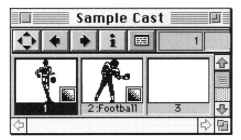

Figure 23. Select the cast member you wish to name.

To name a cast member in the Cast window:

You can give cast members a descriptive name (such as Sunset, Bird, Man 1 and Man 2) so that they're easier to find and manage in the Cast window and throughout your entire movie.

1. In the Cast window, click to select the cast member that you wish to name **(Figure 23)**.

2. Choose Cast Member Info from the Cast menu.

3. In the Cast Member Info dialog box, type the name you wish to assign the selected cast member **(Figure 24)**.

4. Click OK.

Name a Cast Member

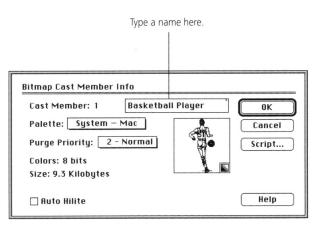

Figure 24. Enter a name in the **Cast Member Info** dialog box.

To find a cast member by its name:

If your Cast window contains a large number of cast members, it can become tedious to search through the window manually to find one cast member out of potentially hundreds. If you've named your cast member, however, you can let Director find it for you automatically. It can also automatically find a range of cast members that share common elements in their names, such as Man 1, Man 2, and Man 3.

1. Choose Find Cast Members from Director's Cast menu.

2. In the Find Cast Members dialog box, click the second radio button labeled "whose name begins with" to select it. **(Figure 25)**.

3. In the adjacent text box, type the name of the cast member(s) you'd like to find. You may type the name partially to find multiple cast members with similar names. For instance, you'd type "Man" to find cast members Man 1, Man 2, and so on.

4. Click Select and Director finds and selects the first cast member with a matching name in the Cast window. Click Select All if you wish to find all cast members with matching names.

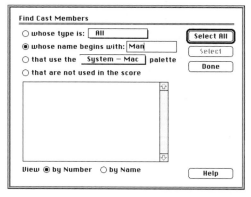

Figure 25. Use the "whose name begins with" option to find cast members by name.

To find a cast member by its color palette:

You can search and find cast members in the Cast window by the color palette they use. This is particularly useful if you have a number of cast members that are mapped to one particular color palette, but must eventually be remapped to another one. To find such a group quickly, you can simply search for all cast members that are linked to a particular palette.

1. Choose Find Cast Members from Director's Cast menu.

2. In the Find Cast Members dialog box, click the third radio button and use the adjacent pop-up menu to select the palette used by the cast members you wish to find **(Figure 26)**.

3. Click the Select All button and Director finds and selects all the appropriate cast members in the Cast window.

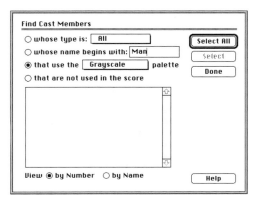

Figure 26. Click the third option and choose a palette to search for.

To sort cast members in the Cast window:

Director can sort cast members by name, type, size, the order they appear in your Score, or the order they appear in the Cast window. Being able to sort cast members is a great way to keep a large, unwieldy cast well organized. When Director sorts cast members, it also removes gaps in the Cast window where you have cut or relocated earlier cast members.

1. Choose Select All from Director's Edit menu **(Figure 27)**.

2. Choose Sort Cast Members from the Cast menu **(Figure 28)**.

3. In the Sort dialog box, select the method of sorting you wish to use **(Figure 29)**.

4. Click Sort.

 Tip

■ When you sort the Cast window, most or all cast members will be reassigned position numbers based on their new location in the window. However, if you have created Lingo scripts that refer to those cast members by number, rather than name, your scripts will no longer be able to find the proper cast members. To avoid this, refer to cast members by name in your scripts.

Figure 27. Choose **Select All** from the **Edit** menu.

Figure 28. Choose **Sort Cast Members** from the **Cast** menu.

Figure 29. Select the method of sorting you wish to use.

Sort Cast Members *(sidebar)*

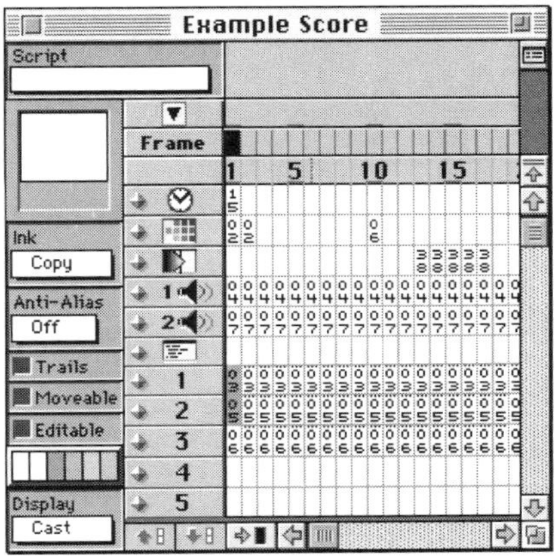

Figure 1. The **Score** window.

Figure 2. Choose **Score** from the **Window** menu.

D irector's Score **(Figure 1)** is similar to the script of a Hollywood movie. It describes what your cast members should do and when they should do it on the Stage. Remember that the **Stage** is where your movie plays out. It usually takes up the full dimensions of your Macintosh's screen, and can be seen in the background behind Director's Cast, Score and other windows.

A Director movie is assembled by assigning cast members, such as graphics and sounds, and events such as visual transitions and tempo changes, to various parts of the Score, which represent various segments of time in your Director movie. You can open the Score window by choosing Score from the Window menu, or by pressing Command-4 **(Figure 2)**.

Frames

The first thing to know about the Score is that it is cut up into small segments of time called frames. Each frame forms a column of cells and the frames are arranged horizontally across the Score window in sequential order **(Figure 3)**. Frames are numbered at the top of their columns. There's no limit to the number of frames you can have in a movie.

Frames in Director are just like the frames you find on a strip of celluloid film—where each frame provides an opportunity to change or continue the action taking place in the movie. For instance, a sound effect in your movie may begin playing at frame 1 but stop playing at frame 15. And in an animation sequence, frame 1 might feature a cast member graphic on the left most side of the Stage. In frame 2, however, that cast member might move a little toward the right. It will appear to move even farther in frame 3, and so on. When a sequence of frames is played in rapid succession, animation occurs. How quickly Director plays the frames of a movie is known as **Tempo**, which you can set in frames per second. *(See page 200 in the Tempo chapter)*

Playback head

The position of the **Playback head** in the Score indicates which frame is currently displayed on the Stage **(Figure 3)**. You can drag the Playback head to display any single frame of your movie on the Stage.

Playback head

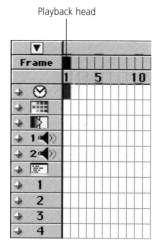

Figure 3. Each frame forms a column of cells and the frames are arranged horizontally across the **Score** window in sequential order.

Score Channels

A large number of events can occur in any frame of Director's Score. For instance, several cast member graphics can appear, a sound effect or two can play, and a transition to a new color palette can begin. You manage and direct these elements and events by placing them each into a **channel** of the Score.

Director's channels run vertically along the left side of the Score window **(Figure 4)**. Each channel forms its own row of cells extending through the frames. The following channel types are available, in this order:

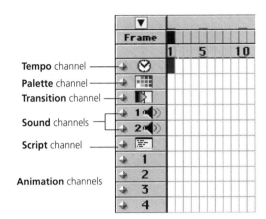

Tempo channel
Palette channel
Transition channel
Sound channels
Script channel

Animation channels

Figure 4. The channels run vertically along the left side of the **Score** window. Each channel forms a row of cells.

- The Tempo channel, which you use to set the speed at which Director plays your entire movie, or just a sequence of frames
- The Palette channel, which you use to set the color palette used to display your movie
- The Transition channel, which you use to set video transition effects between scenes such as dissolves or wipes
- Two sound channels, where you place sound effects, musical scores and voice tracks
- The Script channel, where you place interactive Lingo scripts (which allow you to create buttons, dialog boxes, and hypertext features for interactive movies)
- 48 animation channels to accommodate cast member graphics

Generally, you must place each new cast member or event that you wish to incorporate in a scene in a separate channel of Director's Score. For instance, if you want to place a graphic into the Score, you would place it in the first available animation channel. If you want the scene to feature two cast members on Stage simultaneously, you add the second cast member to the next animation channel—say, channel 2 **(Figure 5)**. If you wish a sound effect to play as well, you place it in one of Director's two sound channels, at the same frame location where your graphics appear **(Figure 6)**. And when you want to change the color palette currently used to display your Director movie, you set a new palette in the Score's palette channel.

In summary, building the Score of a Director movie is mostly a matter of assigning cast members to particular channels in the Score, at particular frames or range of frames within each channel.

Other terms

Before going on, let's define two more terms that will help you understand how Director's Score works. **Cells** are the small units that make up the Score **(Figure 6)**. Each cell contains information about what's happening in a particular channel at a particular frame in your movie. **Sprite** is the term used to describe one instance of a graphical cast member that has been placed in your Score, and now appears on the Stage at one point in time. You could almost use the terms sprite and cast member interchangeably, except that once a cast member has been placed in the Score, its sprite can be stretched and squeezed, or altered with special ink effects, and the original cast member in Director's Cast window is not affected.

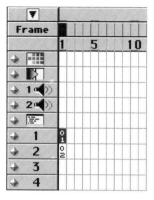

Figure 5. Animation channels 1 and 2 here each contain a graphical cast member in frame 1.

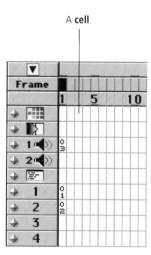

Figure 6. A sound effect is added here to sound channel 1, frame 1.

Cells, Sprites

Figure 7. Choose **Score** from the **Window** menu.

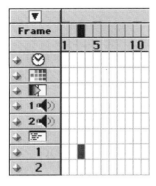

Figure 8. Click a particular frame in a particular channel where you wish to place your cast member.

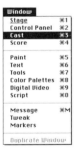

Figure 9. Choose **Cast** from the **Window** menu.

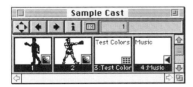

Figure 10. In the **Cast** window, select the cast member(s) you wish to place on the Stage. Cast members 1-4 are selected here.

PLACING CAST MEMBERS IN THE SCORE

A key step to creating any Director movie is assigning a cast member to a particular channel and frame in the Score. You can do so by dragging a cast member from the Cast window to Director's Stage or from the Cast window to particular cells in the Score window. Either method places the cast member in the Score of your movie, although dragging to Director's Stage is generally easier, and it's particular expedient when you're incorporating graphic cast members, since you can immediately position them on the Stage as they should appear in your movie. However, non-visible cast members, such as sounds, color palettes, or scripts are just as easily placed by dragging them to their destination cells in Director's Score.

To place cast members on Director's Stage:

1. Open the Score window by choosing Score from Director's Window menu **(Figure 7)**.

2. In the Score window, click the particular frame, in the particular channel where you wish to place your cast member. **(Figure 8)**.

3. Open Director's Cast window by choosing Cast from the Window menu **(Figure 9)**.

4. In the Cast window, click the cast member that you wish to place on the Stage. If you wish to place multiple cast members, select them together by Shift-clicking **(Figure 10)**.

Place Cast Members on the Stage

5. Drag your cast member selection to the Stage (the area outside the Cast window). The mouse cursor becomes a hand. **(Figure 11)**.

6. Release the mouse button to place the cast members on the Stage. If you selected just one cast member, it is assigned to the frame and channel that you selected in step 2. If you dragged multiple cast members, they are all placed in the frame you selected in step 2, but each cast member is assigned to a different channel in the Score window **(Figure 12)**, unless you held down the option key while dragging *(see the Tip below)*.

✔ **Tip**

■ When you drag multiple cast members from the Cast window to the Stage, Director normally places each cast member in the same frame of your Score, but in different channels of that frame **(Figure 12)**. Sometimes, however, you'll want a collection of cast members to be assigned to the same channel, but placed in separate frames of the Score **(Figure 13)**. For instance, this would be desirable if you're placing a group of cast members that make up an animation sequence, where each cast member should be displayed one after the other in sequential frames. To place a collection of cast members into the Score over time (into separate frames), follow steps 1–6 above, but hold down the Option key as you drag the selected cast members from the Cast window to the Stage.

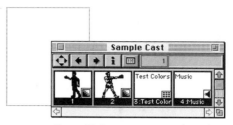

Figure 11. Drag your cast member selection to the Stage as shown here by the dotted outline.

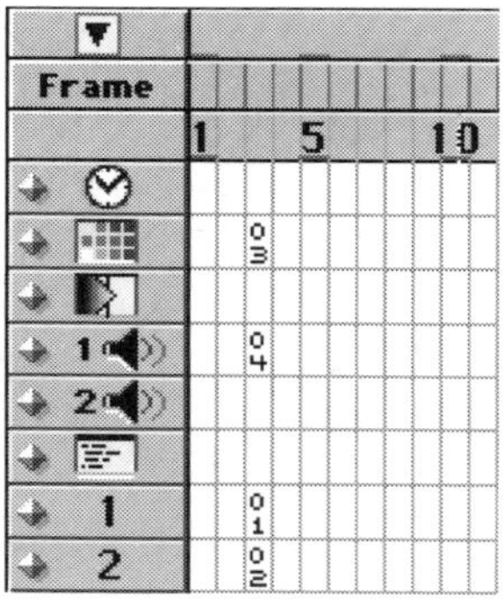

Figure 12. If you drag multiple cast members to the Stage, each cast member is normally assigned to the same frame but a different channel in the Score.

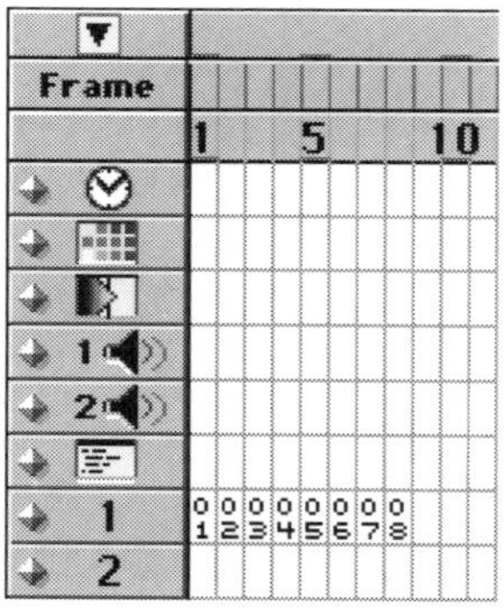

Figure 13. To place a collection of cast members in a series of frames, hold down the Option key while dragging selected cast members from the **Cast** window to the Stage.

Place Cast Members on the Stage

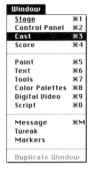

Figure 14. Choose **Score** from the **Window** menu.

Figure 15. Choose **Cast** from the **Window** menu.

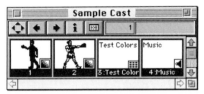

Figure 16. In the **Cast** window, select the cast member(s) you wish to place in the Score. Cast members 1-4 are selected here.

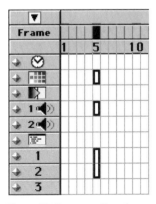

Figure 17. Director outlines the range of cells that your cast member selection will occupy in the Score.

To drag a cast member directly to the Score:

Rather than dragging cast members to Director's Stage, you can place them immediately into the Score window.

1. Open the Score window by choosing Score from Director's Window menu **(Figure 14)**.

2. Open the Cast window by choosing Cast from the Window menu **(Figure 15)**.

3. In the Cast window, click the cast member that you wish to place in the Score, so that it's selected. If you wish to place multiple cast members, you can select them together by Shift-clicking **(Figure 16)**.

4. Drag your cast member selection from the Cast window to a cell in the Score. As you drag, Director outlines the range of cells that your cast member selection will occupy **(Figure 17)**. Director outlines only cells that will accommodate your cast members (for instance, sounds can be dragged only to cells in Director's sound channels).

5. Release the mouse button to place the cast member(s) in the Score. If you dragged just one cast member, it is assigned to the frame and channel that you dragged it to. If you dragged multiple cast members, they are all placed in the frame you dragged them to, but each cast member is assigned to a different channel in the Score window.

Drag Cast Members to the Score

✓ **Tip**

■ To place the cast members over time (into different frames of the same channel, rather than different channels of the same frame, which is the default), hold down the Option key while dragging the cast members from the Cast window to the Score.

To assign Lingo scripts directly to the Score:

If your movie features interactivity, you'll probably create a variety of Lingo scripts that can be assigned to certain frame sequences in the Score's script channel *(see page 210 for details on Frame scripts)*. You assign these scripts by using the Script pop-up menu in the Score window, located at the upper left-hand side. Note that this pop-up menu only allows you to assign Score scripts to the Score.

1. In the script channel of the Score window, select the cells you wish to assign a Lingo script **(Figure 18)**.

2. Use the Script pop-up menu to select an existing script. Scripts are numbered and identified by their first line of Lingo code **(Figure 19)**.

3. You can choose New from the Script pop-up menu to open a new Script window. *(See page 207 for details on Script windows)*

Assign Lingo Scripts to the Score

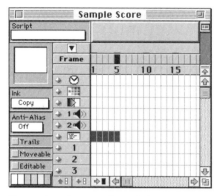

Figure 18. In the Script channel of the **Score** window, select the cells you wish to assign a Lingo script.

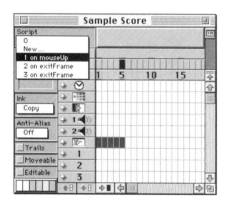

Figure 19. Use the **Script** pop-up menu to select an existing script.

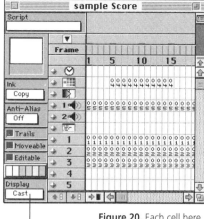

Display pop-up menu.

Figure 20. Each cell here displays the last two digits of its cast member's position number from the Cast window. The Cast display mode is selected.

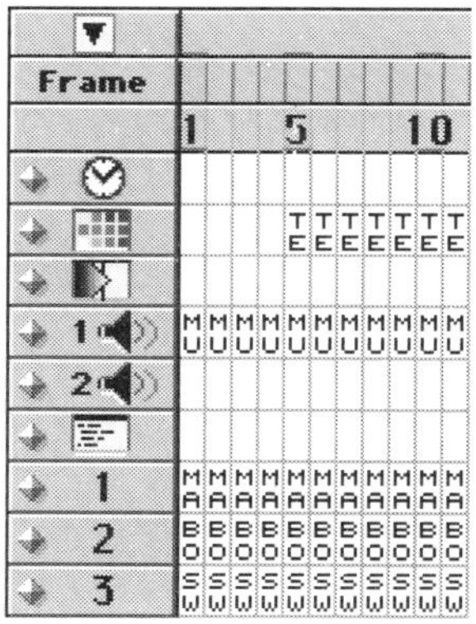

Figure 21. Each cell here displays the first two letters of the cast member's name.

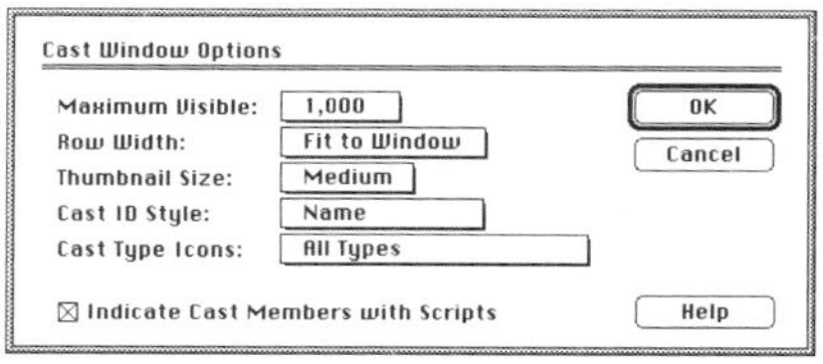

Figure 22. The Cast ID Style setting in the **Cast Window Options** dialog box controls whether cells in the Score display cast member names or numbers when the Cast display mode is selected.

SCORE NOTATION

When you place cast members into the cells of the Score you'll notice that those cells become filled with small letters and numbers. These characters are called **cell notation** and they offer important information about what role the cell plays in the overall Score.

Director can display one of many different types of cell notation in its Score, with each type offering different information about the cells' characteristics. You can choose which display mode Director uses by clicking the Display button in the lower-left corner of the Score **(Figure 20)**, and choosing from the pop-up menu that appears.

Following are explanations of each type of cell notation that Director offers.

Cast notation

Cast notation is the default notation used in Director's Score. In Cast notation, each cell identifies the cast member that it contains. In this mode, each cell displays either the last two digits of its cast member's position number in the Cast window **(Figure 20)**, or the first two letters of the cast member's name **(Figure 21)**. Which specific form is used depends on the Cast ID Style setting in the Cast Window Options dialog box **(Figure 22)**, under the Cast menu.

Blend notation

Cells displayed in Blend notation show the blend percentage that's been assigned to the cell's cast member sprite using the Set Sprite Blend command under the Score menu. For instance, a 35 refers to a 35% blend and two square symbols indicate a 100% blend **(Figure 23)**.

Ink notation

Cells displayed in Ink notation show which ink effect has been applied to the cast member sprite that's contained by the particular cell. The top character in the notated cell indicates the type of cast member contained—B is for bitmap cast members, Q stands for QuickDraw cast members, T stands for QuickDraw text cast members, P stands for PICT cast members, and a bullet symbol indicates a film loop, QuickTime movie, or embedded Director movie. The bottom character in the cell indicates the type of ink effect at work **(Figure 24)**. A small dotted line placed between the top and bottom characters indicates that trails have been turned on. *(See page 59 about trails)*

Motion notation

Cells displayed in Motion notation show the direction in which their sprites are moving, if any **(Figure 25)**. The top character in the notated cell indicates the type of cast member contained—B is for bitmap cast members, Q stands for QuickDraw cast members, T stands for QuickDraw text cast members, P stands for PICT cast members, and a bullet symbol indicates a film loop, QuickTime movie, or embedded Director movie. A dash indicates that the cast member type is the same as in the previous frame. The bottom character in the notated cell indicates the direction in which the cast member sprite is moving relative to the sprite's previous position. Small arrows

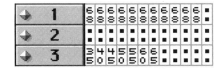

Figure 23. Cells displayed in Blend notation show the blend percentage that's been assigned to the cell's cast member sprite.

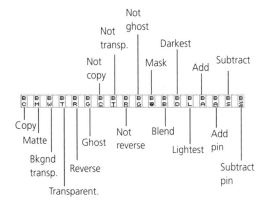

Figure 24. In Ink notation, the character at the bottom of the cell indicates which ink effect has been applied to the cast member sprite. The top character indicates the type of cast member contained as follows:
B - bitmap cast members.
Q - QuickDraw cast members.
T - QuickDraw text cast members.
P - PICT cast members.
A bullet indicates a film loop, QuickTime movie, or embedded Director movie.

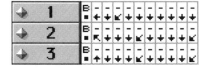

Figure 25. Cells displayed in Motion notation show the direction in which their sprites are moving.

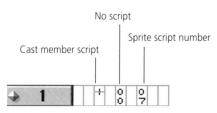

Cast member script

No script

Sprite script number

Figure 26. In Script notation, a number indicates the number of the Score script assigned to the cell. A plus sign indicates a cast member script is present, while 00 indicates that the cell has no script tied to it.

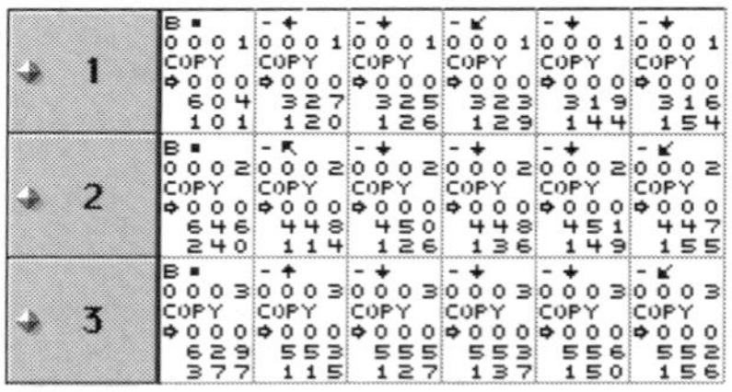

Figure 27. Score cells displayed in Extended notation.

denote the direction, while a square bullet symbol tells you that there is no movement for that cell.

Script notation

Cells displayed in Script notation show the number identifier of any Score script that has been assigned to a cell **(Figure 26)**. Each Score script you create is given an identifying number, and it's this number that is displayed when such scripts are present. A double zero symbol indicates a cell has no script tied to it, while a plus sign tells you that a cast member script is present.

Extended notation

Extended notation offers a wealth of detailed information about the characteristics of each particular cell in the Score window **(Figure 27)**. In fact, this notation type is useful only for the most detailed and meticulous fine-tuning of your score, and is out of the scope of a Visual QuickStart Guide. For more information about Extended notation, see your Director documentation.

Score Notation

Foreground/Background Priorities

MANAGING AND ORGANIZING THE SCORE

To set the foreground and background priorities of sprites in the Score:

If you plan to place and animate a number of sprites simultaneously on Director's Stage, you'll need to control each sprite's **foreground/background priority**. For instance, in animating a character walking down a street, you may want the character to appear to walk in front of background buildings **(Figure 28)** but behind certain sprites such as parked cars, street lamps, and signposts. To accomplish this, you must set the appropriate foreground/background priority of all sprites in the scene, which is determined by the way you order sprites in the 48 animation channels of the Score. Basically, a sprite that's assigned to an earlier animation channel in the Score (for instance, channel 1) will always appear *in the background* when overlapping a sprite that's assigned to a later animation channel (say, channel 15).

As you build a scene in Director's Score, you'll probably find it necessary to relocate certain sprites to earlier or later animation channels in the Score, to give them the proper foreground/background priorities. You can always cut and paste the appropriate cells to new animation channels, but Director provides an easy way to shuffle selected cells from one channel to the next.

1. In the Score window, select the cells that you wish to shuffle from their current animation channel to a new channel **(Figure 29)**. You can either select a finite range of cells within a channel, or double-click the channel's number to select all the cells within that channel.

Figure 28. A sprite's foreground/background priority is determined by its order in the 48 animation channels. Here, the person is in the foreground, while the city sprite is in the background.

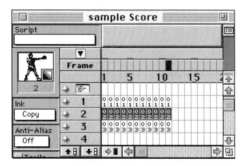

Figure 29. Select the cells that you wish to shuffle from their current animation channel to a new channel. Here, all the cells in channel 2 are selected.

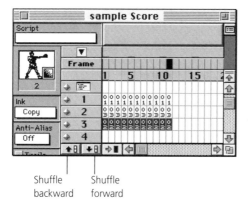

Shuffle backward   Shuffle forward

Figure 30. Click Shuffle forward or Shuffle backward to shift the selected cells one level closer to the foreground or background respectively.

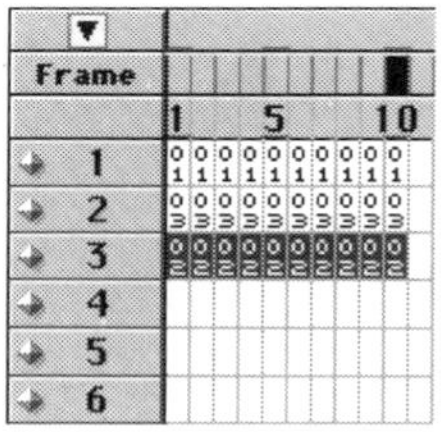

Figure 31. Select the cell or range of cells that you wish to move.

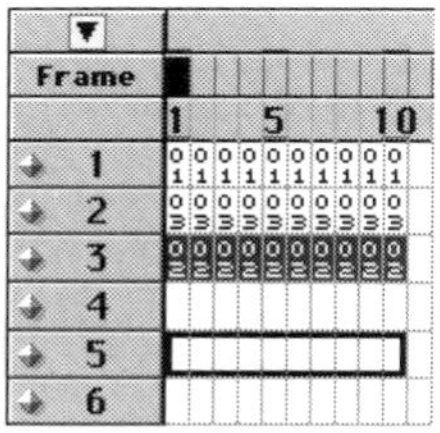

Figure 32. Drag the selected cells to a new cell position in the Score.

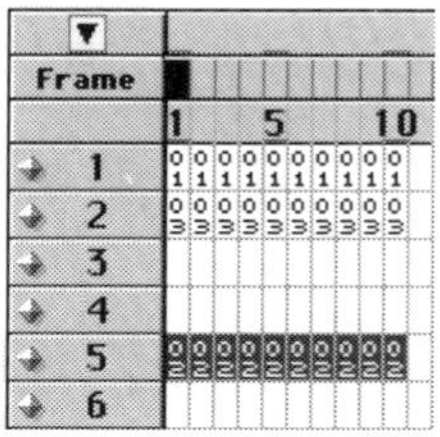

Figure 33. Release the mouse button, and the selected cells will be relocated.

2. Click either the Shuffle forward or Shuffle backward buttons at the bottom left corner of the Score window. Shuffle forward switches the selected cells with the corresponding cells in the channel directly below it, pushing the sprites in the selected cells one level closer to the foreground **(Figure 30)**. Shuffle backward switches the selected cells with the corresponding cells in the channel directly above it, pushing the sprites in the selected cells one level closer to the background.

To move cells within the Score:

1. In the Score window, select the cell or range of cells that you wish to move **(Figure 31)**. The cursor becomes a hand.

2. Drag the selected cells to a new position in the Score window **(Figure 32)**. If you wish to move a copy of the selected cells rather than the originals, hold down the Option key while dragging the cells.

3. Release the mouse button, and Director moves the selected cells to the new location **(Figure 33)**. The contents of the selected cells automatically replaces whatever was present before.

✔ Tip

■ You can also move cells within the Score window by using Director's Cut, Copy, and Paste features. First select the cells you wish to move and then choose Copy Cells or Cut Cells from the Edit menu. Select a new cell location in the Score window, and choose Paste Cells from the Edit menu to place your cells in their new location.

Move Cells within the Score

To insert new frames in the Score:

Sometimes you'll find that you want to add or insert information into the Score in a place where there are no empty cells to accommodate the new information. You can always use Director's cut and paste or drag cell features to shift existing cells to the right, leaving an empty region in the Score, but this can become tedious, especially if you're not sure how many cells must be vacated. It's easier simply to insert new frames in the Score.

1. In the Score, select the existing cells that you wish to insert into another segment of the Score **(Figure 34)**.

2. Use the Cut or Copy features (listed under the Edit menu) to place the selected cells into memory **(Figure 37)**.

3. Click the frame number in the Score where you wish to insert the cells you've cut or copied **(Figure 35)**. An insertion line appears at the frame location you've picked.

4. Choose Paste Cells from the Edit menu **(Figure 38)** to insert the cut or copied cells **(Figure 36)**. Notice that Director creates the necessary number of new frames in its channels to accommodate the selection.

✔ Tip

■ If you've created Lingo scripts that refer to specific frame numbers in your movie, remember that adding new frames can throw off the frame references made by your scripts, causing problems in your movie. To avoid such problems, consider using markers rather than numerical references in your scripts. *(See page 52 on Markers)*

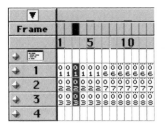

Figure 34. Select the existing cells that you wish to insert into another segment of the Score.

Click the frame number.

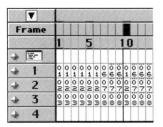

Figure 35. Click the frame number in the Score where you wish to insert the cells you've cut or copied. An insertion line appears.

Figure 36. The selected cells have been inserted into frame 10.

Figure 37. Choose **Cut** or **Copy** under the **Edit** menu.

Figure 38. Choose **Paste Cells** from the **Edit** menu.

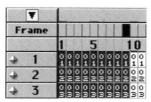

Figure 39. Drag across the cells you wish to cut from the Score.

Figure 40. Choose **Cut Cells** from the **Edit** menu.

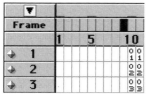

Figure 41. Director removes the selected frames from the Score.

To cut cells from the Score:

1. In the Score, drag across the cells you wish to cut **(Figure 39)**.

2. Choose Cut Cells from the Edit menu to remove the cells from the Score **(Figures 40–41)**. The cells are stored in memory and can be pasted back into the Score.

To move within the Score:

There are a number of ways to move around the Score window.

- Move to a specific frame by dragging the horizontal scroll box and noting the value in its pop-up frame counter **(Figure 42)**.

- Click the Jump button to move the Score to the frame that is currently being displayed on the Stage **(Figure 42)**.

- Double-click the Jump to top button in the top right side of the Score window to display the first channels in the Score **(Figure 43)**.

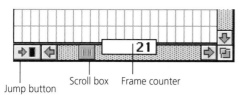

Jump button   Scroll box   Frame counter

Figure 42. Drag the Scroll box to move to a specific frame, or click the Jump button to move to the current frame on the Stage.

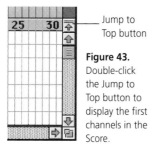

Jump to Top button

Figure 43. Double-click the Jump to Top button to display the first channels in the Score.

To delete cells in the Score:

1. In the Score window, select the cell or range of cells that you wish to delete by dragging the pointer across them **(Figure 44)**.

2. Press the Delete key, or choose Clear Cells from Director's Edit menu **(Figure 45)**.

To add a marker to the Score:

As the Score of your movie grows to hundreds or even thousands of frames, it becomes harder to keep track of which frames do what.

The best way to manage a large Score is to use special markers to label important sections in the Score. For instance, if you're creating an interactive business presentation, you could place a marker called "Main Menu" to mark the beginning of the frames that create the main menu of your presentation. Likewise, you could create "Sales" and "Marketing" markers to identify the frames that contain those respective sections of your movie **(Figure 46)**.

Also when it comes to writing scripts, referring to marker names instead of to changeable frame numbers ensures that Director will always know where to find a particular sequence of frames in your Score. *(See the Interactivity and Lingo chapter for details on scripts)*

1. In the Score window, drag a marker from the marker well and position it above the desired frame **(Figure 47)**.

2. Type the name for your marker, and press Return.

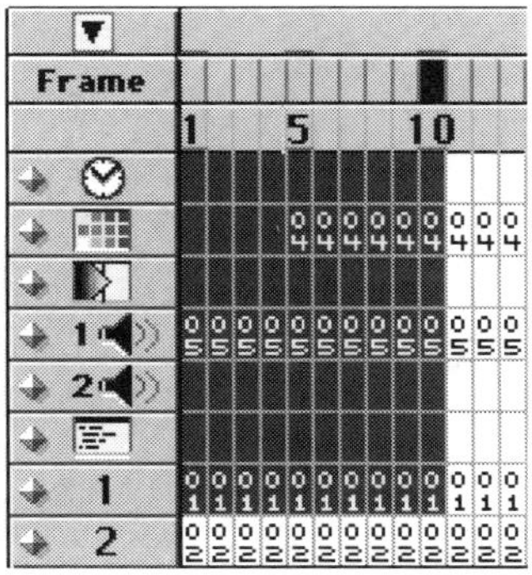

Figure 44. Select the cells in the Score that you wish to delete by dragging the pointer across them.

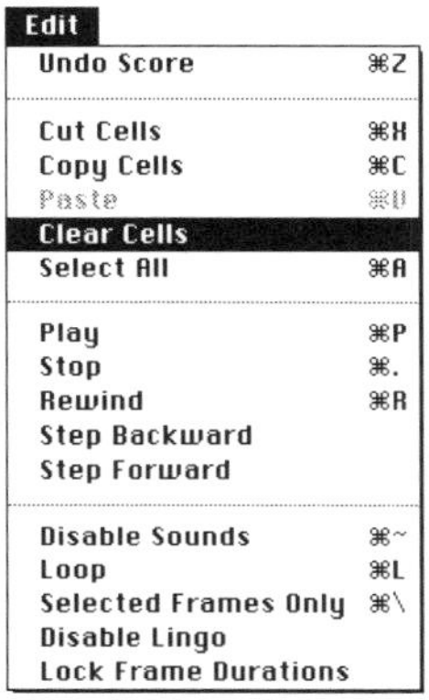

Figure 45. Choose **Clear Cells** from the **Edit** menu.

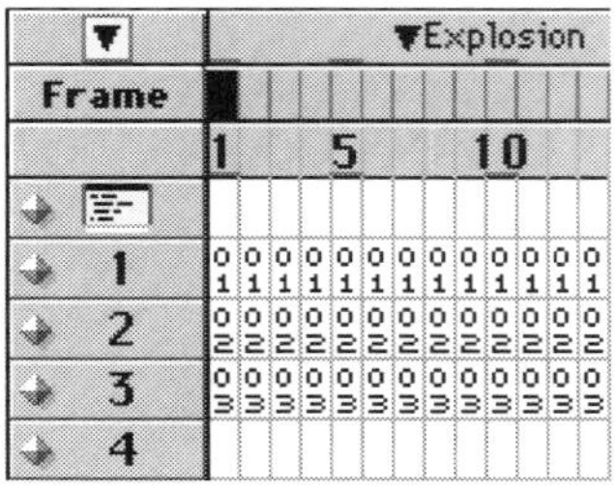

Figure 46. A marker is shown above frame 7 in the Score.

Marker well   Marker placed above frame 7

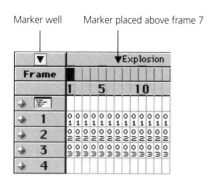

Figure 47. Drag a marker from the Marker well and position it above the desired frame. Type in a name.

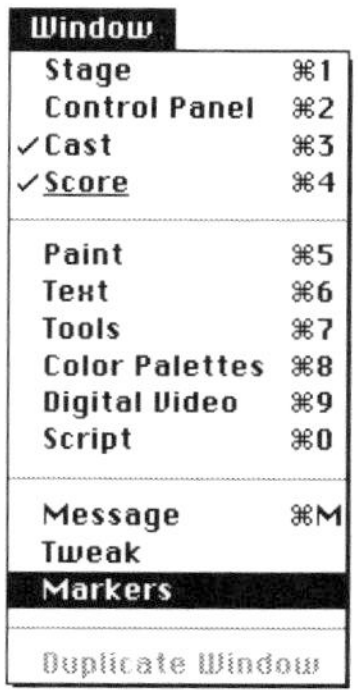

Figure 48. With the **Score** window open, choose **Markers** from the **Windows** menu.

Figure 49. In the **Markers** window, click the marker name that you wish to find or annotate. You can add commentary on the right side of the **Markers** window.

To find and annotate markers in the Score:

Director features a **Marker window** that allows you to search for and jump to existing markers in your Score. You can also use the window to add descriptive comments to markers—for instance, you might add scene descriptions or any other notes that might help someone understand what role the marked frames play in your movie's Score.

1. With the Score window open, choose Markers from the Windows menu **(Figure 48)**.

2. In the Markers window, click the marker name that you wish to find or annotate **(Figure 49)**. In the Score window, Director immediately moves to the part of your movie's Score that contains the selected marker.

3. If you wish to add commentary to the selected marker, click the mouse in the right half of the Marker window to first unselect the marker name that's repeated there. Make sure you then press Return after the marker name before you begin typing the commentary.

Find and Annotate Markers

To color cells in the Score window:

You can add color to cells in the Score window to help you identify distinct parts of your score. For instance, you might color all the cells of a particular animation sequence red, while another sequence would be blue. Having set up such a color code scheme, it's easy to see where each sequence begins and ends.

1. In the Score window, select the cells that you wish to color **(Figure 50)**.

2. In the Cell color selector in the bottom left corner of the Score window, click the color you'd like to apply to the selected cells **(Figure 50)**.

✔ Tip

■ Colored cells can sometimes slow down scrolling performance of the Score window. To avoid this, you can tell Director to show or hide colored cells by choosing Score Window Options from the Score menu, and selecting or deselecting the Colored Cells option **(Figures 51–52)**.

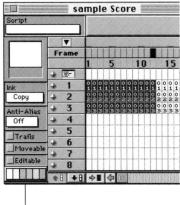

Cell color selector

Figure 50. In the **Score** window, select the cells that you wish to color and click on a color in the Cell color selector.

Figure 51. Choose **Score Window Options** from the **Score** menu.

Colored Cells option

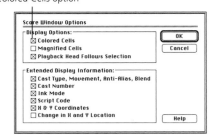

Figure 52. Select or deselect the **Colored Cells** option in the **Score Window Options** box to show or hide colored cells in the Score.

SETTING SPRITE ATTRIBUTES

To set an ink effect for a sprite in the Score:

Director features a variety of ink effects that can be applied to sprites to change the way they appear on the Stage. For instance, you can use ink effects to make sprites appear transparent, to darken or

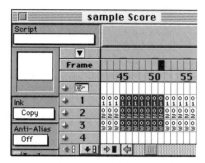

Figure 53. Select the cells in the Score that contain the sprites to which you wish to apply a new ink effect.

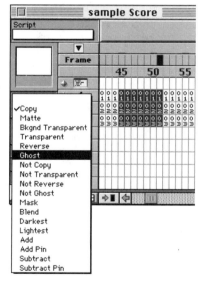

Figure 54. Use the **Ink** pop-up menu to select the desired ink effect.

lighten sprites, and especially to determine how the colors of sprites should change when they overlap one another on the Stage.

1. In the Score window, select the cells that contain the sprites to which you wish to apply a new ink effect **(Figure 53)**.

2. Use the Ink pop-up menu on the left side of the Score window to select the desired ink effect **(Figure 54)**.

The following list describes the effects that various inks have on your sprites. Although the following explanations will help you determine the differences from one effect to another, the best way to understand them is through trial and error.

Copy   This is the default ink effect. Sprites painted with this ink are surrounded by a rectangular bounding box. This box appears invisible on a white Stage, but when the sprite is on a colored Stage, or passes in front of another sprite, the bounding box is visible. Director animates sprites painted in the Copy ink more quickly than any other ink.

Matte   Sprites appear without the white bounding box associated with the Copy ink effect. Sprites painted in this ink use more memory, and animate less quickly, than those in the Copy ink.

Bkgnd Trans Pixels in the sprite that were painted in the background colors are transparent, so you can see the background through them.

Transparent Sprite pixels painted in the background color are transparent, so that you can see any artwork behind them.

Reverse White pixels in the sprite become transparent, so the background shows through.

Ghost When two sprites overlap, any black pixels in the foreground sprite turn the pixel beneath of the sprite white. Any white pixels in the foreground sprite become transparent.

Not Copy
Not Transp.
Not Reverse
Not Ghost These inks act like the standard Copy, Matte, Transparent, and Ghost effects, except that they reverse foreground sprite's colors first.

Mask When applied to foreground artwork, any holes in the sprite can be seen through to background artwork. To do this, however, you need to design your cast members with a mask effect in mind, creating a duplicate of the masked cast member and placing that duplicate in the next position of the Cast window, immediately to the right of the original cast member. *(See page 107 on creating masks)*

Blend The colors of sprites painted in this ink will blend with the colors of the background sprite they pass over. This blend is created on the fly, which can significantly reduce Director's animation performance. Director creates the blend based on the percentage specified with the Set Sprite Blend command.

Darkest With this ink effect, Director compares the pixel colors of foreground and background sprites, and uses whichever pixels of the two are darker to color the foreground sprite. In other words, the darker colors of two overlapping sprites are made visible, even if those colors belong to the background sprite.

Lightest   Works like the Darkest ink
effect, except that the
lighter pixels of two overlapping sprites are visible.

Add   When two sprites overlap,
Director calculates the original colors of the overlapping pixels and repaints
those pixels in a new color
that is created by adding
the two original colors
together. If the value of the
two new colors is greater
than the Mac's maximum
color value, then Director
wraps the new color value
around to the beginning of
the color scale.

Add Pin   Works the same way as the
Add ink effect, except the
new color value can't
exceed the Mac's maximum
color value, and no wrap
occurs.

Subtract   Works the same way as the
Add ink effect, except the
new color for overlapping
sprites is created by *sub-
tracting* the foreground
sprite's color value from the
background sprite's color
value, rather than adding. If
the value of the two new
colors is less than the Mac's
minimum color value,
Director wraps the new
color value around to the
top of the color scale.

Ink Effects in the Score

Subtract Pin   Works the same way as the Subtract ink effect, except the new color value can't be less than the Mac's minimum color value, and no wrap occurs.

✓ **Tip**

■   Remember that using ink effects other than the default Copy ink can slow down your movie's animation performance, so try to use them in strategic places, rather than across the board, if spry animation is important.

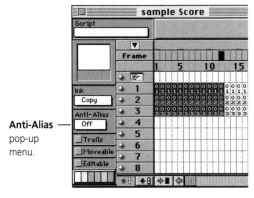

Anti-Alias pop-up menu.

Figure 55. In the **Score** window, select the sprites that you wish to anti-alias. Use the **Anti-Alias** pop-up menu to select the degree of anti-aliasing desired.

To apply anti-aliasing to sprites on the Stage:

Anti-aliasing is a process in which Director attempts to reduce or remove the rough, jagged edges that can often appear on bitmap graphics and text cast members. Reducing these "jaggies," as they're often called, makes your sprites seem more smooth and polished when appearing on the Stage. The trade-off is that anti-aliased sprites can slow down Director's animation performance, so you may want to use this feature sparingly.

1. In the Score window, select the cells that contain the sprites you wish to anti-alias **(Figure 55)**. It would be a good idea to arrange the Score window so that you can also see the Stage behind it, where your sprites appear.

2. Use the Anti-Alias pop-up menu on the left side of the Score window to select the degree of anti-aliasing desired **(Figure 55)**. Your choices are Off, Low, Middle, and High. Note how each level affects the sprites on the Stage.

Anti-Aliasing

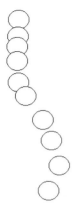

Figure 56. You can set a sprite to leave behind a trail of images as it's moved around, by selecting the **Trails** box in the **Score** window.

✓ **Tips**

■ Anti-aliasing 8-bit cast members with gradient color fills can actually make them look worse, not better.

■ Remember that heavy anti-aliasing can significantly slow down Director's animation performance. One way for improving performance is to anti-alias only a few key frames in an animation (such as the first, middle, and last), which can fool the eye into thinking that the entire sequence has been anti-aliased. Another tip is to use a paint program such as Adobe Photoshop to anti-alias bitmap graphics before importing them as cast members, so Director will not have to do it on the fly.

To apply trails to sprites:

From the Score window, you can set Director to animate a sprite so that it leaves a trail of images as it's moved around the screen from frame to frame **(Figure 56)**. This feature is wonderful for creating an animated hand-writing effect, where a trace is left wherever a cast member happens to move, as if someone were writing with a pencil.

1. In the Score window, select the cells that contain the sprites to which you wish to apply trails **(Figure 57)**.

2. Click the Trails box on the left side of the Score window to select it.

The Trails box.

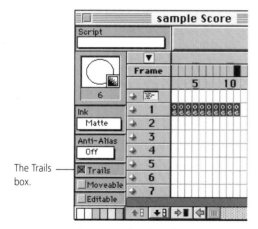

Figure 57. Select the cells in the **Score** window that contain the sprites you wish to apply trails to, and click the Trails box.

To make sprites moveable during movie playback:

It's possible to set Director to allow the sprites in your movie to be dragged on the Stage while the movie is actually playing. An example where this might be useful would be in an educational game in Director, where children can rearrange a variety of items on the screen.

1. In the Score window, select the range of cells that contain the sprites that you wish to render moveable by the user **(Figure 58)**. Remember that the sprites will be moveable only when Director is currently playing through the cells that you have selected in this step.

2. Click the Score window's Moveable checkbox so that it's selected **(Figure 58)**.

3. If you wish to cancel the moveable effect, simply select the cells whose sprites have been rendered moveable, and deselect the Moveable checkbox.

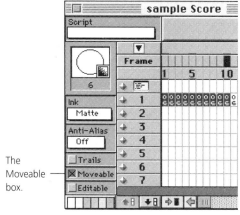

The Moveable box.

Figure 58. Select the range of cells in the Score that contain sprites you wish to render moveable, and click the **Moveable** checkbox.

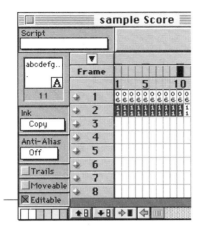

The Editable box.

Figure 59. Select the range of cells in the Score that contain the text sprites you wish to render editable, and click the **Editable** checkbox.

To make text sprites editable during movie playback:

Director allows you to select and edit QuickDraw text sprites on the Stage while the movie is actually playing.

1. In the Score window, select the range of cells that contain the text sprites that you wish to render editable by the user **(Figure 59)**. Remember that the sprites will be editable only when Director is currently playing through the cells that you have selected in this step.

2. Click the Score window's Editable checkbox. **(Figure 59)**.

3. If you wish to cancel the editable effect, simply select the cells whose sprites you've rendered editable, and deselect the Editable checkbox.

Make Text Sprites Editable During Playback

To stretch and squeeze sprites on Director's Stage:

You can change the shape and look of a sprite by stretching and squeezing it. The change affects only the sprite image of the cast member that appears on Stage; the original cast member in the Cast window is not changed by this operation. Stretching and squeezing sprites can lead to some interesting effects, especially when you combine the effect with Director's In-between animation capabilities *(see page 164)*, which allow you to apply stretches and squeezes over multiple frames in your movie.

1. In Director's Score window, select the cell or range of cells that contains the sprite you wish to stretch or squeeze **(Figure 60)**. Director responds by displaying the sprite on the Stage as it appears in the last cell of the selection. The sprite will be encased by a selection rectangle with handles at its corners and edges **(Figure 61)**.

2. Drag any of the selected sprite's handles to stretch or squeeze it **(Figure 62)**. If you selected just one cell in the Score in step 1, only the sprite in that single cell will be affected. If you selected a range of cells that contain the same sprite, the sprites in all of those cells will be changed.

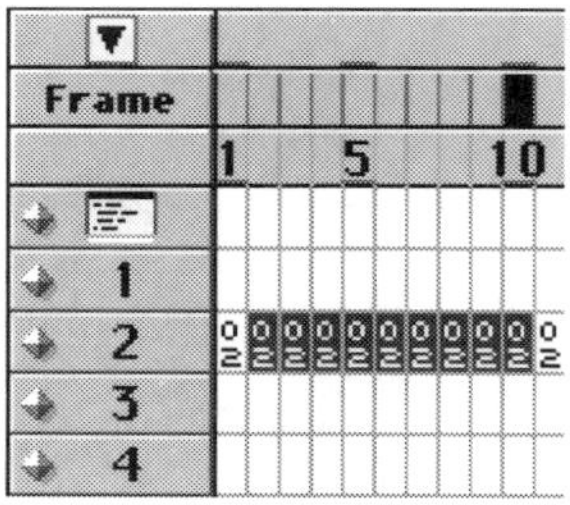

Figure 60. Select the cell or range of cells in the Score that contains the sprite you wish to stretch or squeeze.

Figure 61. A sprite on the Stage encased by a selection rectangle.

Figure 62. Drag any of the selected sprite's handles to stretch or squeeze it. The sprite has been stretched vertically here.

Stretch and Squeeze Sprites

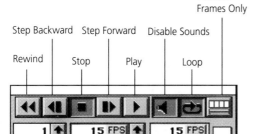

Step Backward Step Forward Disable Sounds

Selected Frames Only

Rewind Stop Play Loop

Figure 1. The **Control Panel**. The buttons of the Control Panel correspond to commands in the **Edit** menu.

Director's Control Panel is used to control the playback of your movie **(Figure 1)**. Much like the controls on a VCR, you can play, rewind, step forward, or step backward through the frames of your movie. The Control Panel also allows you to set and lock the playback rate of your movie, adjust the background color of the Stage, disable sounds, and loop the movie. Open the Control Panel by selecting Control Panel from the Window menu **(Figure 2)** or by pressing Command-2. The buttons of the Control Panel correspond to commands in the Edit menu.

CONTROL PANEL BUTTONS

Figure 2. Choose **Control Panel** from the **Window** menu.

Figure 3. The Rewind button.

Rewind

Click the Rewind button (Command-R) to reset the movie to frame 1 **(Figure 3)**. Doing so during playback automatically stops the movie and rewinds to frame 1.

Figure 4. The Step Backward button.

Step Backward

Step Backward (Command-Left Arrow) steps the movie back one frame at a time **(Figure 4)**. Holding down this button steps backward continuously.

Figure 5. The Stop button.

Stop

Stop (Command-.) stops the movie **(Figure 5)**.

Step Forward

Step Forward (Command-Right Arrow) steps the movie forward one frame at a time **(Figure 6)**. Hold down this button to step forward continuously.

When a Score channel is in Step Recording mode, click Step Forward to copy the contents of the current frame to the next frame. *(See page 157 on Step Recording)*

Figure 6. The Step Forward button.

Play

Play (Command-P) starts the movie **(Figure 7)**. Holding down the Shift key while clicking Play hides all windows and the menu bar until the movie is stopped.

Figure 7. The Play button.

Disable Sounds

Click Disable Sounds (Command-~) to alternately turn your movie's sound off and on **(Figure 8)**.

Sound enabled   Sound disabled

Figure 8.

Loop

Loop (Command-L) controls whether your movie will repeat over and over **(Figure 9)**. If this button is selected, your movie will automatically start over from frame 1 each time it reaches the last frame. Loop is on by default.

Loop enabled (default)

Loop disabled

Figure 9.

Selected Frames Only

Selected Frames Only (Command-\) allows you to play a portion of the current movie **(Figure 10)**. First, open the Score window and select the frames you wish to playback. Then click the Selected Frames Only button. A green bar appears in the Score window above the selected frames. Now when you click the Play button, only these marked frames will play. Click the Selected Frames Only button again to remove the green bar and turn off the selection.

Selected Frames Only enabled

Selected Frames Only disabled

Figure 10.

Control Panel Buttons

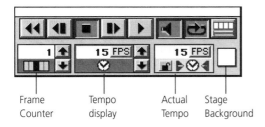

Frame Counter   Tempo display   Actual Tempo   Stage Background

Figure 11. The Frame Counter.

Figure 12. The Tempo display.

CONTROL PANEL INDICATORS

Frame Counter

The Frame Counter indicates which frame of your movie is currently displayed on the Stage **(Figure 11)**. This corresponds to the Playback head indicator in the Score window *(see page 38)*. Click the up or down arrows to step forward or backward through the frames just like the Step Forward and Step Backward buttons. Hold down the up or down arrows to step forward or backward continuously through the frames. You can also enter a frame number to jump to by clicking the displayed frame number and typing a value.

Tempo display

The Tempo display indicates the preset tempo that the current frame should play at, in frames per second **(Figure 12)**. Director will never play a given frame faster than this tempo, but may play slower because of performance limitations of your computer *(see the "Actual Tempo" section on page 66)*. You can change this target tempo setting for each frame by clicking the up or down arrows, or by clicking the displayed tempo number and typing a value. If a tempo setting has been entered in the tempo channel of the Score at a certain frame, that value will be indicated here *(see page 199 for details on the Tempo channel)*. If no such tempo setting has been made, the Tempo display field displays a default value.

ACTUAL TEMPO

The Actual Tempo display **(Figure 13)** indicates the *actual* duration of the current frame in frames per second. The actual tempo of your frames can fall behind the set or desired tempo shown in the Tempo display, due to speed limitations of your computer.

Figure 13. The Actual Tempo display.

To compare the set tempo to the actual tempo:

You can step through a movie frame-by-frame and compare the set tempo in the Tempo display to the actual tempo. Since Macintosh computers can vary in speed performance, some of them may not keep up with your set tempo. If you plan to run your movie on a wide range of Macintoshes, comparing the set tempo to the actual tempo on a slower Macintosh allows you to set appropriate tempo values for the frames, so that the actual tempo never falls below the set tempo. *(See the Tempo chapter for more details)*

1. Open the Control Panel by choosing Control Panel from the Window menu **(Figure 14)**.

2. Click Rewind to reset the movie to the first frame.

3. Click the Step Forward button and compare the number shown in the Tempo display to the number in the Actual Tempo display **(Figure 15)**.

4. Use the arrows in the Tempo display to set new tempo values for the frames.

Figure 14. Choose **Control Panel** from the **Window** menu.

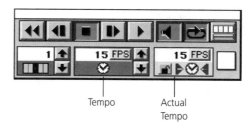

Tempo   Actual Tempo

Figure 15. In the **Control Panel**, compare the set tempo value of each frame to the *actual* tempo of each frame.

Actual Tempo vs. Set Tempo

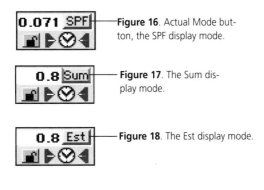

Figure 16. Actual Mode button, the SPF display mode.

Figure 17. The Sum display mode.

Figure 18. The Est display mode.

Figure 19. Two dashes in the Actual Tempo Display indicate that no tempo value was recorded previously for the current frame.

Figure 20. Choose **Control Panel** from the **Window** menu.

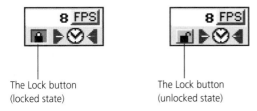

The Lock button (locked state)

The Lock button (unlocked state)

Figure 21. Use the Lock button to lock or unlock your movie's playback speed.

Actual Mode button:

Click the Actual mode button to change the Actual Tempo display to seconds per frame (SPF) **(Figure 16)** instead of frames per second (FPS). Click it again for the Sum display **(Figure 17)**, which indicates the total elapsed time in seconds from the start of your movie to the current frame. Click once more for the Est display **(Figure 18)**, which is similar to the Sum display but more accurate since it includes palette changes and transitions in its calculation of the frame durations. The display mode you select is saved with your movie.

✔ Tip

■ Don't leave your Actual Tempo display in Est mode while playing back your movie, since Est mode can lower playback speed due to its more intensive calculations.

To lock and unlock your movie's playback speed:

If your movie's playback speed is locked during playback, the Actual Tempo display shows previously recorded tempo values for each frame and the frames play at those tempo values. If no values were recorded previously, two dashes are displayed **(Figure 19)**. *(See pages 202-204 in the Tempo chapter for more details on locking your movie's playback speed)*

1. Open the Control Panel by choosing Control Panel from the Window menu **(Figure 20)**.

2. Click the Lock button in the Control Panel to lock or unlock your movie's playback speed **(Figure 21)**.

Actual Mode Button, Lock Playback Speed

Stage Background

Use the Stage Background color chip to change the Stage's background color **(Figure 22)**. Click and hold the color chip to display the color palette **(Figure 23)**, and select a new color for the background using the pointer.

Figure 22. The Stage Background color chip.

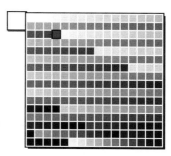

Figure 23. Click the Stage Background color chip to display and select from the current color palette.

Paint Window.

The Paint window is used throughout this chapter. Choose Paint from the Window menu to open it **(Figure 1)** or press Command-5.

Window	
Stage	⌘1
Control Panel	⌘2
Cast	⌘3
Score	⌘4
Paint	⌘5
Text	⌘6
Tools	⌘7
Color Palettes	⌘8
Digital Video	⌘9
Script	⌘0
Message	⌘M
Tweak	
Markers	
Duplicate Window	

Figure 1. Choose **Paint** from the **Window** menu.

D irector's Paint window provides numerous tools such as the Air brush, Paint Bucket, and Lasso for creating and editing bitmap cast member graphics **(Figure 2)**. These tools aren't elaborate as the Adobe Photoshop or MacDraw Pro tools, but are robust enough to create many of the cast members you're likely to showcase in your movies. Use Director's Tools window **(Figure 3)** to create QuickDraw graphics. *(See page 109 in the Tools window chapter for details)*

The Paint window offers an **Effects** menu, containing numerous special-effects commands that can be applied to your artwork, such as Rotate, Distort, Slant, and Perspective.

This chapter covers all the tools in the Paint window tool palette as well as the commands in the Effects and Paint menus.

Figure 2. The **Paint** window.

Figure 3. The **Tools** window.

The Paint Window

THE PAINT WINDOW

The link between the Paint and Cast windows:

It's important to know that when you create a graphic in Director's Paint window, that graphic also becomes a cast member in Director's Cast window **(Figures 4-5)**.

In fact, the Paint window shares a dynamic link with the Cast window. From the Cast window, you can double-click a bitmap cast member and it automatically opens in the Paint window. And from the Paint window, you can access all the bitmap cast members in the Cast window by clicking the Previous and Next buttons in the window's upper left corner **(Figure 4)**.

To add a new cast member in the Paint window:

1. Click the Add button to create a new cast member **(Figure 4)**. Director displays an empty easel in the Paint window and the image you draw is placed into the first available position in the Cast window as soon as you close the Paint window.

To place a graphic onto the Stage from the Paint window:

1. Drag the Place button onto the Stage and Director places the image from the current easel onto the Stage and into the Score.

To work with multiple cast members in the Paint window:

Director's Paint window allows you to work with either one or multiple cast members at a time. Each cast member is displayed in what's known as an **easel**—the area of the Paint window in which

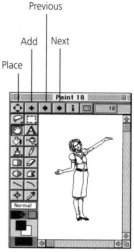

Figure 4. Objects drawn in the Paint window automatically become new cast members, as shown below in the Cast window.

Figure 5. The Cast window.

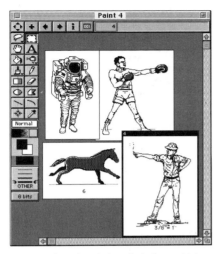

Figure 6. The Paint window displaying multiple easels.

Figure 7. Choose **Paint Window Options** from the **Paint** menu.

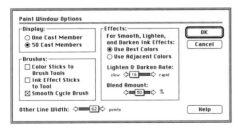

Figure 8. In the **Paint Window Options** dialog box, click the **50 Cast Members** radio button.

you draw **(Figure 6)**. To work with multiple cast members in the Paint window, follow these steps:

1. Open the Paint window by choosing Paint from the Window menu.

2. Choose Paint Window Options from the Paint menu **(Figure 7)**.

3. In the Paint Window Options dialog box, click the 50 Cast Members radio button to select it **(Figure 8)**.

4. Click OK to close the dialog box. Now up to 50 cast members can be displayed in the Paint window.

5. You make an easel active by clicking it; you can reposition an easel by dragging it by the thick bar at the top.

6. To create additional easels, click the Add button in the upper-left corner of the Paint window.

PAINT TOOL PALETTE

Director provides an assortment of painting tools used to create and modify bitmap cast members. These tools are located in the Paint tool palette, which is found on the left side of the Paint window **(Figure 9)**.

Figure 9. The Paint tool palette is found on the left side of the Paint window.

Lasso and Selection Rectangle tools:

Like most Macintosh paint programs, Director's Paint window features a Selection Rectangle and a Lasso that allow you to select all or just parts of cast member artwork. Once artwork has been selected, you can use the Paint window's other tools to modify the selection—for instance, drag it to another region of the Paint window, cut or copy it, rotate it, change its colors, distort it, and so on.

While the two tools work similarly, there is one important difference between them: The Selection Rectangle allows you to select only rectangular regions of artwork, while the Lasso selects any region you "draw" with the mouse, which gives you much greater flexibility in making artwork selections. Another difference is that some of Director's other paint features work only with artwork selected by the Selection Rectangle, not by the Lasso (or vice versa). These instances are identified later in the chapter.

Figure 10. The Selection Rectangle tool.

To select artwork with the Selection Rectangle

1. Click the Selection Rectangle tool in the Paint tool palette **(Figure 10)**.

2. The mouse pointer becomes a crosshair. Position the crosshair wherever you want to begin your selection.

3. Drag the pointer up or down and to one side to outline a rectangular selection around your artwork **(Figure 11)**.

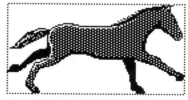

Figure 11. Drag the pointer to outline a rectangular selection or "marquee" around your artwork.

Figure 12. To stretch or compress an artwork selection, hold the Command key, click anywhere in the selection and drag.

Figure 13. Click and hold the Selection Rectangle tool until the **Options** pop-up menu appears.

You'll see a dotted line called a "marquee" encase your artwork selection.

4. Release the mouse button to select the artwork within the marquee.

✔ **Tips**

- You can reposition your artwork selection by moving the mouse to the selection marquee (the crosshair becomes a pointer again) and dragging the artwork to a new area.

- Hold down the Option key while dragging an artwork selection to drag a copy of it, leaving the original in place.

- To stretch or compress an artwork selection, hold down the Command key, click anywhere in the selection and drag **(Figure 12)**. To stretch or compress while keeping the image's original proportions, hold down the Command and Shift keys while dragging.

- To erase a selection, press the Backspace or Delete key. Also, you can double-click the Selection Rectangle tool to select the entire visible portion of the Paint window.

To choose Selection Rectangle options:

You can control how the Selection Rectangle behaves when selecting artwork.

1. Click the Selection Rectangle tool in the Paint tool palette. Hold the mouse button down until the Options pop-up menu appears **(Figure 13)**.

2. Drag to select one of the four options in the menu. Your choices are Shrink, No Shrink, Lasso, and See Thru Lasso.

Shrink makes the selection marquee tighten around whatever object you've selected, although the selection still keeps its rectangular shape. Director identifies an object's border within a selection by looking for color differences between pixels.

No Shrink selects all the artwork that you encased with the selection marquee.

Lasso makes the selection marquee tighten around whatever object you've selected but allows the selection area to take on an irregular shape, as if you had actually used the Lasso tool.

See Thru Lasso is similar to the Lasso option, but it makes all white pixels in your selection become transparent.

To select artwork with the Lasso tool:

1. Click the Lasso tool icon in the Paint tool palette **(Figure 14)**.

2. The mouse pointer turns into a lasso when you move it inside the Paint window. Position the Lasso wherever you want to begin your selection.

3. Drag the Lasso to draw a line around the art you wish to select **(Figure 15)**. Try to end your selection at the point where you started it.

4. Release the mouse button and Director highlights the selected area with the marquee. If you did not entirely encase your selection, Director automatically connects its starting and ending points.

✔ Tips

■ You can use the Lasso tool to select a polygonal shape. Hold the Option key while dragging the Lasso to create an anchor point and draw a straight selection line. Repeat this step to encase your artwork with such lines. double-click to end your selection.

Figure 14. The Lasso tool.

Figure 15. Drag the Lasso to draw a line around the artwork you wish to select.

■ You can reposition your artwork selection by positioning the Lasso within the selection (the Lasso becomes a mouse pointer again), and dragging the artwork to a new location. If you hold down the Option key, you drag a copy of the artwork, leaving the original in place.

To choose Lasso options:

You can control how the Lasso behaves when selecting artwork.

1. Click the Lasso tool icon in the Paint tool palette. Hold the mouse button down until the Options pop-up menu appears **(Figure 16)**.

2. Drag to select one of the three options in the menu. Your choices are Shrink, No Shrink, and See Thru.

Shrink, which is the default setting for the Lasso tool, makes the selection marquee tighten around whatever object you've selected. Director tries to identify an objects border by looking for color differences between pixels. The idea is to "fine-tune" the selection you made by hand.

No Shrink selects all the artwork that you encase with the Lasso and does not fine-tune the selection.

See Thru makes all the white pixels in your selection become transparent.

Figure 16. Click and hold the Lasso tool to display the **Options** pop-up menu.

Hand tool

The Hand tool is used to move an image around in the Paint window **(Figure 17)**. Click the Hand tool then drag the image in the Paint window to move it in any direction. A shortcut for selecting the Hand tool is pressing the spacebar in the Paint window and clicking the mouse.

Figure 17. The Hand tool.

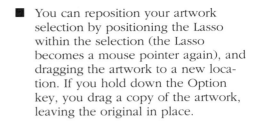

Lasso Options, Hand Tool

Text tool

The Text tool allows you to enter bitmap text anywhere within the Paint window **(Figure 18)**. Simply click the Text tool icon and then click the desired location in the Paint window where text should be entered. A blinking cursor box appears. The text's font, size, and style can be modified in the text menu *(see the Creating Text chapter on page 177 for details on setting text attributes)*. Once the bitmap text has been entered, there is no way of changing the font, size, or style of the text. Any effects or color changes can be applied to bitmap text just like to a regular bitmap image.

Figure 18. The Text tool.

Paint Bucket

Position the Paint bucket **(Figure 19)** over empty space in your artwork and click to fill the space with the selected foreground color.

Figure 19. The Paint bucket tool.

Air Brush

Drag the Air brush **(Figure 20)** to "spray" paint in the selected foreground color, and pattern if any. A variety of Air brush settings allow you to specify the size and density of the Air brush's spray. *(See page 101)*

Figure 20. The Air bush tool.

Paint Brush

The Paint brush tool **(Figure 21)** allows you to paint in the selected foreground color and pattern by dragging the mouse across the Paint window. You can choose from a variety of brush shapes and design your own as well. *(See page 99)*

Figure 21. The Paint brush tool.

Pencil

Drag the Pencil tool **(Figure 22)** to draw single pixels in the selected foreground color. Drawing over existing pixels in the foreground color will change the pixels to the selected background color.

Figure 22. The Pencil tool.

Figure 23. The Rectangle tool.

Figure 24. The Erase tool.

Figure 25. The Ellipse tool.

Figure 26. The Polygon tool.

Rectangle tool

Select the Rectangle tool **(Figure 23)**, then drag the pointer to outline a rectangle shape. Hold down the Shift key while dragging to draw a perfect square. When you release the mouse button, the rectangle is drawn in the Paint window. Notice that the Rectangle tool icon is hollow on the left side, and filled on the right. Click either side of this icon to choose whether the rectangle will be hollow—just a border—or filled with the selected foreground color, and pattern if any.

Eraser

Erase a portion of an image by dragging the Eraser tool **(Figure 24)** across it. Double-click the Eraser tool to clear the entire image in the Paint window.

Ellipse tool

Select the Ellipse tool **(Figure 25)**, then drag the mouse to size the ellipse's outline. Hold down the Shift key while dragging to draw a perfect circle. When you release the mouse button, the ellipse is drawn in the Paint window. Notice that the Ellipse tool icon is hollow on the left side, and filled on the right. Click either side of this icon to choose whether your ellipse will be hollow—just a border—or filled with the selected foreground color and pattern, if any.

Polygon tool

Select the Polygon tool **(Figure 26)**, then click the mouse to draw straight lines that make up a polygon. Each mouse click draws a new line in the polygon, starting from the last line's ending point and ending where the mouse pointer is positioned. Double-click to draw the polygon's final line segment that connects the first and last lines together. Notice that the Polygon tool icon is hollow on the left side, and filled on the right. When selecting the tool, click either side of this icon to choose whether the polygon will be hollow—just a border—or filled with the selected foreground color and pattern, if any.

Line tool

The Line tool **(Figure 27)** is used to draw straight lines. Drag to set any angle for your line. Hold the Shift key while dragging to draw 45 degree lines, and hold the Option key while dragging to drag lines in the currently selected pattern. Click the Line width selector in the tool palette to change the thickness of the line.

Figure 27. The Line tool.

Arc tool

The Arc tool **(Figure 28)** draws one quarter of an ellipse. Drag to preview the length and angle of your arc, and release the mouse button to draw it. Hold the Shift key while dragging to draw 45 degree arcs, and hold the Option key while dragging to draw an arc in the currently selected pattern.

Figure 28. The Arc tool.

Registration Points

When you create a number of different cast members for an animation, there's a chance that the cast members will not all be aligned exactly, so that when they are animated in a sequence, they may appear to jump and shift from one frame to the next. To avoid this problem, you can set a registration point by which all cast members in an animation are aligned. These registration points help ensure that an animation plays smoothly throughout all its frames. For instance, if you were animating several frames of an athlete running, you could set registration points where the character's feet touch the ground. The frames of the animation could then be aligned to these points, ensuring that the runner's feet never hit

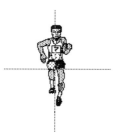

Figure 29. A cast member with its registration point shown in the Paint window.

Figure 30. The Registration tool.

Figure 31. The Registration point here has been moved downward.

above or below groundlevel. (See *"To align cast members' registration points"* on *page 80)*

Every graphical cast member in your movie already has a registration point, which is placed directly at its center **(Figure 29)**. You can view the point by opening a cast member in the Paint window and then clicking the Registration tool **(Figure 30)** located toward the bottom of the Paint tool palette. You can easily reset the registration point to appear at any other given point.

To set a new registration point:

1. Open a cast member within Director's Paint window. If the Paint window is set to display multiple easels, *(see pages 70-71)*, click the particular easel containing the cast member you wish to register.

2. Click the Registration tool in the Paint tool palette to select it **(Figure 30)**. The current registration point assigned to the cast member appears at the intersection of the dotted lines.

3. Move the crosshair pointer to a new location in the Paint window, and click to place the registration mark in this new location **(Figure 31)**.

✔ Tip

■ If you ever want to reset a registration point to its default position (that is, directly at the center of the cast member), double-click the Registration tool in the Paint tool palette.

To align cast members' registration points:

You can align multiple cast members so that their registration points line up exactly on top of each other. Once you have done so, you can use the Paint window's Previous and Next buttons to flip back and forth between the cast members and test the smoothness of the animation they create. If the cast members still need better registration, you can readjust their registration points individually, realign the entire lot, and test again.

1. Choose Cast from the Window menu **(Figure 32)**.

2. Select the cast members that you wish to align by Shift-clicking them to make multiple selections. The cast members of a particular animation sequence should be arranged together in the Cast window, with no unrelated cast members positioned between them. To reposition cast members in the Cast window, simply drag them to new positions.

3. Choose Align Bitmaps from the Cast window **(Figure 33)**. You can now open Director's Paint window, and use the Previous and Next buttons to test how well the cast members are aligned with one another.

Eyedropper

The Eyedropper tool is used to "pick up" and match colors **(Figure 34)**. Click the Eyedropper anywhere in the Paint window, and the color it is positioned on becomes the new foreground color. Hold the Control key while clicking to change any tool into the Eyedropper. *(See page 86 on switching colors with the Eyedropper)*

Figure 32. Choose **Cast** from the **Window** menu.

Figure 33. Choose **Align Bitmaps** from the **Cast** window.

Figure 34. The Eyedropper tool.

The Ink effects selector.

Figure 35.

Figure 36. Click and hold the Ink effects selector to display the **Ink effects** pop-up menu.

To choose an Ink effect:

Director features a wide variety of **Ink effects** that can be applied to the artwork you create in the Paint window (some of the effects include Reverse, Transparent, Smooth, Smear, Smudge, Darken, and Lighten). These effects are applied through a specific paint tool (such as the Paint bucket or Paint brush), and Director remembers which Ink effect each tool paints with.

1. In Director's Paint window, select the tool in the Paint tool palette that you wish to apply an Ink effect with (for instance, the Paint brush or Air brush).

2. Click and hold the Ink effects selector in the Paint tool palette. The Ink effects pop-up menu appears **(Figures 35-36)**.

3. From the pop-up menu, choose the Ink effect that you wish to use with the selected paint tool and release the mouse button. *(For a description of the various Ink effects available, see below)*

Note: You can also apply Ink effects to cast members via the Score window. This is different from using Ink effects in the Paint window, where you apply the effects through a particular paint tool. Applying Ink effects via Director's Score affects an entire sprite and can create a very different visual effect. *(See page 54-58 about using Ink effects in the Score window)*

Normal

Normal is the default ink setting. The current foreground color and pattern are used with the tools in the Paint window.

Ink Effects in Paint Window

Transparent

Transparent ink makes the background color used in patterns transparent. This allows you to see objects behind the pattern.

Reverse

Reverse ink reverses the foreground color, that is, black pixels become white, and white pixels turn black as they are painted over. Reverses other colors as well.

Ghost

Ghost ink paints with the current background color.

Gradient

Gradient allows you to paint with a blend of colors, ranging from the current foreground color to the current gradient destination color. The gradient options are set in the Gradient dialog box.

Reveal

Reveal ink makes use of the previous cast member. As you paint with reveal ink, you uncover the previous cast member in its original foreground color.

Cycle

Cycle ink works only with the Paint brush tool. As you paint, the color cycles through all the colors in the color palette between the current foreground color and destination color. Choose black and white for the foreground and destination colors to cycle through the entire color palette.

Switch

As you paint with Switch ink, any pixels in the current foreground color that you paint over are changed into the destination color.

Blend

Blend is a transparent ink. As you paint over your artwork, it will still be visible, but its colors are blended with the current foreground color. You can set the percentage of blend in the Paint Window Options dialog box.

Darkest

As you paint over an image with Darkest ink, Director compares the level of darkness of the foreground color to the pixels that you are painting over. If the foreground color is darker, the pixels of the image are replaced with its color.

Lightest

As you paint over an image with Lightest ink, Director replaces the pixels with the foreground color where the foreground color is lighter than the pixels of the image.

Darken

Darken ink reduces the brightness of artwork as you paint over it. You can set the rate of this Ink effect in the Paint Window Options dialog box.

Lighten

Lighten ink increases the brightness of artwork as you paint over it.

Smooth

Smooth ink blurs artwork as you paint over it. It has an effect only on existing artwork.

Smear

Smear ink causes the paint of your artwork to spread or smear as you drag the Paint brush across it. The smear occurs in the direction you drag the Paint brush.

Ink Effects in Paint Window

Smudge

Similar to Smear ink, except the colors fade faster as they are smudged.

Spread

Spread ink works with the Paint brush. As you drag the brush across your artwork, whatever image is originally under the brush is picked up and becomes the new shape for the Paint brush.

Clipboard

Uses the contents of the clipboard as the pattern for your brush.

To set the width of a line or border:

You can easily change the width of a line or border drawn by the Paint window's Line, Rectangle, Arc, Ellipse, and Polygon tools.

1. In Director's Paint tool palette, click a line style in the Line width selector (arrows will border the line currently selected) **(Figure 37)**. Click the dotted line item in the selector to draw filled shapes with no border. The **OTHER** selection will use a custom line thickness that you can define in the Paint window's Options dialog box.

2. From the tool palette, select one of Director's shape tools (either the Line, Rectangle, Arc, Ellipse, or Polygon tools will work). When you begin to draw with the tool, it will use the line thickness you just selected.

✔ Tip

■ To create a custom line width, choose Paint Window Options from the Paint menu, and use the scroll bar at the bottom of the dialog box to set the line thickness **(Figures 38-39)**. This value will be used when you choose **OTHER** from the Line width selector in step 1. You can double-click the Line width selector to open the Paint Window Options box.

Figure 37. The Line width selector.

Figure 38. Choose **Paint Window Options** from the **Paint** menu.

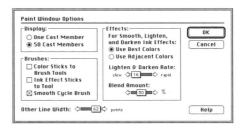

Figure 39. In the **Paint Window Options** dialog box, use the scroll bar at the bottom to set the custom line width.

COLORS, PATTERNS, AND GRADIENTS

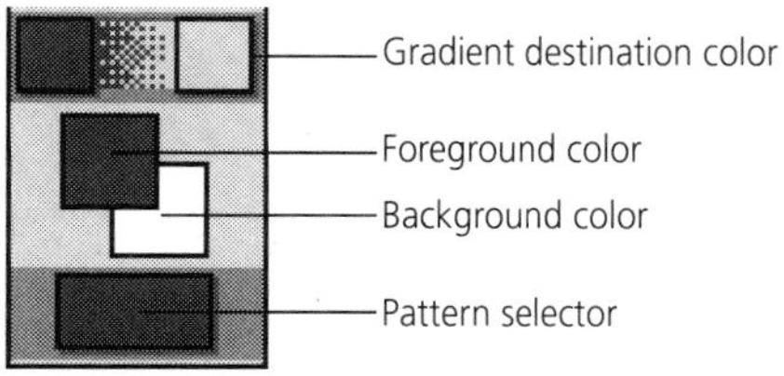

Color Basics

There are three kinds of color specifications that you can use to color cast member artwork. **Foreground** color is Director's primary color specification: Whatever color is selected as your foreground color will be used to color all the artwork you create with Director's Paint tools (for instance, the Paint brush, the Air brush, and the Pencil). The foreground color is also used to color solid patterns, and used as the primary color in multicolored patterns. Director's **background** color, on the other hand, is used as the secondary color in multicolored patterns. Finally, the **gradient destination** color is used in conjunction with the foreground color to create a blended color spectrum.

The current foreground color, background and gradient destination colors, and the pattern selector are all displayed in the Paint tool palette **(Figure 40)**.

Gradient destination color

Foreground color

Background color

Pattern selector

Figure 40. Color and Pattern selectors are displayed in the Paint tool palette.

Foreground color chip

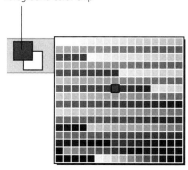

Figure 41. Click and hold the Foreground color chip until the pop-up color palette appears.

To choose the foreground color:

1. Click the Foreground color chip in Director's Paint tool palette and do not release the mouse button. A pop-up color palette appears **(Figure 41)**.

2. Drag to the desired color and release the mouse button. The highlighted color becomes Director's new foreground color, and is displayed by the Foreground color chip in the Paint tool palette.

✔ Tip

■ You can also double-click the Foreground color chip to display its pop-up color palette.

Set Foreground Color

To choose the background color:

1. Click and hold the Background color chip in the Paint tool palette. A pop-up color palette appears **(Figure 42)**.

2. Drag to the desired color and release the mouse button. The highlighted color becomes Director's new background color and is displayed by the Background color chip.

✔ Tip

■ You can double-click the Background color chip to display its pop-up color palette.

To choose the gradient destination color:

1. In Director's tool palette, click and hold the rightmost side of the gradient destination selector. A pop-up color palette appears **(Figure 43)**.

2. Drag to the desired color and release the mouse button. The highlighted color becomes the new gradient destination color and is displayed on the rightmost side of the gradient destination selector.

To switch a particular color in a cast member:

Director makes it easy to isolate a particular color in a cast member and then switch that color with any color of your choice.

1. Make sure that your cast member is displayed in Director's Paint window.

2. Click the Eyedropper in the tool palette **(Figure 44)**.

3. Move the Eyedropper over the particular color in your cast member that you wish to switch and click the mouse **(Figure 45)**. The Eyedropper "picks up" the color and designates it the new foreground color in the Paint window. You can look at the

Background color chip

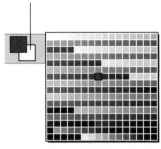

Figure 42. Click and hold the Background color chip until the pop-up color palette appears.

Gradient destination selector

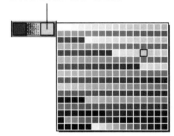

Figure 43. Click and hold the Gradient destination selector until a pop-up color palette appears.

Figure 44. The Eyedropper tool

Figure 45. Place the Eyedropper over the particular color that you wish to switch and click the mouse.

Background & Gradient Destination Colors

Figure 46. Choose **Switch Colors** from the **Effects** menu.

Figure 47. Choose **Transform Bitmap** from the **Cast** menu.

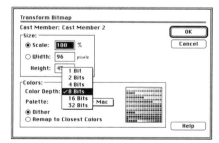

Figure 48. In the **Transform Bitmap** dialog box, use the **Color Depth** pop-up menu to select the desired cast member color depth.

Foreground color chip in the tool palette to make sure that it now displays the color that you want to switch.

4. In the tool palette, click and hold the rightmost side of the gradient destination selector. A pop-up color palette appears.

5. Drag the pointer to the color you wish to select and release the mouse button. You have now chosen the new color that you wish to switch your cast member to.

6. Use the Selection Rectangle or Lasso tool to select the portion of your image where the color switch should take place.

7. Choose Switch Colors from Director's Effects menu **(Figure 46)**. Director switches all colors that match the Foreground color chip to the gradient destination color (which you just set).

To set a cast member's color depth:

Director allows you to set a cast member's **color depth**—in other words, it lets you define how many colors the cast member will be painted in. The common choice is 8-bit or 256 colors. Also available are 1-bit (black and white), 2 bit (four colors), 4-bit (16 colors), 16-bit (about 65,000 colors), and 32-bit (about 16 million colors). The lower the cast member's color depth, the less memory it uses, and the quicker it animates.

1. With the Paint window open, choose Transform Bitmap from the Cast menu **(Figure 47)**.

2. In the Transform Bitmap dialog box, use the Color Depth pop-up menu to select the new depth for the cast member currently in the Paint window **(Figure 48)**.

3. Click OK to apply the new color depth to your cast member.

✓ **Tip**

■ Remember that if you would like to
create a cast member in a high color
depth such as 16 or 32 bits, your
Macintosh must be capable of displaying that many colors. To set your
Macintosh to work at the desired
color depth, choose Control Panels
from the Apple menu **(Figure 49)**,
and double-click the Monitors icon. In
the Monitors dialog box, set your
monitor to display the number of colors that matches the color depth of
your cast member **(Figure 50)**.

To choose a pattern:

You can use some of Director's paint
tools (such as the Paint bucket, Paint
brush, and Air brush) to paint with a certain pattern instead of with a solid color.

1. Click and hold the Pattern selector in
Director's Paint tool palette. A pop-up
Pattern palette appears **(Figure 51)**.
There are four different pattern
palettes that you can choose from. To
change the palette that the Pattern
selector displays, set a new palette in
Director's Patterns dialog box. *(See
page 89 for more information)*

2. Drag to the desired pattern and
release the mouse button. The highlighted pattern becomes selected and
is displayed by the Pattern selector in
the Paint tool palette.

✓ **Tip**

■ Double-click the Pattern selector to
open Director's Patterns dialog box,
where you can edit patterns or select
a different pattern palette to work
with.

Figure 49. Choose
Control Panels
from the **Apple**
menu.

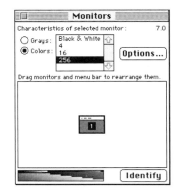

Figure 50. In the **Monitors** dialog
box, set your monitor display to
match the color depth of your cast
member.

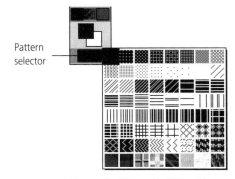

Pattern
selector

Figure 51. Click and hold the Pattern
Selector to display the pop-up **Pattern**
palette.

Pattern Selector

Figure 52. Choose
Patterns from the **Paint**
menu.

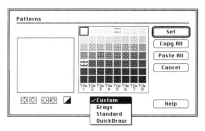

Figure 53. In the **Patterns** dialog box, click
the pop-up menu and select the Custom menu
item.

Pattern edit box

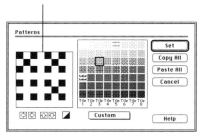

Figure 54. Click the custom pattern that you
wish to edit. An enlarged version of the pattern appears in the pattern edit box.

To edit or create a pattern:

1. With Director's Paint window open,
choose Patterns from the Paint menu
(Figure 52). As a shortcut, you can
double-click the Pattern selector icon
in the Paint tool palette.

2. In the Patterns dialog box, click the
pop-up menu and select the Custom
menu item **(Figure 53)**. Director features four sets of patterns: Three
sets—Grays, Standard and
QuickDraw—are always available to
you and cannot be changed and a
Custom set that can be edited.

3. Click a custom pattern that you wish
to edit. An enlarged version of the
selected pattern appears in the pattern
edit box **(Figure 54)**.

4. In the pattern edit box, click any open
space to place a black pixel in the pattern. Click an existing pixel to make it
white.

5. Click the directional arrows to move
the pattern shape up, down, and sideways.

6. When you're happy with your custom
pattern, click the Set button, and
Director adds the edited pattern to its
custom pattern library.

Edit or Create a Pattern

You can store sets of custom patterns by copying them to and from the Macintosh Scrapbook **(Figure 55)**.

To copy your custom pattern library to the Scrapbook:

1. Click the Copy All button in the Patterns dialog box **(Figure 56)**; this stores the pattern information in the Clipboard

2. Click Cancel

3. Open the Scrapbook (choose Scrapbook under the Apple menu).

4. Choose Paste under the Edit menu to store the patterns there.

To reinstall stored patterns from the Scrapbook:

1. Open the Scrapbook and find the Scrapbook entry that contains the desired patterns.

2. Choose Copy from the Edit menu.

3. Return to Director's Paint window, open the Patterns dialog box, and click the Paste All button to install the copied pattern set.

✔ Tips

■ Even though you can't directly edit the patterns contained in Director's Grays, Standards, and QuickDraw patterns, you can copy those predefined patterns into Director's Custom set, and edit them from there. From the Patterns dialog box, use the pattern pop-up menu to select one of Director's noneditable pattern sets, and then click the Copy All button. Choose the Custom pattern set from the pattern pop-up menu. Click the Paste All button, and Director copies the first set of patterns to the Custom set. You can now edit them freely.

■ Director lets you "pick up" a pattern displayed in its Paint window, and edit it in the Patterns dialog box. To do so, open the Patterns dialog box and click any pattern outside the box.

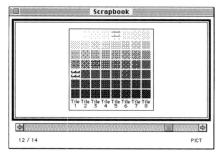

Figure 55. Your custom patterns can be stored in the Macintosh Scrapbook.

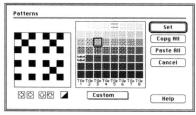

Figure 56. Click the Copy All button in the **Patterns** dialog box.

Figure 57. A sample gradient.

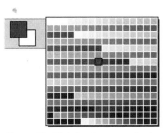

Figure 58. Click the Foreground color chip and select a color to begin the gradient with.

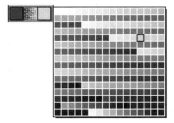

Figure 59. Click the right chip of the gradient destination selector, and choose a color that your gradient will blend to.

Normal
Transprnt
Reverse
Ghost
Gradient
Reveal
Cycle
Switch
Blend
Darkest
Lightest
Darken
Lighten
Smooth
Smear
Smudge
Spread
Clipboard

Figure 60. Click the Ink effects Selector and choose Gradient from the pop-up menu.

To create a gradient:

You can paint your artwork with a **gradient**, which is a blend of many colors that you define. Setting up a gradient is simple: You define the foreground color, which is the color that Director begins the blend with, and then define a gradient destination color, which is the color that the foreground color will be blended through. Director can then automatically blend the two colors to display all the colors in between **(Figure 57)**. A good use of a gradient would be to create a sunset, where the colors blend from red to yellow.

Gradient colors can be used with a number of Director's paint tools, including the Paint brush, Paint bucket, Ellipse, Rectangle, and Polygon tools.

1. In Director's Paint window, select the painting tool that you wish to apply the gradient color to (for instance, the Paint brush or Paint bucket).

2. Click the Foreground color chip in the Paint window and select a color from the pop-up color palette **(Figure 58)**. This will be the color that the gradient begins with.

3. Click the right side of the gradient destination selector and choose a color from the pop-up color palette. This is the color that your gradient will blend to **(Figure 59)**.

4. Click the Ink effects selector in the Paint window, and choose Gradient from the pop-up menu **(Figure 60)**. The paint tool that you selected in step 1 will now paint with a gradient rather than a solid color.

✔ Tip

■ To stop painting with a gradient, simply choose the Normal Ink effect from the Ink effects pop-up menu.

Create a Gradient

To specify additional settings for a gradient:

Director gives you a significant degree of control over the type of color gradient it produces. For instance, you can control the direction in which the gradient fills a given area (from the top, the bottom, the side, and so on), and the "spread" of the gradient (whether the colors are spread evenly throughout the area, or concentrated in certain areas).

1. In the Paint window, choose Gradients from the Paint menu **(Figure 61)**.

2. In the Gradients dialog box, use the Foreground color chip and gradient destination selector to select the colors used to create your gradient **(Figure 62)**. *(See "To create a gradient" on page 91 for more information)*

3. Use the dialog box's pop-up menus to fine-tune the behavior of your gradient. Gradient options are described below:

Direction

Use the Direction pop-up menu to control the direction in which your gradient fills a particular area **(Figure 63)**. The directional possibilities include straightforward selections such as **Top to Bottom** and **Bottom to Top**, as well as three unique options. **Directional** allows you to set a custom direction for the gradient with whatever paint tool you are using to apply the gradient. For instance, if you are using the Paint bucket to fill an area with a gradient, a directional line appears as soon as you click the Paint bucket in the Paint window. Move the directional line in the desired direction, and click to begin your gradient fill. **Shape Burst** creates a gradient that starts at the outer edges of an area, and then fills inward while following the contours of the area **(Figure 64)**.

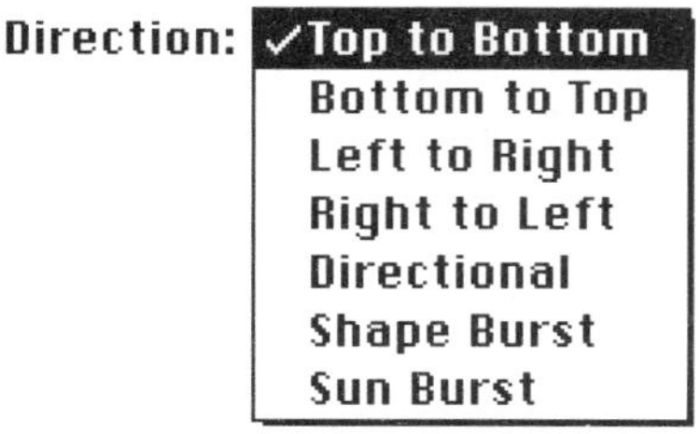

Figure 61. Choose **Gradients** from the **Paint** menu.

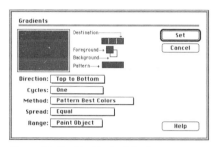

Figure 62. The **Gradients** dialog box.

Figure 63. The **Direction** pop-up menu.

Figure 64. A Shape Burst gradient.

Figure 65. A Sun Burst gradient.

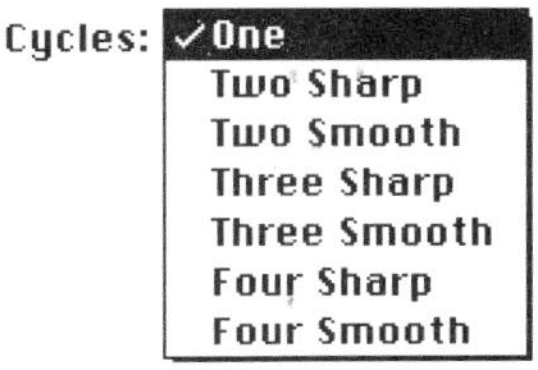

Figure 66. The **Cycles** pop-up menu.

Figure 67. A Two Sharp gradient.

Figure 68. A Two Smooth gradient.

Method: ✓**Pattern Best Colors**
Pattern Best Colors See Thru
Pattern Adjacent Colors
Pattern Adjacent Colors See Thru
Dither Best Colors
Dither Adjacent Colors
Dither Two Colors
Dither One Color
Standard Dither
Multi Dither

Figure 69. The **Method** pop-up menu.

Sun Burst begins a gradient at the outer edges of an area, and moves toward the center in concentric circles **(Figure 65)**.

Cycles

Use the Cycles pop-up menu to specify how many times a gradient repeats within an area **(Figure 66)**. You can set the gradient to cycle through its color spectrum up to four times in a given area. You also specify whether the gradient is sharp, meaning the gradient cycles from foreground to destination color, and then again from foreground to destination **(Figure 67)**, or smooth **(Figure 68)**, which makes the gradient cycle from foreground to destination color, and then in the next cycle, from the destination color to the foreground color.

Method

Use the Method pop-up menu to control how Director blends colors to create its gradient **(Figure 69)**. The first four options listed create the gradient with whatever pattern has been selected from Director's Pattern selector in the Paint window, while the last six options create a generic pattern through a process called "dithering." Here are the options:

Pattern Best Colors ignores the arrangement of colors in the palette you're using, and uses only colors that create a continuous blend between your foreground and destination colors based on whatever pattern has been selected. The **See Thru** version of this option makes any white pixels in this blend transparent.

Pattern Adjacent Colors creates the gradient blend by using all the colors in the selected palette that occur between the gradient's foreground and destination colors, even if those in-between colors do not create a smooth blend.

Dither Best Colors ignores the arrangement of colors in the current color palette, and uses only colors that create a continuous blend between your foreground and destination colors, using a dithered pattern.

Dither Adjacent Colors creates the gradient blend by using all the colors in the selected color palette that occur between the foreground and destination colors, even if those in-between colors do not create a smooth blend.

Dither Two Colors blends only the foreground and destination colors with a dithered pattern.

Dither One Color simply fades the foreground color with a dithered pattern.

Standard Dither blends the foreground and destination colors, ignoring the colors between them and adds several blended colors having a dithered pattern.

Multi Dither—similar to Standard Dither, except the dithered pattern is randomized.

Spread. Use the Spread pop-up menu to control how Director distributes the colors of your gradient within an area **(Figure 70)**. **Equal** spaces the gradient's blended colors evenly throughout an area, while **More Foreground (Figure 71) or More Destination (Figure 72)** increases the amount of foreground or destination color in a gradient. **More Middle** devotes more space to the gradient's middle colors.

Range. Use the Range pop-up menu to decide whether the full range of blended colors in your gradient should be applied over a cast member, a paint object, or over the entire Paint window **(Figure 73)**. Choosing **Paint Object** ensures that the full range of the gradient's colors will be seen in any sized brush stroke or fill area **(Figure 74)**, while the full range of colors may not be seen with the Cast member or Window options **(Figure 75)**.

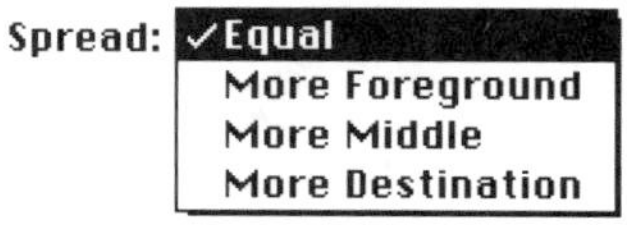

Figure 70. The **Spread** pop-up menu.

Figure 71. A More Foreground gradient.

Figure 72. A More Destination gradient.

Figure 73. The **Range** pop-up menu.

Figure 74. A Paint Object gradient.

Figure 75. A Window gradient.

Figure 76. Choose **Show Rulers** from the **Paint** menu.

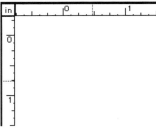

Figure 77. To change the ruler's units of measurement, click the upper- left corner of the ruler.

Figure 78. Choose **Zoom In** from the **Paint** menu.

PAINT MENU COMMANDS

To show/hide Rulers in the Paint window:

You can display a set of horizontal and vertical rulers in the Paint window to help you align and measure your artwork. The rulers can display their measurement values in either inches, centimeters, picas, or pixels.

1. Choose Show Rulers from the Paint menu. Director displays its rulers at the top and left sides of the Paint window **(Figures 76-77)**.

2. When you'd like to turn the rulers off (they take up extra room in the Paint window that could otherwise display artwork), choose Hide Rulers from the Paint menu.

✔ Tips

■ You can set a ruler's zero point by clicking the ruler and dragging to the point where you'd like the new zero point to be.

■ To display the ruler's measurements in a new unit (inches, centimeters, picas, etc.), click at the upper-left corner where the horizontal and vertical rulers meet **(Figure 77)**.

To magnify artwork in the Paint Window:

Director lets you zoom in on artwork to get a closer look at its detail and work with greater accuracy.

1. Choose Zoom In from the Paint menu **(Figure 78)**. Director responds by increasing its magnification. Director will continue displaying the artwork at 100 percent in a small view box in the Paint window's upper-right corner.

2. To increase the level of magnification even further, choose Zoom In from the Paint menu again.

3. To return to normal magnification, choose Zoom Out from the Paint menu until you cannot select it anymore **(Figure 79)**. Or, just click the mouse anywhere in the 100 percent viewing box in the upper-right corner of the Paint window.

✔ Tip

■ Two shortcuts for magnifying artwork in the Paint window: Double-click the Pencil tool icon in the Paint tool palette or hold down the Command key and click anywhere in the Paint window.

Figure 79. Choose **Zoom Out** from the **Paint** menu.

To create a tile from a cast member:

Tiles are similar to patterns in that you can apply them as textures or "fillers" to artwork created in Director. The difference between a tile and a pattern is that the tile is created from an existing cast member in your movie. For instance, if you have a cast member of a brick, you can turn it into a tile that can be used to paint a brick wall. Since tiles are based on an existing cast member, they can feature more than the simple foreground/background color combination that limits traditional patterns. A tile features as many colors as the cast member on which it's based.

1. Make sure that the cast member you wish to base your tile on has already been placed in the Cast window. Creating the tile will have no effect on the cast member.

2. With Director's Paint window open, choose Tiles from the Paint menu **(Figure 80)**.

Figure 80. Choose **Tiles** from the **Paint** menu.

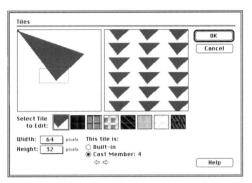

Figure 81. Click the Cast Member radio button in the **Tiles** dialog box.

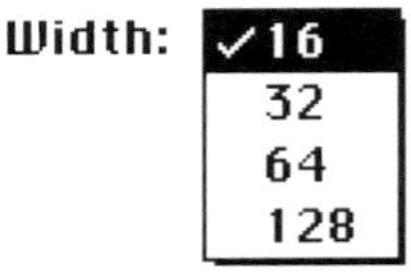

Width:

✓16
32
64
128

Figure 82. The **Width** pop-up menu.

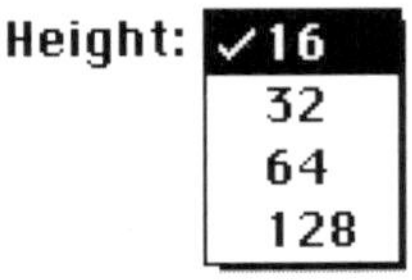

Height:

✓16
32
64
128

Figure 83. The **Height** pop-up menu.

3. In the Tiles dialog box, click the Cast member radio button to select it **(Figure 81)**. The Cast member radio button will be dimmed if your Director movie has no color cast members. You can also choose from a set of built in tiles by clicking the Built-in radio button. Cast members must be saved in at least two bits of color (four colors total) to be turned into a tile.

4. Click the left and right arrows next to the Cast member radio button to cycle through all of the cast members in your movie and choose the particular cast member you wish to turn into a tile. All the cast members appear in the left side of the Tiles dialog box. The right side of the box displays what the particular cast member will look like in tiled form.

5. Use the Width and Height pop-up menus to determine the pixel dimensions that the cast member should conform to as a tile **(Figures 82-83)**. The range of dimensions goes from 16 by 16 to 128 by 128 pixels.

6. On the left side of the Tiles dialog box, notice the dotted border that surrounds the current cast member on display. To create your tile from just a portion of that cast member, drag the dotted border to encompass only the portion that you desire.

7. Click OK to create a new tile based on the selected cast member. Your new tile will now be displayed at the bottom of the Paint window's Pattern palette, which is displayed by clicking the Pattern selector chip.

Patterns

(See page 88)

To choose a Paint brush shape:

Director's Paint brush offers five different shapes—labeled Brush 1 through Brush 5—you can choose from each time you select the brush tool. You can change and customize these brush shapes through Director's Brush Shapes dialog box. *(See page 99 for details)*

1. Click the Paint brush tool in the Paint tool palette, and do not release the mouse button. A pop-up menu appears, listing the different brush shapes that you can choose from **(Figure 84)**.

2. Drag to select the brush shape you wish to use, and release the mouse button. Director will now paint with this particular brush shape.

Optional

Only five brush shapes can be selected from the brush's pop-up menu, although Director can actually store a much wider variety of shapes. You can assign different shapes (probably ones that you have customized yourself) to the pop-up menu, replacing the default styles that are initially assigned. To do so, first follow steps 1 and 2 above to select a brush shape that you wish to replace from the pop-up menu.

3. Once you've selected a brush shape (Brush 1 through Brush 5), choose Brush Shapes from the Paint menu **(Figure 85)**.

4. In the Brush Shapes dialog box, select the new brush shape that you wish to substitute **(Figure 86)**.

5. Click the Set button, and Director will remember to use this new brush shape whenever you select the respective brush number (Brush 1 through Brush 5) from the pop-up menu.

Figure 84. Click and hold the Paint brush tool in the Paint tool palette to display the pop-up menu.

Figure 85. Choose **Brush Shapes** from the **Paint** menu.

Set button

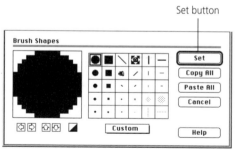

Figure 86. In the **Brush Shapes** dialog box, select a new brush shape to use.

Choose a Paint Brush Shape

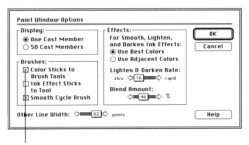

Color Sticks to Brush Tools check box

Figure 87. Choose **Paint Window Options** under the **Paint** menu and check the Color Sticks to Brush Tools check box.

Figure 88. Choose **Brush Shapes** from the **Paint** menu.

Brush shape edit box

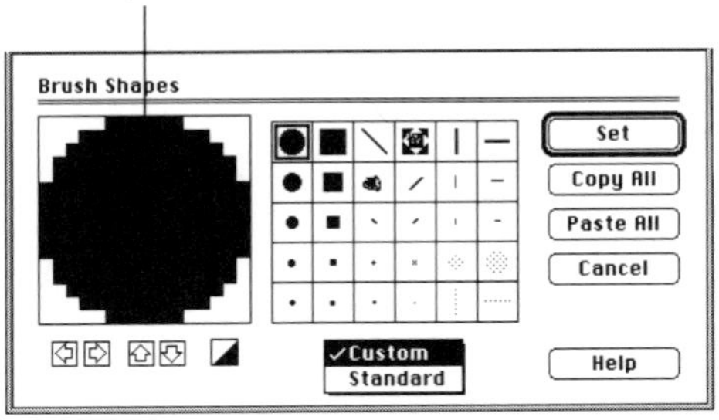

Figure 89. In the **Brush Shapes** dialog box, click the pop-up menu and select the Custom menu item.

✔ **Tips**

■ Double-clicking the Paint Brush tool automatically opens the Brush Shapes dialog box.

■ You can tell Director to automatically select a particular color when you paint with a particular brush—for instance, red for Brush 1, green for Brush 2, and so on. To make Director remember the particular color settings you've associated with each brush shape, choose Paint Window Options under the Paint menu, and check the Color Sticks to Brush Tools setting in the Options dialog box **(Figure 87)**.

To edit a Paint brush shape:

While Director features a variety of existing Paint brush shapes, you can edit them to form your own custom brush styles. Editing is a matter of rearranging the individual pixels that make up the brush's shape.

1. With Director's Paint window open, choose Brush Shapes from the Paint menu **(Figure 88)**.

2. In the Brush Shapes dialog box, click the pop-up menu and select the Custom menu item **(Figure 89)**. Director recognizes two varieties of brush shapes: Standard shapes, which are always available to you and cannot be changed and Custom shapes, which you can edit.

3. Click the custom brush shape that you wish to edit. An enlarged version of the selected brush appears in the brush shape edit box.

4. In the brush shape edit box, click any open space to place a new pixel in the brush. Click an existing pixel to erase it.

Edit a Paint Brush Shape

5. Click the directional arrows in the Brush Shapes dialog box to move the brush shape up, down, and sideways.

6. When you're happy with your new brush design, click the Set button, and Director adds the new brush to its custom brush library.

✔ Tips

- You can store and retrieve sets of custom brush shapes by copying them to and from the Macintosh Scrapbook **(Figure 90)**. To store your custom brush set, first click the Copy All button in the Brush Shapes dialog box; this stores the brush information in the Clipboard. Now leave the dialog box (click Cancel), open the Scrapbook (choose Scrapbook under the Apple menu), and choose Paste under the Edit menu to store the brush shapes there. To reinstall these stored brushes, open the Scrapbook, find the Scrapbook entry that contains the desired brush set, and choose Copy from the Edit menu. Return to Director's Paint window, open the Brush Shapes dialog box, and click the Paste All button to install the copied brush set.

- Director lets you "pick up" any pattern displayed in the Paint window and use it as a brush shape. To do so, open the Brush Shapes dialog box, and click any pattern outside the dialog box to pick it up.

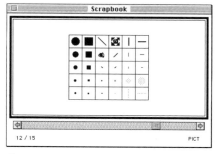

Figure 90. You can store and retrieve your custom brush shapes from the Macintosh Scrapbook.

Store Custom Brush Shapes in Scrapbook

Figure 91. Choose **Air Brushes** from the **Paint** menu.

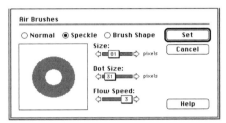

Figure 92. In the **Air Brushes** dialog box, drag the Size, Dot Size, and Flow Speed scroll bars to adjust the Air brush.

Figure 93. The Normal Air brush setting.

Figure 94. The Speckle Air brush setting.

Figure 95. The Brush setting of the Air brush.

To adjust the Air brush spray pattern:

Director lets you adjust the size of the Air brush's spray area, the size of the ink dots it sprays into that area, and the speed at which it sprays them.

1. With Director's Paint window open, choose Air Brushes from the Paint menu **(Figure 91)**.

2. In the Air Brushes dialog box, drag the Size, Dot Size, and Flow Speed scroll bars to adjust the size of the Air brush's spray area, the size of the dots it sprays into the area, and the speed at which it sprays them **(Figure 92)**. As you adjust the scroll bar values, Director displays a preview of how your new settings will affect the Air brush tool. The gray circle indicates the current size of the Air brush's spray area, while the white circle inside represents the size of the dots themselves.

3. Click either the Normal, Speckle, or Brush Shape radio buttons to indicate how the Air brush should spray. At the Normal setting, your Air brush sprays dots of identical size, while the Speckle setting randomly varies the size of dots sprayed. The Brush Shape radio button causes the Air brush to spray in the shape that's currently selected for the Paint brush tool **(Figures 93–95)**.

4. Click the Set button so that your new Air brush settings take effect.

Adjust Air Brush Spray Pattern

To choose an Air brush shape:

Director remembers five different Air brush settings—labeled Air 1 through Air 5—for you to choose from when you select the Air brush tool. You can change and customize these settings through the Air Brushes dialog box.

1. Click and hold the Air brush tool in the Paint tool palette. A pop-up menu appears **(Figure 96)**, listing the different brush settings that you can choose from.

2. Drag to the setting you wish to use, and release the mouse button. Director will now paint with this particular Air brush setting.

Optional

You can replace each of the five Air brush settings with your own custom ones. To do so, first follow steps 1 and 2 above to select the Air brush setting that you wish to customize (again, Air 1 through Air 5).

3. Choose Air Brushes from Director's Paint menu **(Figure 97)**.

4. In the Air Brushes dialog box, change the brush's size, dot size, and speed settings **(Figure 98)** to the new desired values. *(See page 101 for more about these settings)*

5. Click the Set button, and Director will remember to use these new settings whenever you select the same brush setting (Air 1 through Air 5) from the Air brush tool's pop-up menu.

Gradients

(See page 91)

Figure 96. Click and hold the Air brush tool in the Paint tool palette to display the pop-up menu.

Figure 97. Choose **Air Brushes** from the **Paint** menu.

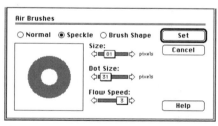

Figure 98. In the **Air Brushes** dialog box, drag the Size, Dot Size, and Flow Speed scroll bars to adjust the Air brush.

Figure 99. Select the artwork that you wish to rotate with the Selection Rectangle tool.

Figure 100. Choose either **Rotate Right** or **Rotate Left** from the **Effects** menu.

Figure 101. The artwork after using Rotate Right.

Figure 102. The artwork after using Rotate Left.

Figure 103. Drag one of the handles to rotate your art selection in 1-degree increments.

EFFECTS

Director's Effects menu offers a variety of effects and functions that can be applied to existing artwork. These features include flips and rotations of cast members, edge traces, color reversals, and image distortions. You can perform an effect on any portion of an image, rather than the whole thing. For most of these effects, you must use Director's Selection Rectangle, not its Lasso, to make the selection.

To rotate artwork left and right by 90 degrees:

Director lets you rotate entire images or parts of images in 90-degree increments.

1. In Director's Paint window, click the Selection Rectangle tool and use it to select the artwork that you wish to rotate **(Figure 99)**.

2. Choose either Rotate Right or Rotate Left from the Effects menu **(Figure 100)** to rotate the selected artwork 90 degrees **(Figures 101-102)**.

To freely rotate artwork in 1-degree increments:

The Free Rotate command lets you rotate artwork in 1-degree increments.

1. In Director's Paint window, click the Selection Rectangle tool and use it to select the artwork that you wish to rotate.

2. Choose Free Rotate from the Effects menu. Notice that Director places little "handles" at each corner of your selection.

3. Drag one of the handles to rotate your art selection in 1-degree increments **(Figure 103)**.

Rotate Left, Rotate Right, Free Rotate

To flip artwork horizontally or vertically:

Director lets you "flip" an artwork selection to create a mirror-image **(Figure 104)**.

1. In Director's Paint window, click the Selection Rectangle tool and use it to select the artwork that you wish to flip.

2. Choose either Flip Horizontal or Flip Vertical from Director's Effects menu **(Figure 105)**.

Figure 104. You can "flip" an artwork selection to create a mirror-image.

To distort artwork:

You can alter the shape and dimensional appearance of artwork using Director's Perspective, Slant, and Distort commands **(Figures 106–109)**. Distort allows you to bend and stretch artwork; Slant gives the artwork a parallelogram shape; and Perspective makes the artwork seem as if it is being viewed from a particular vantage point, with one part of the image appearing to be closer than the other.

1. In the Paint window, click the Selection Rectangle tool, and use it to select the artwork that you wish to alter.

2. Choose Perspective, Slant, or Distort from Director's Effects menu. Notice that Director places little "handles" at each corner of your selection.

3. Drag one of the handles to apply the desired effect to the artwork.

✔ Tip

■ You may want to make a copy of your artwork before distorting it. To do so, select the image with the Selection Rectangle tool, move the mouse pointer within the selection marquee, hold down the Option key, and drag an identical copy of the original artwork to a new location.

Figure 105. Choose either **Flip Horizontal** or **Flip Vertical** from the **Effects** menu.

Figure 106. Unaltered artwork.

Figure 107. The Perspective effect.

Figure 108. The Slant effect.

Figure 109. The Distort effect.

Figure 110. The **Effects** menu.

Figure 111. The **Invert Colors** effect reverses the colors of an image.

Figure 112. The Trace Edges effect creates an outline around the edges of your selected artwork.

To apply other special effects to artwork:

Invert Colors, Trace Edges, Fill, Lighten, Darken, Smooth, and Switch Colors are additional commands from the Effects menu that you can apply to your artwork.

1. In Director's Paint window, click the Selection Rectangle or Lasso tool, and use it to select the artwork that you wish to affect (note that you cannot use the Lasso tool with the Trace Edges command).

2. Choose Invert Colors, Trace Edges, Fill, Lighten, Darken, Smooth, or Switch Colors from Director's Effects menu **(Figure 110)**.

The **Invert Colors** effect reverses all the colors in the selected artwork. If the artwork is black and white, white pixels turn to black, and vice versa, which creates a negative image **(Figure 111)**. If the artwork uses more than two colors, Director reverses the order in which the colors are displayed. The artwork's color palette is effectively flipped, so that the colors that were assigned to the top of the palette are placed at its bottom. *(See the Color in Director chapter for details on palettes)*

The **Trace Edges** effect creates an outline around the edges of the artwork you've selected **(Figure 112)**. Select Trace Edges repeatedly to increase the number of outlines in the trace.

Invert Colors, Trace Edges

The **Fill** command fills the selected area in the Paint window with the foreground color and pattern.

The **Lighten** and **Darken** commands respectively increase and decrease the brightness of the selected artwork.

The **Smooth** command softens the edges of your artwork **(Figure 113)** by adding pixels that blend the colors between edges.

The **Switch Color** command changes the foreground color in the selected area to the current destination color.

Figure 113. The Smooth command softens the edges of your artwork.

To create a sequence of in-between images of an artwork selection:

Director's **Auto Distort** command creates a number of in-between images for artwork that you transform with the Slant, Distort, Perspective, or Free Rotate commands. Let's say you use the Free Rotate command to rotate a picture by 350 degrees—almost a full circle. You can then use Auto Distort to create versions of the artwork in a number of rotated positions between 0 and 350 degrees—for instance, at 60 degrees, 120 degrees, 180, 240, and so on **(Figure 114)**. Director then places each of these in-between images into Director's Cast window, where they can be incorporated in your movie as an animation sequence.

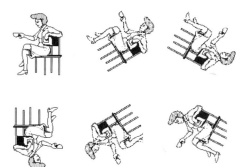

Figure 114. The Auto Distort command has been used here in combination with the Free Rotate command to create a series of in-between rotated images.

1. In the Paint tool palette, click the Selection Rectangle tool, and use it to select the artwork that you wish to transform.

2. Choose Perspective, Slant, Distort, or Free Rotate from the Effects menu. Notice that Director places little "handles" at each corner of your selection.

3. Drag one of the handles to rotate or distort the selected art.

4. While the Selection Rectangle is still active, choose Auto Distort from the Effects menu **(Figure 115)**.

Figure 115. Choose **Auto Distort** from the **Effects** menu.

Figure 116. In the **Auto Distort** dialog box, enter the number of in-between cast members you wish to create.

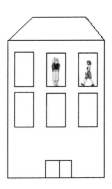

Figure 117. The windows of this house cast member are transparent, allowing you to see the characters behind them.

Figure 118. Choose **Duplicate Cast Member** from the **Cast** menu.

5. In the Auto Distort dialog box, type the number of in-between cast members you wish to create **(Figure 116)**. In other words, how many new cast members should be created to transform the original artwork to the altered state created in step 3 above.

6. Click OK. Director creates the new in-between cast members and adds them into the next available positions in the Cast window.

Ink Masks

Using an ink mask allows certain parts of a cast member to be transparent—in other words, you can see through it to other artwork in the background—while other parts of the cast member remain opaque. Why would you ever want a cast member to behave that way? Imagine creating a scene in which a house is viewed from outside, and animated characters can be seen through its windows **(Figure 117)**. In such a scene, the house itself would be opaque but the windows transparent, allowing you to see the characters behind them. Another good example is a scene inside a moving car. The car is opaque, but its windows are transparent so that you can see the passing scenery.

To create a mask:

1. Make sure that you've already placed the cast member you wish to mask in Director's Score.

2. Open the cast member you wish to mask in the Paint window. A quick way to do this is to double-click it in the Cast window.

3. Choose Duplicate Cast Member from the Cast menu **(Figure 118)**.

Ink Masks

4. While viewing the cloned cast member, choose Transform Bitmap from Director's Cast menu, and select 1-Bit in the Color Depth pop-up menu. You are changing the cloned cast member to black and white (1-bit color depth), which is required to make a mask **(Figure 119)**.

5. Click OK to leave the Transform Bitmap dialog box.

6. From the Paint tool palette, select either the Paint bucket or Paint brush tool.

7. Fill in the parts of the cloned cast member that should be opaque (that is, that should not be seen through). Be sure not to paint outside the borders of the cloned cast member; doing so could create a ghosting effect when you place the mask in your movie.

8. Open Director's Cast window by choosing Cast from the Windows menu.

9. In the Cast window, make sure that the cloned cast member you've created is positioned immediately following the original version of the cast member **(Figure 120)**. If it is not already there, drag the clone to the appropriate location.

10. Choose Score from the Window menu.

11. Select the frames in the Score that contain the cast member you wish to mask.

12. In the Score, click and hold the Ink effects selector to display a pop-up menu, and choose Mask. **(Figure 121)**. Director displays your masked cast member in the selected frames.

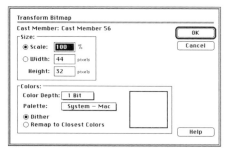

Figure 119. Select 1-Bit in the **Color Depth** pop-up menu in the **Transform Bitmap** dialog box.

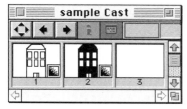

Figure 120. In the **Cast** window, make sure the cloned cast member is positioned immediately following the original cast member.

Ink effects selector

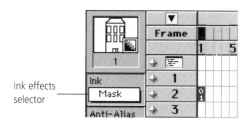

Figure 121. In the Score window, choose **Mask** in the **Ink effects** pop-up menu.

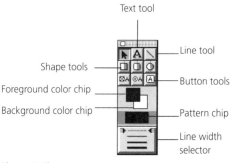

Text tool

Line tool

Shape tools

Button tools

Foreground color chip

Background color chip

Pattern chip

Line width selector

Figure 1. The **Tools** window.

Figure 2. The Text tool.

Figure 3. The Line tool.

Director's Tools Window allows you to create text and shape graphics directly on the Stage **(Figure 1)**. These type of graphics are called **QuickDraw** graphics. They offer several advantages over bitmap graphics created in Director's Paint window: QuickDraw shapes and text can be resized and edited on the Stage. They consume a lot less memory than bitmap images, and print much cleaner to laser printers. On the down side, QuickDraw graphics animate slower, so if speed is an issue, use bitmap text and graphics. QuickDraw graphics are automatically placed into the Score and Cast windows once created on the Stage. You cannot edit QuickDraw graphics in the Paint window. QuickDraw text can be edited in the Text window.

Text Tool

Use the Text tool to create text as an alternative to using the Text window under the Window menu **(Figure 2)**. Text created with the Text tool is visible in the Text and Cast windows.

Select the Text tool, then click the Stage where you wish to create and position some text. Click the arrow in the Tools window to select text on the Stage that you wish to edit. *(See pages 180-185 in the Creating Text in Director chapter for more information on the Text tool and creating text with the Text window)*

Line Tool

Use the QuickDraw Line tool to draw lines on Director's Stage **(Figure 3)**. Drag it to size your line. The line width can be changed by using the Line width selector at the bottom of the Tools window.

Text Tool, Line Tool

Shape Tools

The QuickDraw Shape tools work very much like the Shape tools in the Paint window tool palette **(Figure 4)**. Click the left or hollow side of a Shape tool to draw an outline of that shape on the Stage by dragging (you can set the thickness of the outline by using the Line width selector at the bottom of the Tools window). The right sides or shaded sides of the Shape tools produce solid shapes using the current foreground color and pattern.

Figure 4. The Shape tools.

✔ Tip

■ Hold the Shift key while dragging a Shape tool on the Stage to constrain its shape to a perfect square or circle. Hold the Shift key while dragging the Line tool to constrain it to 45-degree lines.

Button Tools

Director allows you to create standard buttons, checkboxes, and radio buttons by using the Button tools provided in the Tools window **(Figure 5)**. Select the appropriate Button tool, then drag a rectangle on the Stage where the button should be placed. You can then type in the text that should appear on or next to your button. The font, size, and style of the button text can be set from the Text menu. Once placed onto the Stage, a button cast member is created. Button text can be edited directly on the Stage. You can attach a script to a button so that some action takes place when it is clicked. *(See page 206 for information on scripts)*

Figure 5. The Button tools.

Shape Tools, Button Tools

Foreground color chip

Background color chip

Figure 6. The Foreground and Background color chips.

Figure 7. Select a QuickDraw line or shape on the Stage.

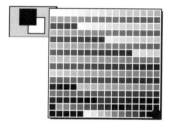

Figure 8. Click and hold the Foreground or Background color chips to select a new color from the pop-up menu.

This is a sample of some QuickDraw Text

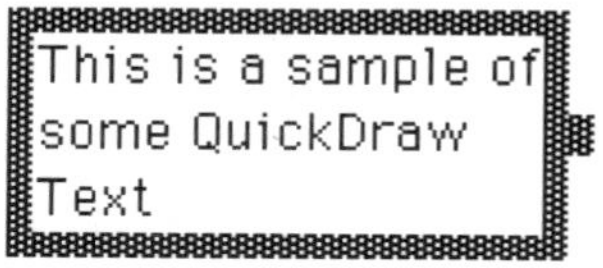

Figure 9. Select a block of QuickDraw text on the Stage.

FOREGROUND AND BACKGROUND COLOR CHIPS

Use the Foreground and Background color chips in the Tools window **(Figure 6)** to set the color of QuickDraw lines, shapes, text typed in Text and Script windows, and set the color of sprites.

To set the color of QuickDraw lines or shapes:

1. Select a QuickDraw line or shape on the Stage. A thick border appears around the image **(Figure 7)**.

2. Click and hold the Foreground or Background color chips in the Tools window to select a new color from the pop-up menu for the foreground or background colors **(Figure 8)**. The background color has no effect on a QuickDraw line, but does effect the color of hollow and solid QuickDraw shapes if a pattern for them is selected.

To set the color of QuickDraw text:

1. Select a block of QuickDraw text on the Stage. A thick border appears around it **(Figure 9)**.

2. Select a foreground color using the Foreground color chip **(Figure 8)**. Additional text now typed will have this color, but to change existing text color, select the actual text first by dragging across it, and then click the Foreground color chip.

3. Select a background color for the text block by using the Background color chip.

To set the color of text in Text and Script windows:

1. Select a Text or Script window so that it is the active window **(Figure 10)**.

2. Select a foreground color using the Foreground color chip in the Tools window **(Figure 11)**. Additional text now typed will have this color, but to change the color of existing text, select the actual text first by dragging across it and then click the Foreground color chip.

3. Select a background color for the Text or Script windows by using the Background color chip in the Tools window.

To set the color of sprites:

1. Select a sprite on the Stage or in the Score.

2. Choose a new foreground or background color using the Foreground and Background color chips in the Tools window **(Figure 11)**. Unless the foreground color of the sprite is originally black, changing its foreground color in this manner can result in unpredictable colors.

Pattern chip

Click and hold the Pattern chip to select a new pattern from the pop-up menu **(Figure 12)**.

Line width selector

Allows you to set the line width that's used with the Line tool and hollow Shape tools **(Figure 13)**.

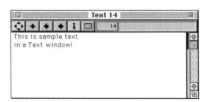

Figure 10. Make a Text or Script window active.

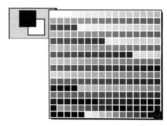

Figure 11. Click and hold the Foreground or Background color chips to select a new color from the pop-up menu.

Figure 12. The Pattern chip.

Figure 13. The Line width selector.

COLOR IN DIRECTOR 8

Color Palette.

The Color Palette is used throughout this chapter. Choose Color Palettes from the Window menu to display it (**Figure 1**).

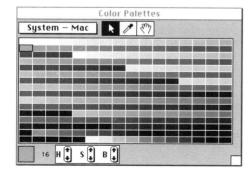

Figure 1. Choose **Color Palettes** from the **Window** menu.

Figure 2. The **Color Palette**.

A **color palette** is a collection of colors that Director uses to paint a particular cast member sprite **(Figure 2)**. Each palette is created by the particular software package used to draw the cast member, such as Adobe Photoshop, Fractal Painter, or even Director itself. Each cast member can have its own unique color palette. Most palettes feature 16 colors, 256 colors, or 16 million colors (also known as 4-bit, 8-bit, and 24-bit color, respectively), although the 256-color variety is the most common.

It's important to understand the nature of palettes in Director and how to work around their limitations to make your movies appear attractive. In this chapter you'll learn how to take the most commonly used colors from a variety of cast member palettes and arrange them into a new "optimal" palette that all cast members can use simultaneously. And you'll learn how to edit existing palettes: rearranging colors, moving colors between palettes, and removing unwanted colors to make room for more useful ones. You also discover how to create impressive visual effects through smooth transitions between palettes and a special technique called "color cycling" that makes cast members appear to animate and pulse.

Color Palette

ASSIGNING PALETTES TO CAST MEMBERS AND FRAMES

To set a default palette:

You can set a default color palette that is used automatically when you create a new Director movie.

1. Choose Movie Info from the File menu **(Figure 3)**.

2. Use the Default Palette pop-up menu to select the palette you wish to use as your movie's default palette **(Figure 4)**.

3. Click OK.

Figure 3. Choose **Movie Info** from the **File** menu.

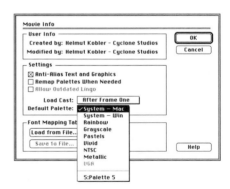

Figure 4. Select your movie's default palette from the pop-up menu.

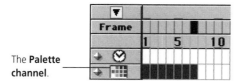

The **Palette channel**.

Figure 5. In the **Palette channel**, select the frame or series of frames whose palette you would like to set.

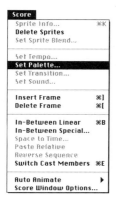

Figure 6. Choose **Set Palette** from the **Score** menu.

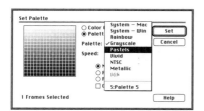

Figure 7. In the **Set Palette** dialog box, use the **Palette** pop-up menu to choose a palette you wish to apply to the selected frames.

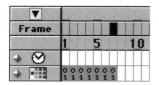

Figure 8. Click set in the **Set Palette** dialog box and Director sets the new palette in selected frames.

To set the current palette in the Score:

When Director plays a movie, it displays its cast members using a color palette specified in the palette channel of the Score. These settings override any default palette set through the Movie Info command *(see page 114)*. Like all of Director's Score channels, the palette channel **(Figure 5)** can be controlled on a frame-by-frame basis—for instance, frame 1 can employ palette A to display cast members, while frame 5 switches to palette B, and frame 15 switches to palette C. By swapping palettes like this you can display a sequence of distinct cast members in their original palettes, and create unique visual effects by changing between palettes over time.

When you drag a cast member from the Cast window onto the Stage, Director automatically assigns that cast member's palette to the palette channel and uses that palette for all subsequent frames until a new palette is set in the channel. Setting a new palette in the palette channel is easy.

1. In the palette channel, select the frame or frames where you wish to set a new color palette **(Figure 5)**.

2. Choose Set Palette from the Score menu **(Figure 6)**.

3. In the Set Palette dialog box, use the Palette pop-up menu to choose the palette you wish to apply to the selected frames. Your choices include all of Director's core palettes (System, Rainbow, Pastels, etc.), plus any you've created **(Figure 7)**.

4. Click Set. Director sets the new palette in the selected frames **(Figure 8)**. Don't be surprised if the cast members in those frames suddenly change colors—they are now displayed in the colors of your new palette.

✔ **Tip**

■ You can double-click a frame in the palette channel to open the Set Palette dialog box.

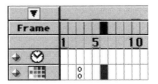

Figure 9. Select the cell in the **palette channel** where the palette transition should take place.

To set the transition of palettes over a single frame:

Switching palettes in a scene can be a little jarring: You see a particular set of colors in one frame, and in the next frame the set is entirely different. Director lets you use a palette transition to control the speed at which colors change, smoothing the switch from one palette to the next.

1. In the palette channel of the Score window, select the cell where you would like your palette transition to take place **(Figure 9)**.

2. Choose Set Palette from the Score menu **(Figure 10)**.

3. In the Set Palette dialog box, use the Palette pop-up menu to choose the palette to which you wish to make a transition **(Figure 11)**. Remember that the palette you set in this frame should be different from the palette used in the channel's previous frames.

4. In the Set Palette dialog box, adjust the Speed scroll bar to determine how fast the transition between the old and new palettes will be. The speed can be set anywhere between 1 and 30 frames per second **(Figure 12)**. Your movie will be paused in this frame while the transition takes place.

5. Click Set to apply the new palette with its transition.

Figure 10. Choose **Set Palette** from the **Score** menu.

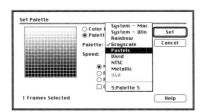

Figure 11. Use the **Palette** pop-up menu in the **Set Palette** dialog box to choose the palette to transition to.

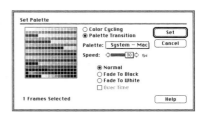

Figure 12. Adjust the Speed scroll bar to determine how fast the transition between the palettes should be.

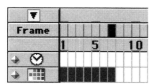

Figure 13. Select a series of cells in the **Palette channel** in which your palette transition will occur.

Figure 14. Choose **Set Palette** from the **Score** menu.

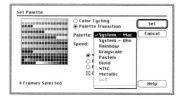

Figure 15. Select the transition palette in the **Palette** pop-up menu.

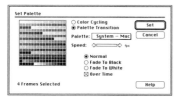

Figure 16. Check the **Over Time** box.

To set the transition of palettes over a series of frames:

Just as you can set a smooth palette transition over one frame, you can set a transition to last over a series of frames. This will make the transition between palettes more subtle, and your animation can continue without interruption.

1. In the Score's palette channel, select the series of cells in which your palette transition will occur **(Figure 13)**.

2. Choose Set Palette from the Score menu **(Figure 14)**.

3. In the Set Palette dialog box, use the Palette pop-up menu to select the palette to which you want to make a transition **(Figure 15)**.

4. Check the Over Time box **(Figure 16)**.

5. Click Set to apply the new palette with its transition.

To import palettes into Director:

You can import color palettes into Director by importing a cast member that already uses the desired palette.

1. Choose Import from the File menu **(Figure 17)**.

2. In the Import dialog box, select the desired cast member and click Import **(Figure 18)**.

3. When you try to import a cast member with a palette that is not currently being used, Director stops the import process and asks whether you'd like to automatically remap the new cast member to the colors of the current palette or keep its original palette and add it to the Cast window. Choose the **Install Palette in Cast** radio button **(Figure 19)**, and click OK to keep the cast member's original palette intact, at least for the time being.

4. Director will ask you to name the new palette that you're importing. Type a name that identifies the palette with its cast member, and then click OK **(Figure 20)**. Director places both the imported cast member and its palette in the Cast window. The new palette can now be assigned to the palette channel, edited, mapped to existing cast members, and so on.

Figure 17. Choose **Import** from the **File** menu.

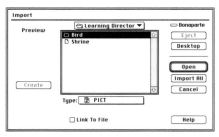

Figure 18. Select the desired cast member and click Import.

Figure 19. Choose the **Install Palette in Cast** radio button to import the cast member's original palette.

Figure 20. Name the new palette that you're importing.

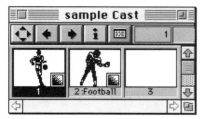

Figure 21. Select the cast member you'd like to remap. Here, cast member 1 is selected.

Figure 22. Choose **Transform Bitmap** from the **Cast** menu.

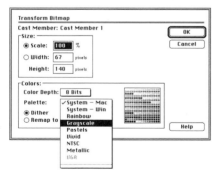

Figure 23. In the **Transform Bitmap** dialog box, select a palette from the **Palette** pop-up menu to which the cast member should be remapped.

To remap a cast member to a different palette:

Director lets you "remap" a cast member to a different palette, allowing you to unite all cast members under the same color palette. When you remap a cast member to a new palette, Director examines the cast member's original colors and decides which colors in the new palette best match the old. This often leads to a close, but not identical match of colors.

1. In the Cast window, select the cast member you would like to remap **(Figure 21)**.

2. Choose Transform Bitmap from the Cast menu **(Figure 22)**.

3. In the Transform Bitmap dialog box, use the Palette pop-up menu to choose the palette to which the cast member should be remapped. Director allows you to choose from all the palettes in the current movie, as well some standard default palettes **(Figure 23)**.

4. Click OK to remap the cast member to the new palette. Now play your movie back to see how the cast member looks in its new color scheme, or examine the cast member more closely in Director's Paint window. *(See page 69)*

✔ Tip

■ Since remapping a cast member to a new palette can skew the cast member's colors, it's a good idea to perform your first remap on a copy of the cast member. This way, you can still revert to an earlier color scheme. To create a copy of a cast member, simply select it in the Cast window, and choose Copy Cast from the Edit menu; then select an empty cast member position and choose Paste from the Edit menu.

✔ Tip

■ If you are not happy with the new color scheme of a remapped cast member, you can manually adjust the colors of that cast member's new palette so that they more closely match the cast member's original colors. *To edit a palette, see page 128.*

To remap the entire cast to a new palette:

Director can automatically remap all cast members to a particular color palette. Note that this feature only affects the appearance of cast members on the Stage, and does not transform the actual cast members' color palettes.

1. Choose Movie Info from Director's File menu **(Figure 24)**.

2. In the Movie Info dialog box, check the Remap Palettes When Needed box **(Figure 25)**.

3. Use the Default Palette pop-up menu to choose a palette. Director will remap all cast members in any frame to this palette as long as it remains the active palette **(Figure 25)**. If you've created an optimal palette *(see page 121)*, you'll probably want to remap your cast members to this one.

4. Click OK.

Figure 24. Choose **Movie Info** from the **File** menu.

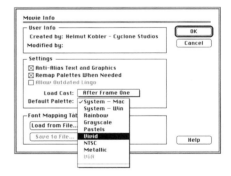

Figure 25. In the **Movie Info** dialog box, check the **Remap Palettes When Needed** box, and choose a new palette from the **Palette** pop-up menu.

Remap Entire Cast to a New Palette

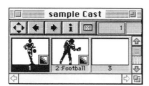

Figure 26. Select a cast member to be used as the basis for your optimal palette.

Figure 27. Choose **Color Palettes** from the **Window** menu.

Figure 28. Choose **Select Used Colors** from the **Palette** menu.

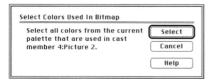

Figure 29. In the **Select Used Colors** dialog box, click the Select button to highlight all colors used by the selected cast member.

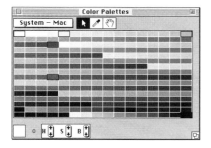

Figure 30. The **Color Palette** with five highlighted colors used by the selected cast member.

To create an optimal palette for all cast members:

It's possible to create a single, specialized palette that incorporates many of the same colors, or similar ones, shared by your entire cast. Once you've created this "optimal" palette, you can remap all of your cast members to it using the steps outlined on page 120. This approach allows your movie to operate from a single common palette, keeping colors consistent throughout.

Remember, however, that remapping a cast member to a new palette—even an optimal one—often leads to a close but not identical match of colors. So don't be surprised if your cast members are colored a little differently once they've been remapped to an optimal palette.

1. In the Cast window, select a cast member whose palette you wish to use as the basis for your optimal palette **(Figure 26)**. It's preferable to choose a cast member that uses only a small number of the colors available in its palette. For instance, a cast member that uses only three colors from a palette of 256 would be ideal.

2. Choose Color Palettes from Director's Window menu **(Figure 27)**.

3. With the Color Palette open, choose Select Used Colors from the Palette menu **(Figure 28)**.

4. In the Select Used Colors dialog box, click the Select button **(Figure 29)**. Director will highlight all the colors used by the cast member you selected earlier. It's often difficult to tell which of the palette's colors are selected. Selected colors have a thin black border, while unselected colors have thin white borders **(Figure 30)**.

Create an Optimal Palette

5. Choose Duplicate Palette from the Palette menu **(Figure 31)**. By copying the original palette, you're free to work without disturbing the cast member's current coloring.

6. In the dialog box, type the name you wish to give this palette **(Figure 32)**. You might want to use something descriptive, such as "Optimal Palette". Click OK.

7. With all the used colors still highlighted in the Palette window, click the hand tool and then drag one of the highlighted colors to the second color position in the first row of colors (the position immediately to the right of white). Director rearranges the selected colors into a continuous range and places them at the top of the palette where they're easier to work with **(Figure 33)**.

Figure 31. Choose **Duplicate Palette** from the **Palette** menu.

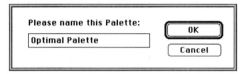

Figure 32. Type the name you wish to give this duplicated palette.

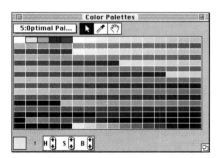

Figure 33. Drag one of the highlighted colors to the second position in the first row. Director rearranges the selected colors into a continuous range at the top of the palette.

Create an Optimal Palette

Figure 34. Choose **Invert Selection** from the **Palette** menu.

Figure 35. Choose **Blend Colors** from the **Palette** menu.

8. Choose Invert Selection from the Palette menu **(Figure 34)**. This selects all the *unused* colors in the palette.

9. Choose Blend Colors from the Palette menu **(Figure 35)**. Director changes all unused colors into a continuous range of similar colors so you can easily tell them apart from the used colors that will be the backbone of your optimal palette **(Figure 36)**. In this area of blended colors (which you don't need, since these colors are not used by the cast member selected in step 1) you can paste additional colors from other cast member palettes.

10. You're now ready to collect additional used colors from other palettes. In the Palette window, click the Palette pop-up menu and select another palette used by other cast members in your movie **(Figure 37)**.

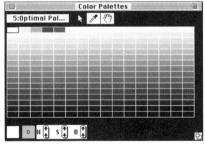

Figure 36. Blending a range of colors changes them into a continuous range of similar colors, so you can easily tell them apart from the used colors.

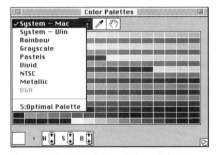

Figure 37. In the **Palette** window, click the **Palette** pop-up menu and select another palette used by other cast members in your movie.

Create an Optimal Palette

11. In the Palette window, click each color chip that you'd like to add to your optimal palette **(Figure 38)**. You can also select a cast member in the Cast window that uses this palette and then choose Select Used Colors under the Palette menu to highlight all the colors the cast member uses. Hold down the Command key to make multiple, discontinuous selections, or the Shift key to select a range. Try to select a handful of colors that best represent the color range of the palette. For instance, pick a couple of reds, a couple of blues, a few grays, greens, and so on.

12. Choose Copy Colors from the Edit menu **(Figure 39)**.

13. In the Palette window, click the Palette pop-up menu and select the optimal palette you created earlier **(Figure 40)**.

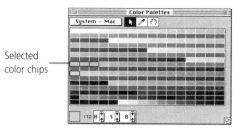

Selected color chips

Figure 38. In the **Palette** window, select the color chips to be added to your optimal palette.

Figure 39. Choose **Copy Colors** from the **Edit** menu.

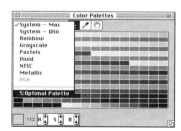

Figure 40. In the **Palette** window, click the **Palette** pop-up menu and select the optimal palette you created earlier.

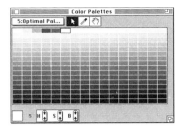

Figure 41. In the optimal palette, highlight one of the blended, unused color chips.

Figure 42. Choose **Paste Into Palette** from the **Edit** menu.

14. In the optimal palette, highlight one of the blended, unused color chips **(Figure 41)**. Try to select the first blended chip that immediately follows the last used color in the palette, so that your new colors will be placed right next to the existing colors. Make sure that you have enough blended, unused color chips to accommodate the new colors.

15. Choose Paste Into Palette from the Edit menu to add the new colors to your optimal palette **(Figure 42)**.

16. Repeat steps 10 through 15 to continue adding colors from other cast member palettes.

17. Close the Palette window when you've filled up your optimal palette.

18. Now you're ready to remap your movie's cast members to the optimal palette you've just created. To do so, follow the steps outlined on page 120, under the heading *"To remap the entire cast to a new palette."*

✔ **Tip**

■ Creating an optimal palette can sometimes require a lot of trial and error. After your first attempt, you may find that the optimal palette's colors are still not true enough to your cast member's original colors. In that case, simply open the optimal palette (choose Color Palettes from the Window menu) and adjust or replace the colors that affect your cast members. *(See page 128 for more details about editing the colors in a palette)*

Create an Optimal Palette

To sample colors directly from artwork:

Director's Eyedropper tool makes it easy to identify specific colors that appear in a cast member on the Stage. With the Eyedropper, you can click any color you see on the Stage, and Director automatically highlights that color in the Color Palettes window. This is especially useful when you want to isolate certain colors in a palette, either for modification or for copying into another custom palette that you're building, such as an optimal palette.

1. In the Score window, select the cell that contains the cast member whose colors you'd like to identify in the current palette. Its cast member should appear on the Stage **(Figure 43)**.

2. Choose Color Palettes from the Window menu **(Figure 44)**.

3. In the Color Palettes window, select the Eyedropper tool **(Figure 45)**.

4. With the Eyedropper tool, click the cast member on the Stage to sample its color at any point **(Figure 43)**. This color becomes highlighted in the Color Palette window **(Figure 45)**. You can now modify the color or copy it to a new palette.

Figure 43. A cast member on the Stage. Use the Eyedropper tool to sample its color at any point.

Figure 44. Choose **Color Palettes** from the **Window** menu.

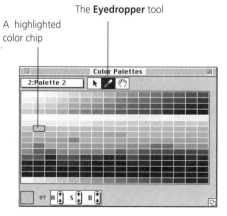

The **Eyedropper** tool

A highlighted color chip

Figure 45. In the **Color Palettes** window, select the eyedropper tool.

HSB and RGB.

You can edit individual colors by using either the Color Palette window or the Color Picker *(see page 129).* In the Color Palette window, colors are defined using the hue, saturation, brightness **HSB** color model. With the Color Picker, you can define colors using either HSB, or the red, green, blue **RGB** model. By adjusting color values in these models, you can create one of the more than 16 million colors that your Macintosh can display. Here are the particular features of each model:

In the HSB model, **hue** refers to the basic color that is created by mixing two primary colors, such as red and green. **Saturation** refers to the amount of white that's mixed into any given color—a fully saturated color is vivid, containing no white, while a less saturated color appears lighter, more pastel. **Brightness** measures how much black is mixed into a color. Lowering the brightness value adds more black, making the color darker and muddier. A brightness value of 0 makes a color solid black.

The RGB model is simpler, defining colors by mixing varying degrees of red, green, and blue. Each color has over 65,000 degrees to choose from.

HSB and RGB Color Models

CUSTOMIZING COLOR PALETTES

To edit a color in the Palette window:

You can easily edit the colors in an existing palette, substituting new colors for old ones.

1. Choose Color Palettes from the Window menu **(Figure 46)**.

2. In the Color Palettes window, use the Palette pop-up menu to select the color palette you'd like to edit **(Figure 47)**. You can enlarge the Palette window by dragging the window's size box in the lower-right corner.

3. With the pointer tool click the color chip you want to edit. The chip is highlighted by a black border, and its color is displayed in the lower-left corner of the Palette window **(Figure 48)**.

4. Use the hue, saturation, and brightness controls (labeled H, S, and B, respectively) at the bottom of the Palette window to adjust the color. Clicking the up and down arrows steps through new values for the color **(Figure 48)**.

or

4. For greater accuracy in your color selection, use Director's Color Picker. The Color Picker allows you to describe a new color by using precise numeric values or simply by clicking the color wheel. With a color chip selected in the Palette window, choose Set Color from the Palette menu **(Figure 49)**.

Figure 46. Choose **Color Palettes** from the **Window** menu.

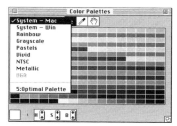

Figure 47. In the **Palette** window, select the palette you would like to edit from the **Palette** pop-up menu.

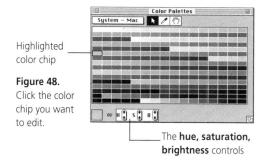

Highlighted color chip

Figure 48. Click the color chip you want to edit.

The **hue, saturation, brightness** controls

Figure 49. Choose **Set Color** from the **Palette** menu.

5. In the Color Picker dialog box, click a desired color on the color wheel **(Figure 50)**. Use the Color Picker's scroll bar to control brightness. To make a precise selection, type values in the Hue, Saturation, and Brightness boxes, or the Red, Green, and Blue boxes.

6. When you're satisfied with the selected color, click OK. Director returns to the Palette window, and places the new color in the palette.

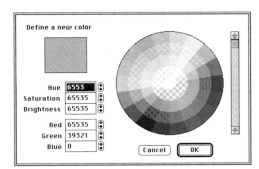

Figure 50. In the **Color Picker** dialog box, click inside the color wheel to select a color, or type values into the Hue, Saturation, Brightness, or Red, Green, Blue boxes for a precise selection.

✔ **Tip**

■ When editing a color chip, you may want to work with a copy of it. This way you can easily return to the original color if you have to, since only its copy will have been changed. To copy a color, select it in the palette and choose Copy Colors from the Edit menu. Then select an unused color chip in the palette and choose Paste to Palette from the Edit menu to copy the color to the new location.

Color Picker

To copy and paste colors in a palette:

You can use Director's Copy and Paste features to move colors from one palette to another or to rearrange colors within a single palette.

1. Choose Color Palettes from the Window menu.

2. In the Color Palettes window, use the pointer or hand tool to select the color chips you wish to copy. Hold down the Command key to make multiple, discontinuous selections, or Shift-click to select a range between two color chips **(Figure 51)**.

3. Choose Copy Colors from the Edit menu **(Figure 52)**.

4. If you are copying the colors to a new palette, use the palette pop-up menu to choose the destination palette.

5. Click the new color chip position in which to paste the copied colors **(Figure 53)**.

6. Choose Paste into Palette from the Edit menu to place the copied colors **(Figure 54)**.

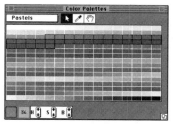

Figure 51. In the **Color Palettes** window, use the pointer or hand tool to select the color chips you wish to copy.

Figure 52. Choose **Copy Colors** from the **Edit** menu.

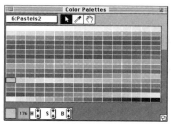

Figure 53. Click the new color chip position where the copied color(s) will be pasted.

Figure 54. Choose **Paste Into Palette** from the **Edit** menu.

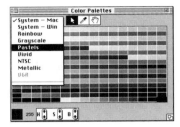

Figure 55. In the **Color Palettes** window, use the **Palette** pop-up menu to select the desired palette.

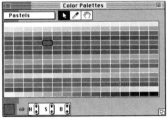

Figure 56. With the pointer tool, select the first color in your blend.

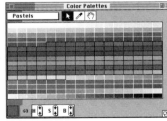

Figure 57. Hold down the Shift key and select your blend's destination color to highlight all colors in this range.

To blend colors within a palette:

Director can blend colors contained in a range of color chips that you specify. The Blend Colors command makes it possible to create palettes featuring a variety of similar colors—especially useful for creating subtle gradient fills and smooth color cycling. For example, if you were creating a sunset backdrop, you might use a palette whose colors were blended from red to yellow.

1. Choose Color Palettes from the Window menu.

2. In the Color Palettes window, use the Palette pop-up menu to select the desired palette **(Figure 55)**.

3. With the pointer tool, select the first color in your blend **(Figure 56)**. For instance, if you want to blend the palette from red to yellow, you would first click the red color chip.

4. Hold down the Shift key and select your blend's destination color **(Figure 57)**. If blending from red to yellow, you'd select the yellow color chip. Holding down Shift allows you to select this destination color along with every color between it and the first selected color.

5. Choose Blend Colors from the Palette menu **(Figure 58)**. The palette will blend in a continuous tone from the first selected color to the second.

Figure 58. Choose **Blend Colors** from the **Palette** menu.

✔ **Tips**

■ Sometimes you'll want to control the number of color chips over which your blend occurs—for instance, you may want a blend to occupy only fifteen or twenty color chips, rather than taking up a hundred valuable chips in an already limited palette. To do this, you may have to move the two blended colors closer together in their palette so that they are separated by the desired number of color chips. To move a color chip, use the Palette window's hand tool to drag it to a new position in the palette.

■ Keep in mind that creating a blend can radically change your palette. For this reason, you may want to work with a duplicate of the original palette so you can always go back to the original if you don't like the results of the blend. To copy the current palette, choose Duplicate Palette from the Palette menu **(Figure 59)**, type a name for the new palette, and click OK.

Figure 59. Choose **Duplicate Palette** from the **Palette** menu.

Blend Colors within a Palette

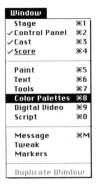

Figure 60. Choose **Color Palettes** from the **Window** menu.

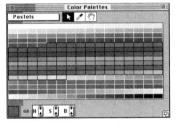

Figure 61. In the **Color Palettes** window, select a range of colors to be reversed.

Figure 62. Choose **Reverse Color Order** from the **Palette** menu.

To reverse the order of a palette's colors:

You can reverse the order of all the colors in a palette, or just within a select range. Reversing colors causes the chips positioned toward the end of the palette to be moved toward the palette's beginning. Doing so can change the coloring of cast members that are based on that particular palette, since the cast members refer to color chip positions in the palette that now hold new colors.

1. Choose Color Palettes from the Window menu **(Figure 60)**.

2. In the Color Palettes window, select a range of colors to be reversed. Using the pointer tool, select the first color chip in the range **(Figure 61)**.

3. Hold down the Shift key and select the last color chip in the range. All color chips between the two colors will also be selected.

4. Choose Reverse Color Order from the Palette menu. Director reverses the order of all the colors selected **(Figure 62)**.

✔ Tip

■ Reversing the color order in a palette will adversely affect the coloring of cast members using that palette. Consequently you may want to work with a duplicate of the palette, and then apply the new palette to cast members selectively. Simply choose Duplicate Palette from the Palette menu before beginning the reverse.

Reverse Order of Palette Colors

To sort colors in a palette:

Director can sort the colors in a palette by their hue, saturation, or brightness values. This feature is helpful when you would like to compare related colors in a palette.

1. Choose Color Palettes from the Window menu.

2. In the Color Palettes window, select a range of colors to sort **(Figure 63)**. Using the pointer tool, select the first color chip in the range.

3. Hold down the Shift key and select the last color chip in the range. All color chips between the two selections will be selected.

4. Choose Sort Colors from the Palette menu **(Figure 64)**.

5. In the Sort Colors dialog box, click either Hue, Saturation, or Brightness to indicate which color type you'd like to sort by **(Figure 65)**. Sorting by hue is recommended, since it arranges similar colors together in the palette.

✔ Tip

■ Like most other changes to a color palette, sorting the color order will adversely affect the coloring of cast members using that palette. Consequently you may want to create a duplicate of the palette, sort your colors in the copied palette, and then apply the new palette to cast members selectively. To do so, choose Duplicate Palette from the Palette menu before beginning the sort.

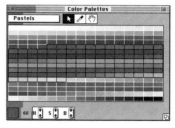

Figure 63. In the **Color Palettes** window, select a range of colors to sort.

Figure 64. Choose **Sort Colors** from the **Palette** menu.

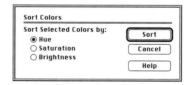

Figure 65. In the **Sort** dialog box, click Hue, Saturation, or Brightness to indicate which color type to sort by.

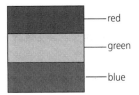

Figure 66. Color cycling, initial colors.

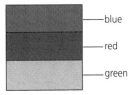

Figure 67. Color cycling, first step.

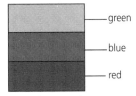

Figure 68. Color cycling, last step.

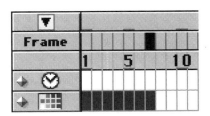

Figure 69. In the **Score's** palette channel, select the frame or series of frames that contain cast member(s) you wish to color cycle.

COLOR CYCLING

To cycle through colors in a palette:

The technique known as **color cycling** achieves the illusion of animation by rotating the colors in a cast member over time. For instance, let's take a cast member that is painted red on top, green in the middle, and blue at its base **(Figure 66)**. Color cycling would rotate these colors so that in the first step of the cycle, the red color would shift to the cast member's middle, the green to its base, and the blue to its top. In the next step of the cycle, the red would shift to the cast member's base, the green to its top, and blue to the middle **(Figures 67-68)**.

Cycling colors is the process used to animate TV weather maps, where a storm front appears to pulsate through a range of dark and light shades of blue. It's also handy for effects such as fire and explosions, where color pulses through a series of reds, yellows, and oranges.

Color cycling in Director is applied to a selected range of colors over a series of frames. Within those frames, any cast members painted in the selected colors will be cycled.

1. Place the cast members that you wish to color cycle in the desired animation channels and frames of Director's Score.

2. In the Score's Palette channel, select the frame or series of frames that contain the cast member(s) you wish to color cycle **(Figure 69)**. You can select a single frame if you would like to cycle through a stationary cast member (in other words, one that won't move while being cycled). Select a range if you would like to cycle throughout an animation.

3. Choose Set Palette from the Score menu **(Figure 70)**.

4. In the Set Palette dialog box, click the Color Cycling radio button to select it **(Figure 71)**.

5. Use the Palette pop-up menu to select the palette you wish to apply and cycle in the frames selected in the Score.

6. Click in the palette to select a range of colors that you wish to cycle. You can Shift-click two color chips to select the range of colors between them **(Figure 71)**.

7. Type the number of cycles in the Cycles box if you wish to make complete color cycles per frame. A cycle is achieved each time Director rotates through all the colors selected in step 6.

8. Check the Over Time box if you want the color cycling to occur over a series of frames **(Figure 72)**. In this case, the Cycles box is not active.

9. Check the Auto Reverse box if you wish the color cycling to reverse itself at the end of a cycle—for instance, to cycle colors from red to blue in the first cycle, and then from blue to red in the second.

10. Click Set to apply your color cycling to the selected frames in your Score.

Figure 70. Choose **Set Palette** from the **Score** menu.

The **Color Cycling** radio button

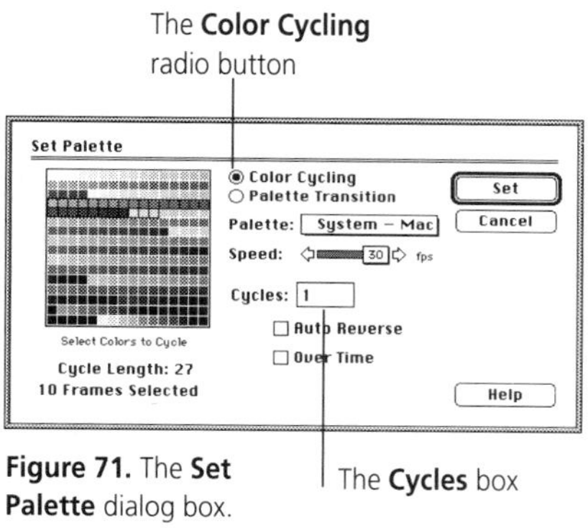

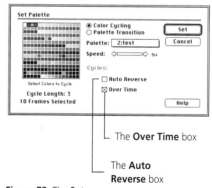

Figure 71. The **Set Palette** dialog box. | The **Cycles** box

The **Over Time** box

The **Auto Reverse** box

Figure 72. The **Set Palette** dialog box with the Over Time box checked.

Color Cycling

Note: Color cycling can occur only over a continuous range of colors in a palette. If you wish to cycle only through several colors that are scattered throughout the palette, you will have to group them first in the palette and then recast the cast members that you wish to color cycle *(see page 130 on "To copy and paste colors in a palette")*. Remember to select colors that are present in the cast members for the color cycling to affect, otherwise no cycling will take place. Also, if your cycling will affect a range of frames and the Over Time box is checked in the Set Palette dialog box, make sure that the number of colors you select for cycling is equal to or less than the number of frames you are color cycling in. If you select more colors to cycle (such as all 256 colors of a palette), and there are only 100 frames in the Score to cycle through, the colors will not fully cycle.

✔ **Tip**

■ Before playing your color cycling animation from the Score, open the Palette window (choose Color Palettes from the Window menu). Leave it open while playing the animation to see exactly how Director cycles through the colors you selected.

Auto Animate.

The Auto Animate command is used throughout this chapter. Choose Auto Animate from the Score menu **(Figure 1)**.

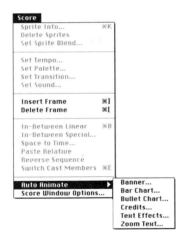

Figure 1. Choose **Auto Animate** from the **Score** menu.

Director's Auto Animate command provides a handful of ready-made animations. These include bullet charts, text banners, scrolling credits, and even straightforward bar charts. You can also use Auto Animate to apply special effects to text, making words zoom in and out, or appear to sparkle.

Animating elements such as these is easy because Director provides you with pre-set animation templates: you simply choose a pre-set animation, and then plug your own information and settings into the template. The problem with this approach is that you lose a degree of control over the animation (for instance, you can move a text heading from left to right, but you can't make it zig-zag). Nonetheless, Auto Animate can be a useful feature for quick and dirty work, and is especially useful for creating multimedia slide presentations that can afford to be straightforward in their appearance.

✔ Tip

■ One of Auto Animate's limitations is that it doesn't let you combine a number of its features into a single animation. For instance, you can't zoom text while making it sparkle at the same time. To overcome this limitation at least partially, look for ways to cleverly string together two or more separate Auto Animations in your Score, so that when played, they all seem to belong to the same sequence. By using this strategy, for example, you could create a zoom text animation that ends in frame 30, and then a sparkle text animation that picks right up at frame 31.

ANIMATING A BANNER

Use the Auto Animate Banner feature to animate a banner of text, like a ticker-tape-style news message, moving from the left to right side of your screen **(Figure 2)**.

1. In the Score window, click the desired frame in the desired animation channel to indicate where your banner animation should begin.

2. Choose Banner from the Auto Animate pop-up menu, under the Score menu.

3. In the Banner dialog box, type in the text you'd like to animate. You can animate only a single line of text (up to 255 characters) at a time **(Figures 3 & 4)**.

4. Click Create to place your banner animation into the Score. Before doing so, you may want to make some other adjustments discussed below.

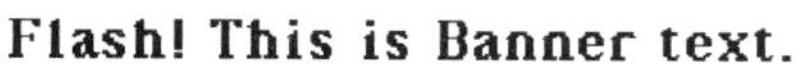

To Set the Text's Style:

1. In the Banner dialog box, click the Text Style button.

2. In the Text Style dialog box, choose the desired font, size, and style from the appropriate pop-up menus **(Figure 5)**. *Note*: You can only set one text style for the entire banner. This is another limitation of the Auto Animate feature.

3. To color the banner text, click and hold the Foreground color chip (the top chip of the overlapping two), and choose the desired color from the pop-up color palette **(Figures 6 & 7)**.

4. To give the banner text a background color as well, so that it's cast within a colored box, choose the color by clicking and holding the Background color chip, and selecting the desired color from the pop-up color palette.

5. Click OK.

Figure 2. An Auto Animate banner.

Figure 3. The Banner dialog box.

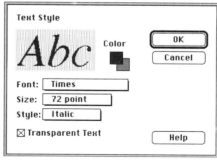

Figure 4. Type banner text into this box.

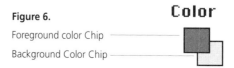

Figure 5. The Text Style box.

Figure 6.

Foreground color Chip ———

Background Color Chip ———

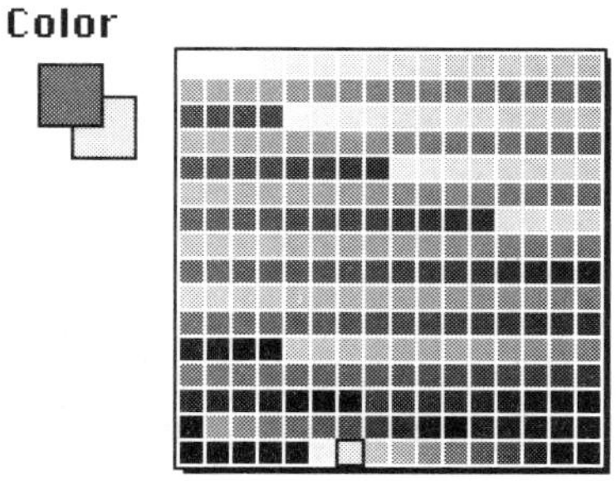

Color

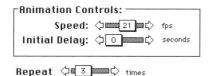

Figure 7. The pop-up color palette.

Figure 8. Use these controls to set the speed of your banner as well as any delays and repeats.

To Set Animation Speed, Delays and Repeats:

1. To set the speed at which your banner is animated, move the Speed slide bar in the Banner dialog box to the desired value, which is measured in frames per second **(Figure 8)**. A higher speed value means a faster banner, but the animation may also look less smooth.

2. To set a pause at the beginning of the banner's animation, move the Initial Delay slide bar to the desired value, measured in seconds.

3. To set the banner animation to repeat itself a certain number of times, move the Repeat slide bar to the desired value.

Set Animation Speed for Banners

ANIMATING BAR CHARTS

Use the Auto Animate Bar Chart feature to bring business bar charts to life. Creating bar charts is straightforward: You place a title heading above the chart (such as "1994 Widget Sales"), and assign labels to the chart's horizontal and vertical axis. You can animate up to six data bars at a time. The bars can be cast in a variety of graphic styles, to appear as stacked coins, bricks of bullion, concrete slabs, pointing fingers, or just solid colors **(Figure 9)**.

1. In the Score window, click the desired frame in the desired channel to indicate where your bar chart animation should begin.

2. Choose Bar Chart from the Auto Animate pop-up menu, under the Score menu.

3. In the Bar Chart dialog box, type your chart's title into the Title text box (e.g. "93/94 Unit Sales") **(Figure 10)**.

4. In the Vertical Label text box (below the Title Style button), type the name given to the chart's vertical axis (such as "In 100's").

5. Type the name given to each of the chart's data bars in the six Bar Label text boxes (for instance, "Q1", "Q2", "Q3", and "Q4") **(Figure 11)**. It's fine to leave some boxes empty if your chart doesn't call for using a full six data bars.

6. In the Value text boxes, type the data value (up to 32,000) that each respective bar should indicate on the chart. This tells Director how tall to make each bar on the chart, in relation to the chart's vertical axis **(Figure 11)**.

7. In the Range box, type the minimum and maximum data values to set a range **(Figure 12)**.

Figure 9. An Auto Animate bar chart.

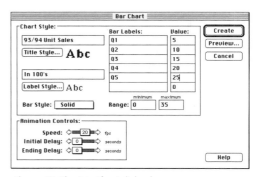

Figure 10. The **Bar Chart** dialog box.

Bar Labels:	Value:
Q1	5
Q2	10
Q3	15
Q4	20
Q5	25
	0

Figure 11. Type in the labels and values for each bar in your chart .

Figure 12. Type in a range for the data values of your bars.

	minimum	maximum
Range:	0	35

Bar Style:

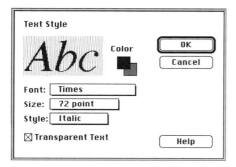

Figure 13. Use the **Bar Style** pop-up menu to choose the graphical style in which your data bars are displayed.

Text Style

Figure 14. The **Text Style** box.

Color

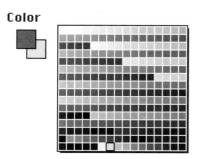

Figure 15.

Foreground color chip

Background color chip

Color

Figure 16. The pop-up color palette.

In general, try setting the minimum value to 0, and the maximum value at a number that's slightly greater than the largest value you assigned to your data bars in step 6.

8. Use the Bar Style pop-up menu to choose the graphic style for your data bars. Choices are Solid, Concrete, Coins, Bullion and Hand. **(Figure 13)**.

9. Click Create to place your chart animation into the Score. Before doing so, you may want to make some other adjustments discussed below.

To Set Text Styles for Bar Charts:

1. Director lets you set the text styles of your chart's title, vertical label, and horizontal label. In the Bar Chart dialog box, click either the Title Style or Label Style buttons to open the Text Style dialog box.

2. In the Text Style dialog box, choose the desired font, size, and style from the appropriate pop-up menus **(Figure 14)**. *Note:* You can only set one text style for the chart's title, and one style for all of its labels. This is a limitation of the Auto Animate feature.

3. To color the chart's title or label text, click and hold the Foreground color chip and choose the desired color from the pop-up color palette **(Figures 15–16)**.

4. To give your chart's text a background color as well, so that it's cast within a colored box, choose the color by clicking and holding the Background color chip and selecting the desired color from the pop-up color palette.

5. Click OK.

To Set Animation Speed and Delays for Bar Charts:

1. To set the speed at which your bar chart is animated, move the Speed slide bar (or click the small arrows on either side of the bar) to the desired value, which is measured roughly in frames per second **(Figure 17)**. A higher speed value means a faster animation, but the animation may also look less smooth.

2. To set a pause at the beginning of the chart's animation, move the Initial Delay slide bar to the desired value, measured in seconds.

3. To pause the action when your bar chart animation has finished, move the Ending Delay slide bar to the desired value, measured in seconds.

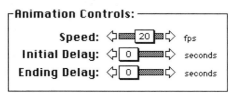

Figure 17. Use these slide bar controls to set the speed of your bar chart animation, as well as any delays.

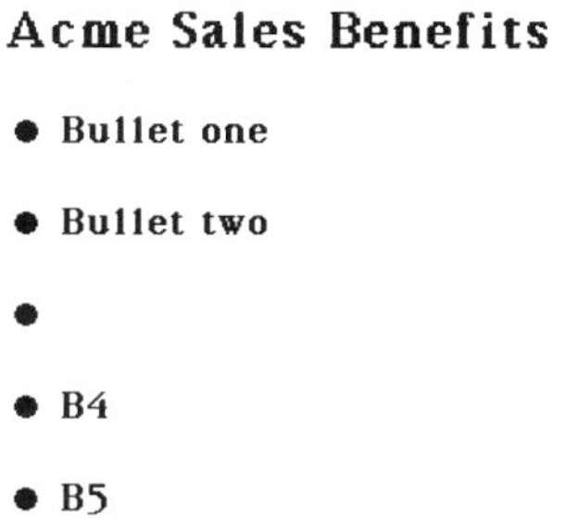

Acme Sales Benefits

- **Bullet one**

- **Bullet two**

-

- **B4**

- **B5**

Figure 18. Use Auto Animate to create a bullet chart where the bullets animate into position.

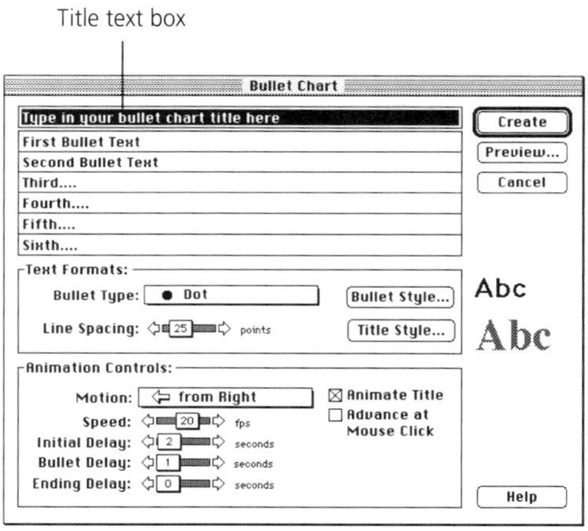

Title text box

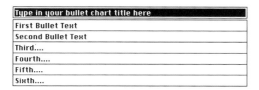

Figure 19. The **Bullet Chart** dialog box.

Type in your bullet chart title here
First Bullet Text
Second Bullet Text
Third....
Fourth....
Fifth....
Sixth....

Figure 20. Type the text for each of your chart's six bullets into these text boxes.

ANIMATING A BULLET CHART

Use the Auto Animate Bullet Chart feature to create a bullet text chart, where each bullet item in the chart can be animated into place in a number of styles **(Figure 18)**.

1. In the Score window, click the desired frame in the desired channel to indicate where your bullet chart animation should begin.

2. Choose Bullet Chart from the Auto Animate pop-up menu, under the Score menu.

3. In the Bullet Chart dialog box, type your chart's title into the Title text box **(Figure 19)** (for instance, "Acme Sales Benefits"). This title will appear at the top of the chart, above the bullet items you create.

4. Type the text for each desired bullet into the six Bullet text boxes. It's fine to leave some boxes empty if your chart doesn't call for six bullet items. **(Figure 20)**.

5. Use the Bullet Style pop-up menu to select the graphical symbol that appears at the left of your bullet text. Your choices include round bullets, check marks, pointing hands, and arrows **(Figure 21 *next page*)**.

6. Use the Motion pop-up menu to choose the direction from which your bulleted text will move onto the screen **(Figure 22 *next page*)**.

7. To set the amount of white space between each bullet item, move the Line Spacing slide bar in the Bullet Chart dialog box to the desired value (from 0 to 72 points).

Animating a Bullet Chart

8. To animate the title of your bullet chart, check the Animate Title box in the Bullet Chart dialog box.

9. Click Create in the Bullet Chart dialog box to place your bullet animation into the Score. Before doing so, you may want to make some other adjustments discussed below.

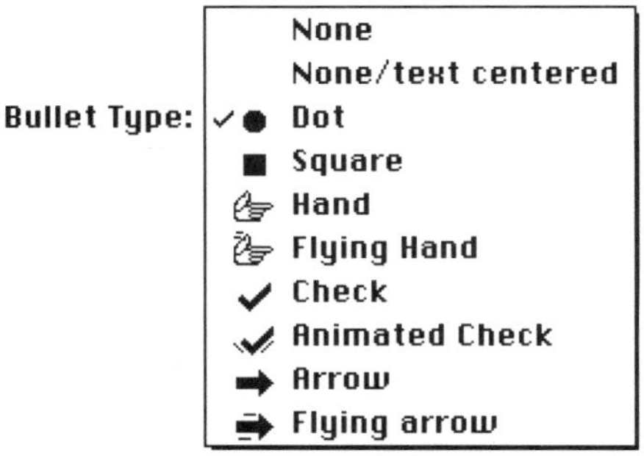

To set text styles of Bullet Charts:

1. Director lets you set the text styles for either your chart's title, or its bulleted text. In the Bullet Chart dialog box, click either the Title Style or Bullet Style buttons to open the Text Style dialog box.

2. In the Text Style dialog box, choose the desired font, size, and style from the appropriate pop-up menus **(Figure 23)**. *Note:* You can only set one text style for the chart's title, and one style for the bullets. This is a limitation of the Auto Animate feature.

3. To color the chart's title or bullet text, click and hold the Foreground color chip (the top chip of the overlapping two) in the Text Style dialog box, and choose the desired color from the pop-up palette **(Figures 24–25)**.

4. To give your chart's text a background color as well, so that it's cast within a colored box, choose the color by clicking and holding the Background color chip, and selecting the desired color from the pop-up color palette.

5. Click OK.

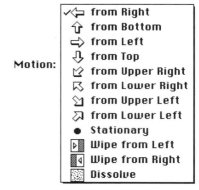

Figure 21. Choose a bullet type from the **Bullet Style** pop-up menu.

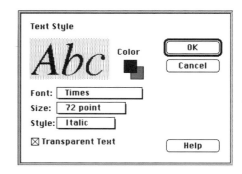

Figure 22. Use the **Motion** pop-up menu to set the direction from which your bullets will animate into place.

Figure 23. The **Text Style** box.

Set Text Styles for Bullet Charts

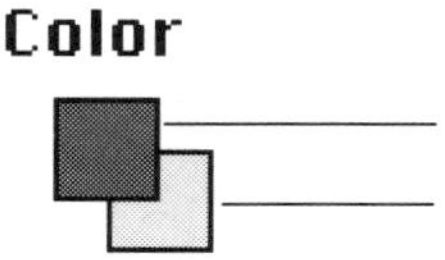

Color

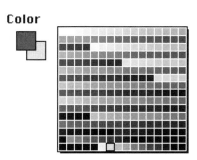

Figure 24.

— Foreground color chip
— Background color chip

Color

Figure 25. The pop-up color palette.

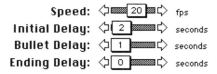

Speed: ◁ 20 ▷ fps
Initial Delay: ◁ 2 ▷ seconds
Bullet Delay: ◁ 1 ▷ seconds
Ending Delay: ◁ 0 ▷ seconds

Figure 26. Use these slide bar controls to set the speed of your bullet chart animation, as well as any delays.

To Set Animation Speed and Delays for Bullet Charts:

1. To set the speed at which your bullet text is animated into place, move the Speed slide bar (or click the small arrows on either side of the bar) to the desired value, which is measured roughly in frames per second **(Figure 26)**. A higher speed value means a faster animation, but the animation may also look less smooth.

2. To set a pause at the beginning of the animation, move the Initial Delay slide bar to the desired value, measured in seconds.

3. To set a pause before each bullet is animated, move the Bullet Delay slide bar to the desired value, measured in seconds.

4. To pause the action when your bullet animation has finished, move the Ending Delay slide bar to the desired value, measured in seconds.

To Preview and Position the Animation:

You can preview the bullet chart you create in order to fine-tune it before placing it in the Score. To do so, click the Preview button in the Bullet Chart dialog box *(see page 154 for more details)*. Director also lets you position your chart to play anywhere on screen. To do so, see page 155.

ANIMATING CREDITS

Use the Auto Animate Credits feature to animate a series of movie-style text credits that scroll from the bottom of the screen to the top **(Figure 27)**.

1. In the Score window, click the desired frame in the desired channel to indicate where your credits animation should begin.

2. Choose Credits from the Auto Animate pop-up menu, under the Score menu.

3. In the Credits dialog box, type the text you'd like to animate into the Credits Text box. You can press the Return key to start a new line in the credits **(Figures 28–29)**.

4. Use the Justification pop-up menu to align your credits to the left or right side of the screen, or to center them. **(Figure 30)**.

5. Click Create to place your credits animation into the Score.

✓ Tip

■ Director accepts up to 255 characters in a credits animation. If your credits require more characters, try creating multiple credit animations, and then arrange them in your Score so that they play sequentially.

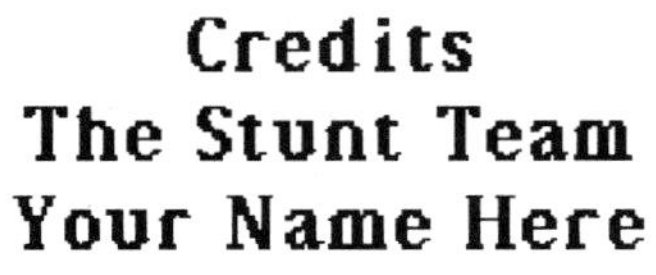

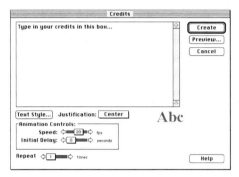

Figure 27. A credits animation.

Figure 28. The **Credits** dialog box.

Figure 29. Type your credits into this text box.

Figure 30. The **Justification** pop-up menu.

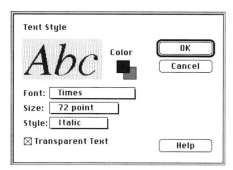

Figure 31. The **Text Style** dialog box.

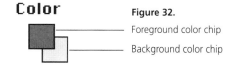

Figure 32.
Foreground color chip
Background color chip

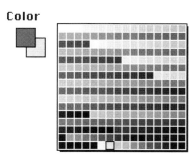

Figure 33. The pop-up color palette.

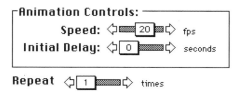

Figure 34. Use these slide bar controls to set the speed of your Credits animation, as well as any delay and repeats.

To set text styles of Credits:

1. In the Credits dialog box, click the Text Style button.

2. In the Text Style dialog box, choose the desired font, size, and style from the appropriate pop-up menus **(Figure 31)**. You can only set one text style for the entire credits animation.

3. To color the credit's text, click and hold the Foreground color chip and choose the desired color from the pop-up palette **(Figures 32–33)**.

4. To give your credit's text a background color, so that it's cast within a colored box, choose the color by clicking and holding the Background color chip, and selecting the desired color from the pop-up color palette.

5. Click OK.

To Set Animation Speed, Delays and Repeats for Credits:

1. To set the speed at which your credits are animated, move the Speed slide bar to the desired value, which is measured roughly in frames per second. A higher speed value means a faster animation, but the animation may also look less smooth.

2. To set a pause at the beginning of the credit's animation, move the Initial Delay slide bar to the desired value, measured in seconds.

3. To repeat a credits animation, move the Repeat slide bar to the desired value **(Figure 34).**

TO ZOOM TEXT

Use the Zoom Text Auto Animate feature to zoom in and out of text on the screen.

1. In the Score window, click the desired frame in the desired channel to indicate where your zoom animation should begin.

2. Choose Zoom Text from the Auto Animate pop-up menu, under the Score menu.

3. In the Zoom Text dialog box, type in the text you'd like to zoom. You can type up to 255 characters, but try to keep the text brief so that it all fits on screen **(Figure 35)**.

4. Use the Zoom Type pop-up menu to select the desired zoom style. Your choices are Zoom In, Zoom Out, or Zoom in, Then Out **(Figure 36)**.

5. Click Create to place your zoom animation into the Score. Before doing so, you may want to make some other adjustments discussed below.

To Set the Text's Style:

1. In the Zoom Text dialog box, click the Text Style button.

2. In the Text Style dialog box, choose the desired font, size, and style from the appropriate pop-up menus **(Figure 37)**. You can only set one text style for the entire zoom animation.

3. To color the zoom text, click and hold the Foreground color chip and choose the desired color from the pop-up color palette **(Figures 38-39)**.

4. To give the zoom text a background color, so that it's cast within a colored box, choose the color by clicking and holding the Background color chip, and selecting the desired color from the pop-up color palette.

5. Click OK.

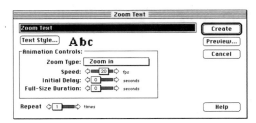

Figure 35. The **Zoom Text** dialog box. Enter zoom text on the first line at the top.

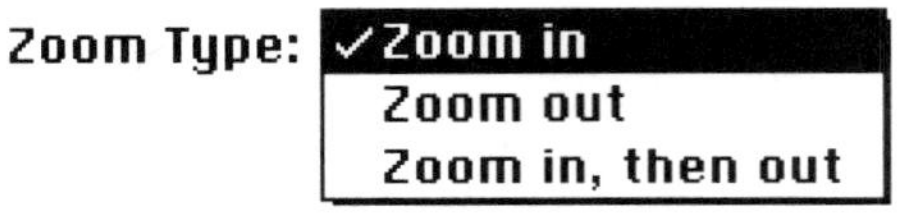

Zoom Type:
✓ Zoom in
Zoom out
Zoom in, then out

Figure 36. Use the **Zoom Type** pop-up menu to select the desired zoom style.

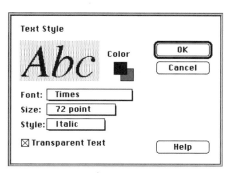

Figure 37. The **Text Style** dialog box.

Color

Figure 38.

Foreground color chip

Background color chip

Color

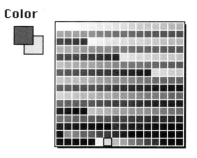

Figure 39. The pop-up color palette.

To Set Animation Speed, Delays and Repeats for Zoom Text:

1. To set the speed at which your zoom is animated, move the Speed slide bar (or click the small arrows on either side of the bar) to the desired value, which is measured roughly in frames per second. A higher speed value means a faster zoom, but the animation may also look less smooth **(Figure 40)**.

2. To set a pause at the beginning of the zoom's animation, move the Initial Delay slide bar to the desired value, measured in seconds.

3. To set a pause when your zoomed text reaches its full size, move the Full-Size Duration slide bar to the desired value, measured in seconds.

4. To repeat a zoom animation—for instance, so that text zooms in and out a few times—move the Repeat slide bar to the desired value.

Set Zoom Text Style and Speed

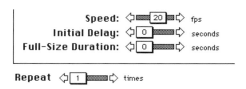

Figure 40. Use these slide bar controls to set the speed of your zoom animation, as well as any delays and repeats.

ANIMATING TEXT EFFECTS

The Auto Animate Text Effects feature lets you animate text with three varieties of special effects: The Sparkle effect makes text appear to glitter on screen; the Letter Slide effect forms a word or series of words by animating each letter into place from the right-hand side of the screen; and the Typewriter effect places letters on screen one at a time, as if they were being typed.

1. In the Score window, click the desired frame in the desired channel to indicate where your effects animation should begin.

2. Choose Text Effects from the Auto Animate pop-up menu, under the Score menu.

3. In the Text Effects dialog box, type the text you'd like to animate **(Figure 41)**.

4. Use the Effect pop-up menu to choose the desired text effect: Sparkle, Letter slide, or Typewriter **(Figure 42)**.

5. Click Create to place your effects animation into the Score. Before doing so, you may want to make some other adjustments discussed below.

To Set the Text's Style:

1. From the Text Effects dialog box, click the Text Style button.

2. In the Text Style dialog dialog box, choose the desired font, size, and style from the appropriate pop-up menus **(Figure 43)**. You can only set one text style for the entire effects animation. This is a limitation of the Auto Animate feature.

3. To color the animated text, click and hold the Foreground color chip and choose the desired color from the pop-up color palette **(Figures 44-45)**.

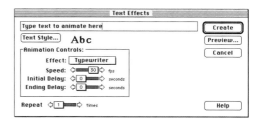

Figure 41. The **Text Effects** dialog box. Type your text on the first line at the top.

Figure 42. Use the **Effect** pop-up menu to select the desired text effect.

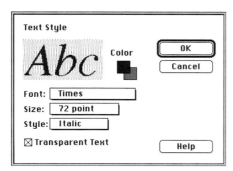

Figure 43. The **Text Style** dialog box.

Color

Figure 44.

Foreground color chip

Background color chip

Color

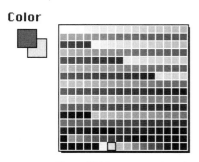

Figure 45. The pop-up color palette.

4. To give the effects text a background color, so that it's cast within a colored box, choose the color by clicking and holding the Background color chip, and selecting the desired color from the pop-up color palette.

5. Click OK.

To Set Animation Speed, Delays and Repeats of Text Effects:

1. To set the speed at which your text effect is animated, move the Speed slide bar (or click the small arrows on either side of the bar) to the desired value, which is measured roughly in frames per second **(Figure 46)**. A higher speed value means a faster effect, but the animation may also look less smooth.

2. To set a pause at the beginning of a text effect animation, move the Initial Delay slide bar to the desired value, measured in seconds.

3. To pause the action when your effects animation has finished, move the Ending Delay slide bar to the desired value, measured in seconds.

4. To repeat the effects animation—for instance, so that your text continues to sparkle—move the Repeat slide bar to the desired value.

Speed: ◁▥▥ 20 ▥▥▷ fps
Initial Delay: ◁ 0 ▥▥▥▷ seconds
Ending Delay: ◁ 0 ▥▥▥▷ seconds

Repeat ◁ 1 ▥▥▥▷ times

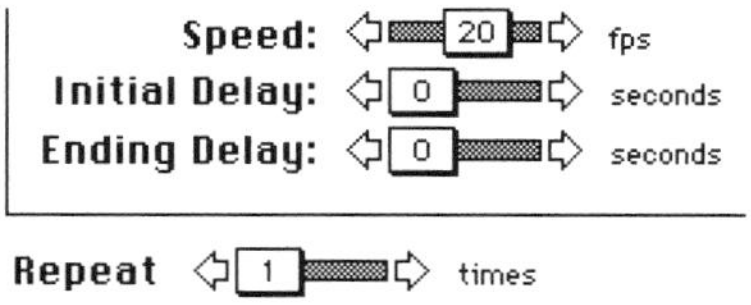

Figure 46. Use these slide bar controls to set the speed of your Text Effects animation, as well as any delays and repeats.

To Preview an Auto Animation:

Once an Auto Animation has been placed into Director's Score, it cannot be modified. To make any adjustments, you must erase the old Auto Animation from the Score, and create a new one. Director provides the opportunity to preview any Auto Animation before placing it in the Score through the Preview dialog box. After seeing a preview, you can go back and fine tune the animation—perhaps change its frame rate to make it more smooth, change its type size or style, and so on.

1. Click the Preview button in the main dialog box of any Auto Animation feature that Director supports—Zoom, Bullets, Text Effects, Banner, and so on (**Figure 47**). Director plays a preview of the Auto Animation and displays the Preview dialog box **(Figure 48** shows the Text Effects Preview box, which is similar to the Preview boxes of all the other Auto Animate features)**.

2. Click the play button in the Preview dialog box to repeat the preview, or click cancel to cancel the preview.

The Preview button.

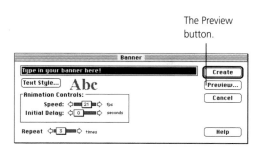

Figure 47. Click the Preview button on the right side of the main dialog box for any Auto Animation feature.

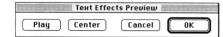

Figure 48. The **Text Effects Preview** dialog box.

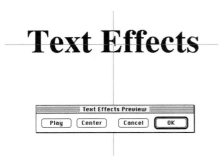

Figure 49. With the **Preview** box open, click anywhere on screen to position the Auto Animation.

To Position an Auto Animation:

Director ordinarily positions Auto Animations to play in the center of your screen. This play position can be changed easily from Director's Preview dialog box.

1. Open the Preview dialog box for your Auto Animation using the steps on page 154.

2. Click anywhere on screen (notice how the mouse pointer becomes a crosshair symbol as you position it). Director now plays the animation directly centered at the point where you clicked **(Figure 49)**.

3. You can reposition the animation again simply by clicking in a new location on the screen.

4. To center an animation to its original position, click the center button in the Preview dialog box.

5. Click OK to return to the Auto Animation dialog box. Director will now play your animation in the last position set from the Preview box.

ANIMATION TECHNIQUES

Score	
Sprite Info...	⌘K
Delete Sprites	
Set Sprite Blend...	
Set Tempo...	
Set Palette...	
Set Transition...	
Set Sound...	
Insert Frame	⌘]
Delete Frame	⌘[
In-Between Linear	⌘B
In-Between Special...	
Space to Time...	
Paste Relative	
Reverse Sequence	
Switch Cast Members	⌘E
Auto Animate ▶	Banner...
Score Window Options...	Bar Chart...
	Bullet Chart...
	Credits...
	Text Effects...
	Zoom Text...

Figure 1. The Auto Animate features are covered in the Auto Animate chapter.

Figure 2. With **Step Recording**, animation is created by manually adjusting and recording cast member positions on a frame-by-frame basis. Each successive frame of the cyclist is slightly shifted to the left on the Stage and Step recorded to form an animation sequence.

Director provides a variety of techniques for creating detailed animations. These can be classified into four basic groups—**Step recording**, **Real-time recording**, **Auto animation**, and **In-betweening**. By understanding the strengths and weaknesses of these approaches, you will learn how to select the most appropriate technique for achieving your animation goal.

This chapter covers the basics of using Step Recording, Real-time recording, and In-betweening. Also covered are the handy commands—Space to Time, Cast to Time, and Paste Relative. Film loops are included as well. The Auto animation features **(Figure 1)**, such as animated banners and bullet charts, are covered in the previous Auto Animate chapter.

Step Recording

Step recording is the most precise method of creating animation in Director—you arrange each frame of an animation by hand. Step recording is also the most labor-intensive method for the same reason: First you arrange your cast members in a given frame, then record the frame, then rearrange the cast members slightly, then record the next frame, then rearrange, then record, and so on **(Figure 2)**. This process of creating a series of frames, all of which feature small differences in the size or position of cast members, is what makes animation possible.

If you're looking to perform quick and painless animation, Step recording is not the method to use. You'd be better served by using techniques such as In-betweening, Real-time recording, Cast to time, or Space to time, which are also detailed in this chapter. But if you want complete, hands-on control over the behavior of cast members from one frame to another, Step recording is the method of choice. Also, if you're new to animation in general, you'll find it useful to master this technique, because it embodies fundamental animation concepts.

To Step-Record an Animation:

1. In the Score window, click the desired frame in the desired animation channel to indicate where in the Score your Step recording will begin. If you don't select a frame, Director will probably start with frame 1 in channel 1 **(Figure 3)**.

2. Drag a cast member onto the Stage. As soon as you do this, a recording light appears beside the channel number to which you have assigned this cast member **(Figure 4)**. The light indicates that the current frame of your animation is being recorded to the Score.

3. Position the cast member as it should appear in the first frame of your animation. Once in position, click the Step Forward button in Director's Control Panel window **(Figure 5)** to record the first frame to the Score, and move the playback head to the second frame of your animation.

4. Position the cast member as it should appear in the next frame (again, you will probably want to move it slightly or change its shape). Once in position, click the Step Forward button in the Control Panel window to record this new frame to the Score.

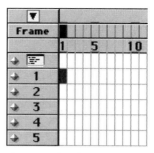

Figure 3. Select the cell in the Score where your Step recording should begin.

Step Record Indicator

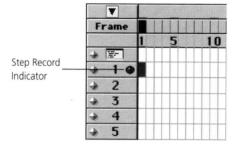

Figure 4. When you drag a cast member onto the Stage, a recording light automatically appears beside the channel number to which the cast member is assigned.

Step Forward button

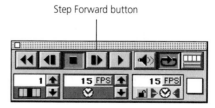

Figure 5. Click the Step Forward button in the Control Panel to record a frame of your animation, and to advance to the next frame.

Rewind button   Play button

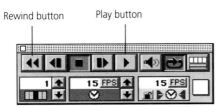

Figure 6. Click Rewind then Play in the Control Panel to play back your full sequence of frames.

Figure 7. By selecting then Option-clicking a sprite on the Stage, you turn on Step recording for the channel that contains this sprite. The sprite is highlighted by a thick border indicating that it's being recorded.

5. Repeat Step 4 as many times as necessary to complete the animation. When you are finished, you can use the Control Panel window to rewind and play back the full sequence of frames **(Figure 6)**.

✓ **Tips**

■ You can turn step recording on or off for a particular channel by holding down the Option key and clicking the channel number to the left of the channel cells.

■ You can record a sprite that's already on the Stage by clicking it first to select it, then clicking it again while holding down the Option key. A thick selection border appears surrounding the sprite, indicating that it is being recorded **(Figure 7)**. Step recording is turned on in the channel that contains this sprite.

■ If you wish to turn on Step recording for multiple sprites on the Stage, Shift-click each of them, then Option-click each of them. The Step record indicator appears in each of the channels containing these sprites and a selection border highlights each sprite on the Stage.

Step Record an Animation

To place cast members into sequential frames using Cast to Time:

The Cast to Time command offers a convenient way to create an animation by moving a series of cast members from the Cast window into sequential frames in Director's Score. Suppose you have ten cast members that form an animation sequence such as a character walking. By placing these ten cast members into sequential frames in the Score, an animation is formed. Normally when you drag a multiple cast member selection from the Cast window into the Score, the cast members are all placed into the same frame, but each into a separate channel. Use the Cast to Time command to place cast members of a multiple cast member selection into sequential frames in the same channel.

1. In the Score window, click a cell to indicate the starting point where your cast members should be placed **(Figure 8)**.

2. In the Cast window, select the cast members that you want to move onto the Stage and into your Score. You can select a sequential range of cast members by clicking the first member in the sequence and while holding down the Shift key, clicking the last member in the sequence. To select cast members in a nonsequential order (for instance, the first, third, and seventh members), hold down the Command key while clicking.

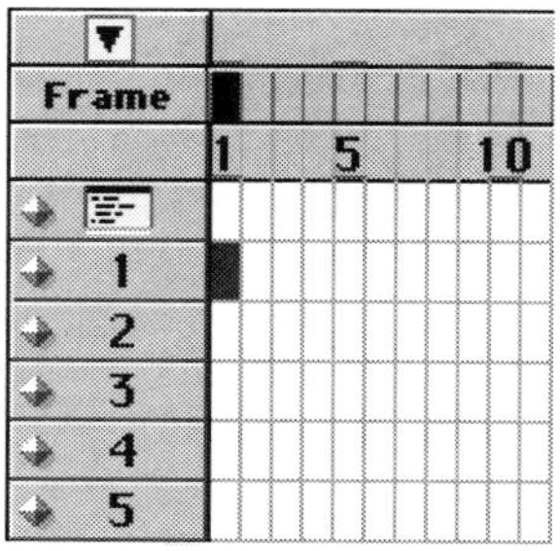

Figure 8. Select the cell in the Score to indicate the starting point where your cast members should be placed.

Cast to Time

Figure 9. Choose **Cast to Time** from the **Cast** menu.

Figure 10. Ten selected cast members placed into sequential frames in the Score using **Cast to Time**.

3. With the Cast window still active, choose Cast to Time from the Cast menu **(Figure 9)**. Director places the selected cast members onto the Stage, and into their respective frames (for instance, if you selected 10 cast members, they will be placed into 10 sequential frames of Director's Score) **(Figure 10)**. You can now rewind and play your new animation using the Control Panel window.

✔ **Tips**

■ As a shortcut, you can place selected cast members across frames in the Score by holding the Option key while dragging them from the Cast window.

■ Before using Cast to Time, make sure that the order of cast members in your selected sequence corresponds to the order the cast members should have in the frames.

■ To reposition an entire sequence of cast members that was placed on the Stage using the Cast to Time command, select all the cells that contain the cast members you'd like to move, and drag the cast member that appears on the Stage to a new position. Although it seems like you've only moved one cast member, Director moves the entire sequence of cast members in the frames that you selected in the Score.

Space to Time

You will find it convenient to initially place cast members that form an animation sequence, such as a dog running across the Stage, into a single frame in the Score, so you can view all of them at once on the Stage for proper positioning. After positioning these cast members, you will probably want to transfer them from the single frame in the Score to multiple frames occupying a single channel, to form an animation sequence. The Space to Time command allows you to do just that.

1. Select a cell in the Score where you wish your animation sequence to begin.

2. Drag the cast members that comprise your animation sequence one by one from the Cast window onto the Stage area. Director automatically places these cast members into sequential channels in the Score, all in the same frame **(Figure 11)**. Be sure to drag them in the order in which your animation sequence takes place.

3. Select the cells in the Score that comprise your animation sequence, and choose Space to Time from the Score menu to rearrange the cells into a single channel **(Figure 12)**.

4. In the Space to Time dialog box, enter the Spread sprites value that indicates how many frames apart the cast members should be placed **(Figure 13)**. Director rearranges your sprites so that they occupy a single channel, instead of a single frame **(Figure 14)**.

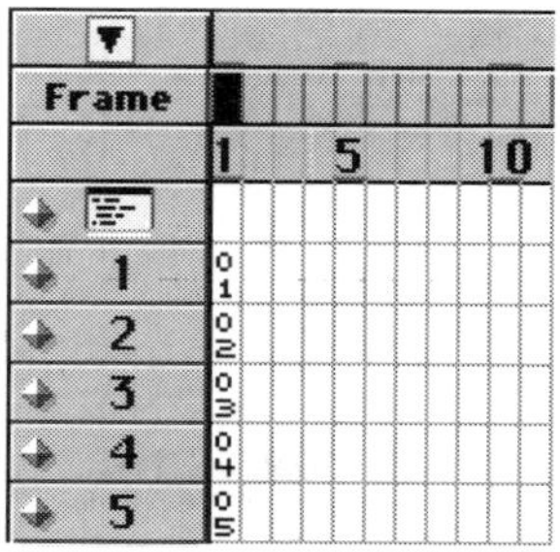

Figure 11. Cast members dragged from the Cast window onto the Stage are automatically placed into sequential channels in the Score.

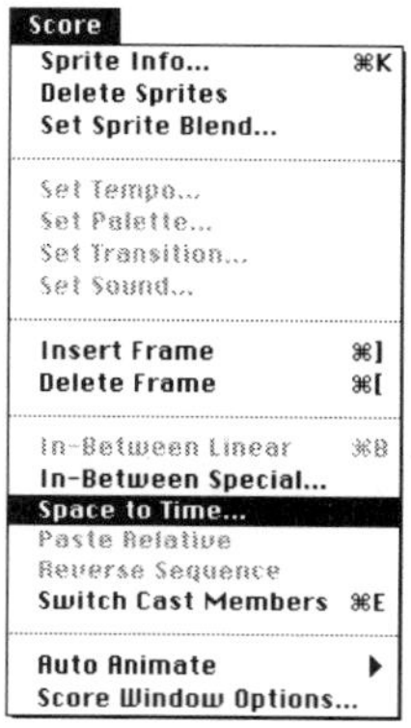

Figure 12. Choose **Space to Time** from the **Score** menu.

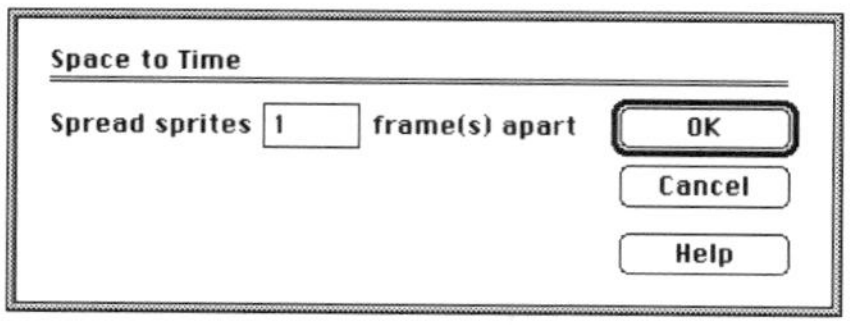

Figure 13. The Spread sprites value in the **Space to Time** dialog box determines how many frames apart sprites will be placed in the Score.

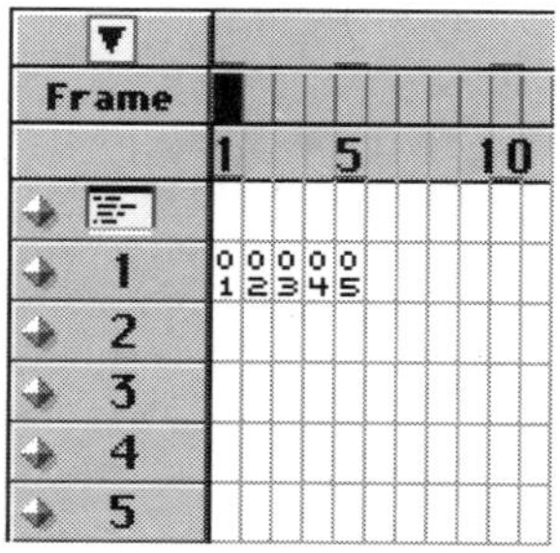

Figure 14. Sprites are shown rearranged into a single channel using **Space to Time**.

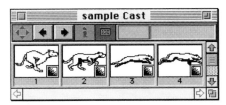

Figure 15. The **Cast** window here shows four cast members that comprise the animated sequence of a running dog.

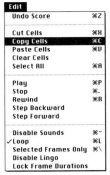

Figure 16. Select the cells in the Score that make up your animated sequence.

Figure 17. Choose **Copy Cells** from the **Edit** menu.

Figure 18. Choose **Paste Relative** from the **Score** menu.

Figure 19. Using **Paste Relative**, a copy of an animated sequence (such as a running dog in this case) is placed on the Stage exactly where the previous sequence ends. The first six frames are shown.

✔ **Tip**

■ Space to Time is a convenient way to set up the points used with the curved In-between feature *(see pages 168-169)*. Place your cast member into the key points on the Stage all in a single frame. Then use Space to Time to transfer these key points into multiple frames. Enter a value of 10 to 20 for the Sprite spread so that your in-between curve consists of enough frames to appear smooth.

To paste an animated sequence relative to another:

A useful technique for creating a long animated sequence involves repeating a shorter sequence of cast members over and over again while moving them across the Stage. Take for example a running dog, with only four distinct cast members in its sequence **(Figure 15)**. Continuously alternating through this short sequence while moving it across the Stage creates the illusion of a much longer animation. Paste Relative allows you to link together a series of short sequences to achieve this effect.

1. In the Score, select the cells that make up your animated sequence **(Figure 16)**.

2. In the Edit menu, choose Copy Cells **(Figure 17)**.

3. Select the cell in the Score immediately following the last cell of your sequence.

4. From the Score menu, choose Paste Relative **(Figure 18)**. A copy of your sequence is placed onto the Stage beginning exactly where the previous sequence ends **(Figure 19)**.

Paste Relative

IN-BETWEEN ANIMATION

Of the various animation techniques that Director supports, **In-between** animation is probably the most practical and convenient to use. That's because creating an In-between animation is only a matter of setting up the first frame of an animation in which a cast member is in location A, and then setting up the last frame of the animation in which the cast member is in location B **(Figure 20)**. Once you've created these so-called **key frames**, you can use the In-between command to automatically draw all the frames necessary to move the cast member from the first key frame to the second. Director creates all the frames *in between* the key frames you just established, with each of the in-between frames featuring the cast member in a slightly different position **(Figure 21)**. It's an extremely quick and painless process, and it creates smooth, fluid motion that in many instances would be difficult to achieve if you were to create each of the animation frames by hand. You can set the number of frames that lie between your key frames. The more empty frames you set up between your key frames, the smoother your animation will be.

To create an In-between animation along a straight path:

1. In the Score window, click the desired frame in the desired channel to indicate where to begin your In-between animation **(Figure 22)**.

2. Drag the cast member you wish to animate from the Cast window onto Director's Stage to create the first key frame of the animation. Be sure to position it at the location where your animation should begin.

Location A

Location B

Figure 20. Locations A and B represent the **key frames** that are used with the In-between command.

Figure 21. The In-between command fills in all the frames *in between* your **key frames**. Ten separate frames are shown here all at once.

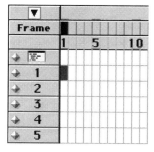

Figure 22. Select the cell in the Score where your In-between animation should begin.

Figure 23. Choose **Copy Cells** from the **Edit** menu.

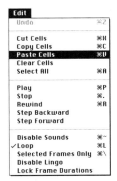

Figure 24. Choose **Paste Cells** from the **Edit** menu.

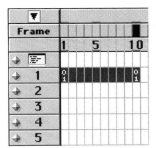

Figure 25. In the Score, select the **key frames** and all the frames between them.

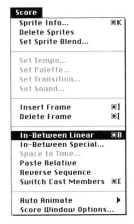

Figure 26. Choose **In-Between Linear** from the **Score** menu.

3. Click the Score window to make it active, and select the cell that contains the cast member you just positioned on the Stage. Choose Copy Cells from the Edit menu **(Figure 23)**.

4. In the Score window, select a later frame in the same channel that the first key frame occupies to set up your second key frame. The more empty frames that are between the first key frame and the second, the smoother your animation will be.

5. Choose Paste Cells from the Edit menu to place your cast member into this second key frame, and onto Director's Stage **(Figure 24)**. Now, on the Stage, move the cast member to the location where your animation should end.

6. In the Score window, select all the frames from the starting point to the ending point of your animation by dragging across them **(Figure 25)**. Be sure to include the key frames in this selection.

7. Choose In-Between Linear from the Score menu **(Figure 26)**. Director fills in all the *in between* frames to create your animation.

In-Between Animation

To add acceleration and deceleration:

You can use the In-between command to animate a cast member so that it speeds up as it begins to move along its path, and then slows down as it nears the end of its path.

1. To do this, follow steps 1-6 on pages 164-165 to create your key frames and select them in the Score window.

2. Instead of choosing In-Between Linear from the Score menu, choose In-Between Special **(Figure 27)**.

3. In the In-Between Special dialog box, use the pop-up menus **Accelerate Over First Frames** and **Decelerate Over Last Frames** to set the number of frames in which the cast member will speed up at the beginning of its animation, and slow down at its end **(Figure 28)**.

4. Click OK to create the animation.

To stretch or squeeze a sprite with In-betweening:

You can use In-betweening to create a sequence of frames that shows your sprite gradually stretching or squeezing. Once again, all you need to do is set up the key frames of your In-between animation. In this case, your first key frame would show your cast member in its original unsqueezed or unstretched state. The second key frame would show the cast member as it would appear in the last frame of your In-between animation in its final stretched or squeezed form.

1. In the Score window, click the desired frame in the desired channel to indicate where to begin your In-between animation.

2. Drag the cast member you wish to stretch or squeeze **(Figure 29)** from the Cast window onto Director's Stage to create the first key frame in your animation.

Figure 27. Choose **In-Between Special** from the **Score** menu.

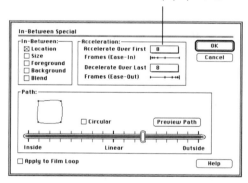

Figure 28. Use the Acceleration pop-up menus in the **In-Between Special** dialog box to set the acceleration and deceleration of your In-between animation.

Figure 29. Drag the cast member you wish to stretch or squeeze from the Cast window onto the Stage.

Accelerate, Stretch Sprites with In-Between

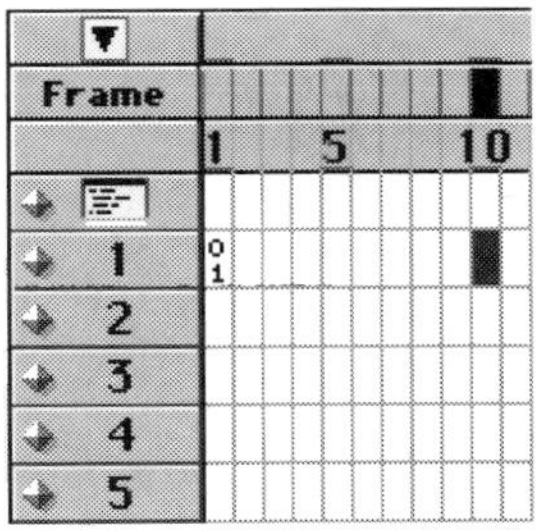

Figure 30. In the Score window, select a later frame in the same channel that the first key frame occupies. This frame will be your second key frame.

Figure 31. Drag the handles on the selection rectangle surrounding your sprite to stretch or squeeze it.

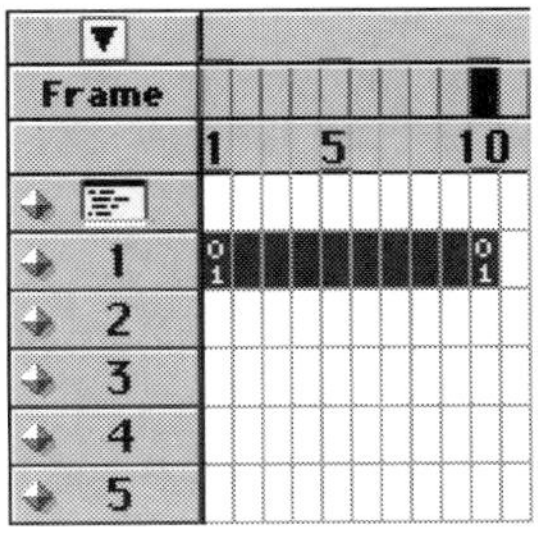

Figure 32. In the Score, select the **key frames** and all the frames between them.

Figure 33. Choose **In Between Special** from the **Score** menu.

3. Click the Score window to make it active, and click the cell that you just created so that it's selected (if not already).

4. In the Score window, select a later frame in the same channel that the first first key frame occupies to set up your second key frame **(Figure 30)**. The more empty frames that are between the first key frame and the second, the more gradual will be your stretching or squeezing.

5. Choose Paste Cells from the Edit menu to place your cast member into this second key frame, and onto the Stage. Now drag the handles on the selection rectangle that surrounds this sprite to stretch or squeeze it **(Figure 31)**.

6. In the Score window, select all the cells from the starting point to the ending point of your animation by dragging across them **(Figure 32)**. Be sure to include the key frames in this selection.

7. Choose In-Between Special from the Score menu **(Figure 33)**.

8. Make sure that Size is the only check box selected in the In-between Special dialog box.

9. Click OK to place the animation into the Score.

✔ Tip

■ You can animate a sprite stretching or squeezing while moving across the Stage by combining two In-betweening aspects at the same time. In step 5 above, move the second key frame sprite to a new location on the Stage in addition to stretching or squeezing it. Also in step 8, select both the Size and Location check boxes.

To Create In-Between Animations That Curve:

In-betweening can be used to animate a cast member along a curved path. The process is similar to the one used to animate cast members in a straight line, but instead of creating only two key frames, you create a whole series of them to describe the cast member's curved path.

1. In the Score window, click the desired frame in the desired channel to indicate where your In-between animation will begin.

2. From the Cast window, drag the cast member you wish to animate onto the Stage to create the first key frame. Be sure to position it at the location where your animation should begin.

3. From the Cast window, drag the same cast member as you did in step 2 onto the Stage, so that the two identical cast members share the Stage **(Figure 34)**. Position it in a new location to set the second key frame of the curved In-between animation.

4. Repeat step 3 as many times as necessary to set all the key frames that define your curved path **(Figure 35)**.

5. In the Score window, select all the sprites that make up the key frames of your curved animation sequence. These cells should all lie in the same frame **(Figure 36)**.

Figure 34. Drag your cast member onto the Stage to a new location to create key frame 2.

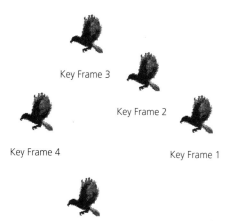

Key Frame 3

Key Frame 2

Key Frame 4

Key Frame 1

Key Frame 5

Figure 35. Five key frames here have been positioned on the Stage to define a curved path for an In-between Special animation.

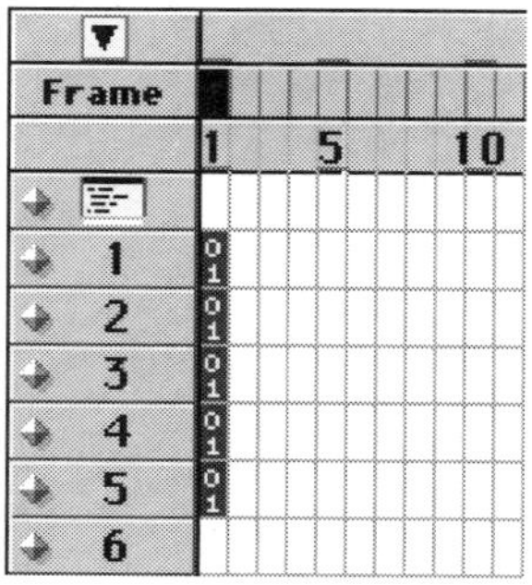

Figure 36. In the Score, select all the key frames of your curved animation sequence.

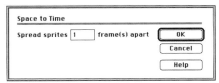

Figure 37. Choose **Space to Time** from the **Score** menu.

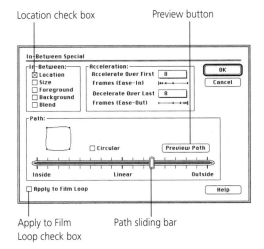

Figure 38. The spread sprites value in the **Space to Time** dialog box determines how many frames apart sprites will be placed in the Score.

Location check box   Preview button

Apply to Film   Path sliding bar
Loop check box

Figure 39. The **In-Between Special** dialog box.

6. Choose Space to Time from the Score menu **(Figure 37)**, which transfers the cast members into the same channel, while assigning each cast member to a different frame in that channel.

7. In the Space to Time dialog box, type the number of empty frames for Director to place between each of the cast member key frames you created **(Figure 38)**. Remember, the more empty frames you place between the key frames, the smoother your animation will be.

8. Click OK.

9. Choose In-Between Special from the Score menu while the key frames are still selected in Director's Score.

10. In the In-Between Special dialog box, click the Location check box to indicate that the In-between operation will apply to the location of the cast members you selected in the Score **(Figure 39)**.

11. If the cast member you're animating is a film loop *(see page 173)*, click the Apply to Film Loop checkbox as well.

12. In the In-Between Special dialog box, drag the Path sliding bar to set the degree of curve that Director uses to animate your cast member from one key frame to the next. Setting the bar to the left flattens the curve. Setting it in the center eliminates the curve altogether, while setting the bar to the right increases the degree of curve in the animation.

13. Click the Preview button to see a preview of the path your animation will follow. Choose In-Between Special from the Score menu again to return to the dialog box.

14. Click OK in the In-Between Special dialog box to place the animation into the Score.

In-Between Animations that Curve

To create a circular animation path with In-Between:

Setting up an In-between animation for a circular path is very similar to setting up a curved In-between animation. The main difference is that the last key frame sprite of your circular animation shares the same position on the Stage as the first key frame sprite. This is necessary for defining a circular path. Follow steps 1-14 on the previous pages for creating a curved In-between animation. When you reach step 10, click the Circular check box instead of the Location check box, and ignore step 12. When you reach step 4, create your last key frame sprite through the following steps:

1. Select the first key frame sprite in the Score of your circular In-between animation **(Figure 40)**.

2. Choose Copy Cells from the Edit menu **(Figure 41)**.

3. Select the cell in the Score below your second to last key frame sprite **(Figure 42)**.

4. Choose Paste Cells from the Edit menu **(Figure 43)**. Your first and last key frame sprites now share the same exact position on the Stage as is required for circular In-betweening.

✔ **Tip**

■ To define the roundest possible circular path, use five key frames arranged on the Stage as shown in **(Figure 44)**. The fifth key frame sprite overlaps the first, so four are only visible.

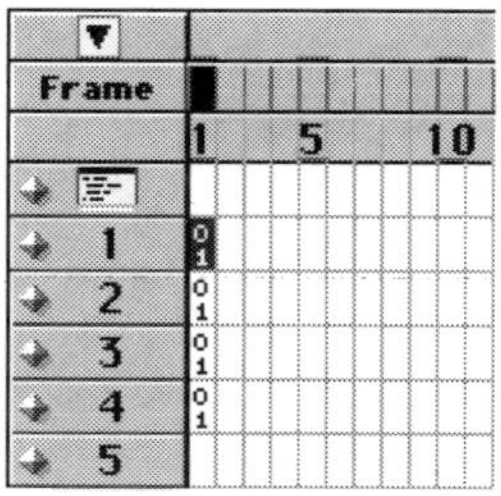

Real-Time Recording

One of the most direct ways to animate objects in Director is to use its Real-time recording feature. With Real-time recording, you move a single cast member or a film loop cast member around the screen using the mouse, and Director records its movement and its movement rate to the

Figure 40. In the Score, select the first key frame sprite of your circular In-between animation.

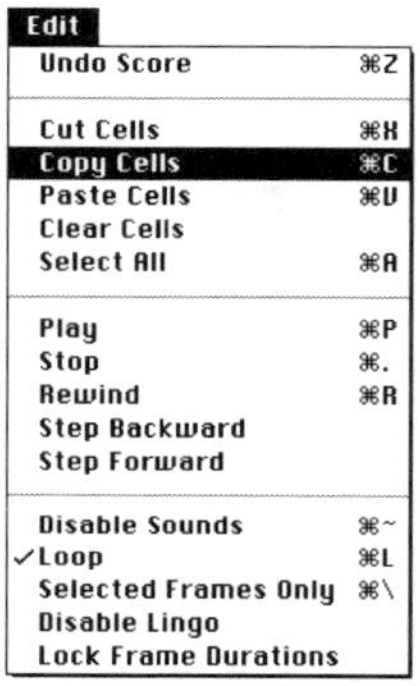

Figure 41. Choose **Copy Cells** from the **Edit** menu.

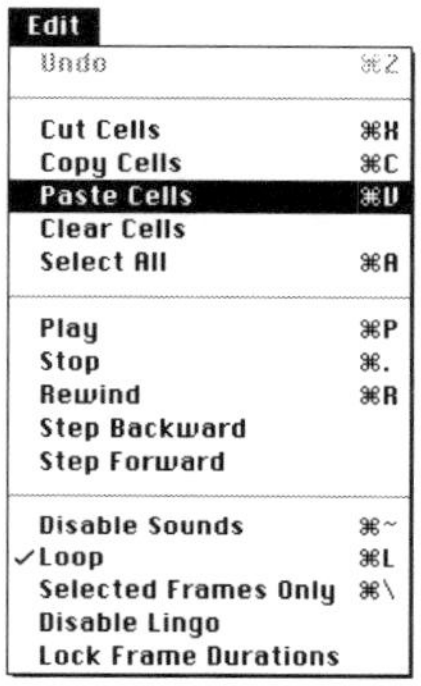

Figure 43. Choose **Paste Cells** in the **Edit** menu.

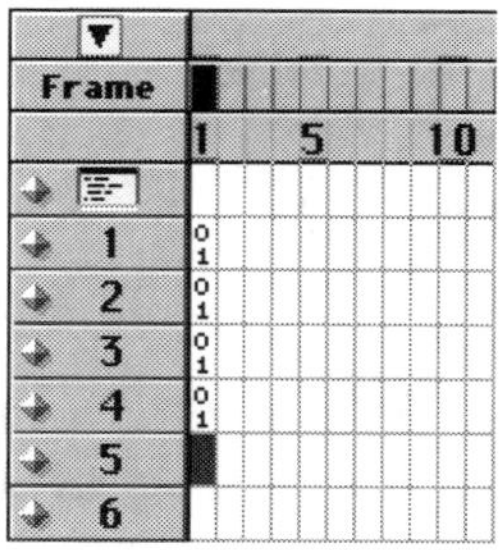

Figure 42. In the Score, select the cell below your second to last key frame sprite.

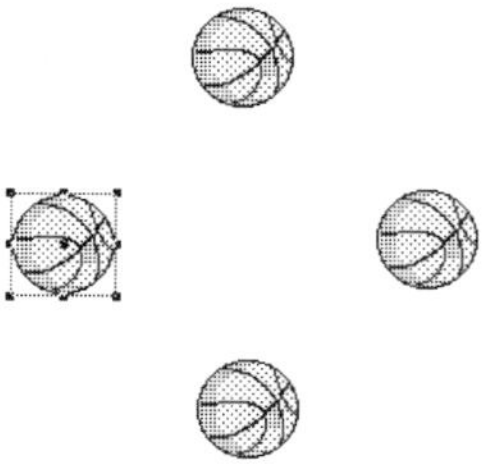

Figure 44. To define the most accurate circular path, use five key frame sprites. The first and fifth key sprites overlap here.

Figure 45. Click the Selected Frames Only button in the Control Panel to record in a specific range of frames.

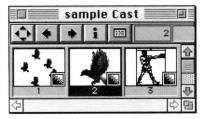

Figure 46. In the Cast window, click the cast member you wish to animate with Real-time recording.

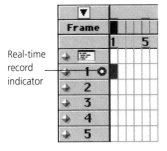

Real-time record indicator

Figure 47. Hold down the Control key and the Spacebar to select Real-time recording

Figure 48. Click the mouse pointer on the Stage and the selected cast member appears.

Edit	
Undo Score	⌘Z
Cut Cells	⌘H
Copy Cells	⌘C
Paste Bitmap	⌘U
Clear Cells	
Select All	⌘A
Play	⌘P
Stop	⌘.
Rewind	⌘R
Step Backward	
Step Forward	
Disable Sounds	⌘~
✓Loop	⌘L
Selected Frames Only	⌘\
Disable Lingo	
Lock Frame Durations	

Figure 49. Choose **Undo** from the **Edit** menu.

Score automatically. This is especially useful if you want to animate an item along a natural, free-flowing path featuring many changes in direction.

The major drawback to this approach is that the motion generated by your hand is often considerably less smooth than you might like. However, after you record a cast member's motion in real-time, you can go back and adjust individual frames in your Score.

1. In the Score window, click the desired frame in the desired channel to indicate where your Real-time recording should begin. To record in a specific range of frames, select those frames and click the Selected Frames Only button **(Figure 45)** in the Control Panel.

2. In the Cast window, click the cast member or film loop that you wish to animate so that it's selected **(Figure 46)**.

3. Move the mouse pointer to the location on the Stage where you will begin your animation.

4. Hold down the Control key and the Spacebar. A Real-time record indicator appears next to the number of the channel that you are recording in **(Figure 47)**.

5. Drag to begin recording your animation path. Notice that as soon as you click the mouse, the cast member you selected appears automatically on the Stage **(Figure 48)**.

6. Release the mouse button to end your Real-time recording session. Director places this animation into the Score.

7. If you don't like the animation, choose Undo from the Edit menu **(Figure 49)** and start again.

✓ **Tips**

■ Remember that Real-time recording requires you to select a cast member from the Cast window, but *not* to drag it on the Stage, as you normally would. If you do drag the cast member on Stage first, you will probably record the cast member twice.

■ If you begin to record your animation from a frame that contains other cast members, those cast members will be recorded in the frames through which you are Real-time recording. To avoid this, you might want to real-time record from a totally empty frame, and then copy and paste your recorded frames into their proper place in the Score.

■ If Real-time recording seems too sensitive to your mouse movements, you can make it less so by slowing down the tempo at which Director records. To do this, set a new tempo in the Control Panel window by entering a new value (in frames per second) in the Tempo Display box **(Figure 50)**. Once recorded, you can reset the tempo value to its higher rate to play back your animation.

■ You can create a handwriting type of effect by selecting the cells of your Real-time recorded animation, then clicking the Trails checkbox in the Score **(Figure 51)**. As your sprite moves across the Stage, it will leave a trail.

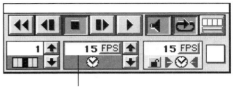

Tempo Display box

Figure 50. In the Control Panel, enter a lower value in the Tempo Display box if the mouse movements are too sensitive while you are Real-time recording.

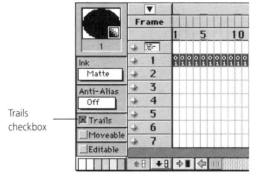

Trails checkbox

Figure 51. Select the cells of your Real-time recorded animation and click the Trails check box in the Score so that your sprite leaves behind a trail on the Stage.

Figure 52. A film loop cast member consists of a sequence of looped frames.

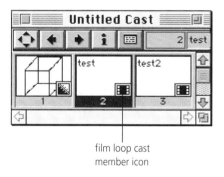

film loop cast
member icon

Figure 53. The **Cast** window.

Creating Film Loops:

A film loop is a special kind of cast member that you can create and animate in Director. Think of a film loop as an animated cast member. Instead of consisting of just one image, it's actually composed of several cast members that create a looping animation—perhaps a dog running **(Figure 52)**, a globe spinning, a helicopter hovering, and so on. The beauty of a film loop is that it can be combined with Director's In-Between Special feature to create an animation within an animation. For instance, the film loop of a bird flapping its wings in place can be "in-betweened" to move from one side of the screen to another (you can also use Director's Real-Time Recording feature to create the motion path for a film loop to follow).

Again, a film loop is simply a collection of conventional cast members that have already been created in some kind of graphics program (such as Photoshop or even Director's Paint window), in which each member is a frame in the film loop animation. Like conventional cast members, a film loop is kept in Director's Cast window, and is identified by the film loop icon **(Figure 53)**. Film loop cast members are similarly dragged onto the Stage to be inserted into your movie.

Note: Even though you've placed a film loop into your movie, it will not appear to animate if you step through its frames using the Control Panel, or if you drag Director's Playback head across the frames in your Score. Film loops animate only when you play your movie.

Note: You cannot apply ink effects—such as the commonly used transparencies or matte settings—to film loops. These effects must first be applied to the individual cast members that make up a film loop, before they are joined together.

Film Loops

To Create a Film Loop:

1. Choose Import from the File menu to import your film loop's individual cast members into Director's Cast window. Be sure to import the cast members in the order in which they should appear in the loop.

2. In the Cast window, select all of the individual cast members that will make up the film loop animation **(Figure 54)**. Hold down the Command key while clicking each cast member to select them together.

3. Drag the selected cast members from the Cast window into a desired position in the Score, where they are automatically placed into a single frame **(Figure 55)**.

4. With the Score window still active, choose Space to Time from the Score menu to transfer your film loop cast members into multiple frames in the Score to create an animation sequence **(Figure 56)**.

5. In the Space to Time dialog box, enter a value of 1 for the sprite spread.

6. Make sure the cells of your animated sequence are selected in the Score, and choose Copy Cells from the Edit menu.

7. In the Cast window, select an empty cast member position, and choose Paste Cells from the Edit menu.

8. A dialog box appears asking you to name the film loop you're creating **(Figure 57)**. Type a name and click OK. The film loop is created in the cast member position you just selected.

To Create a Multichannel Film Loop:

Multichannel film loops consist of more than one channel of animation, where each channel can feature its own animat-

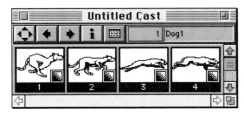

Figure 54. In the Cast window, select all the cast members that will make up your film loop animation, as shown here for a running dog film loop.

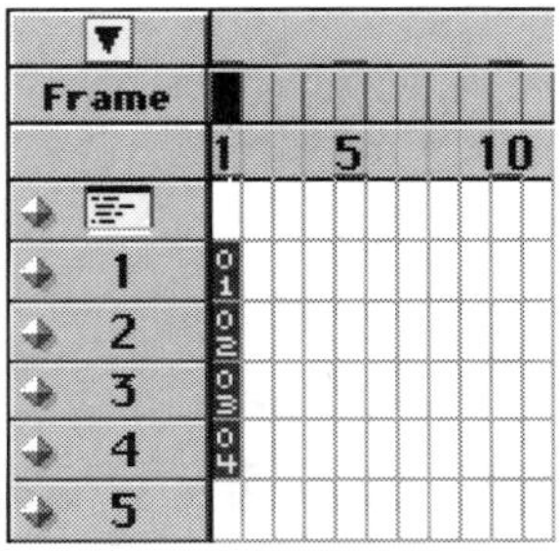

Figure 55. Drag the selected cast members from the Cast window into the Score.

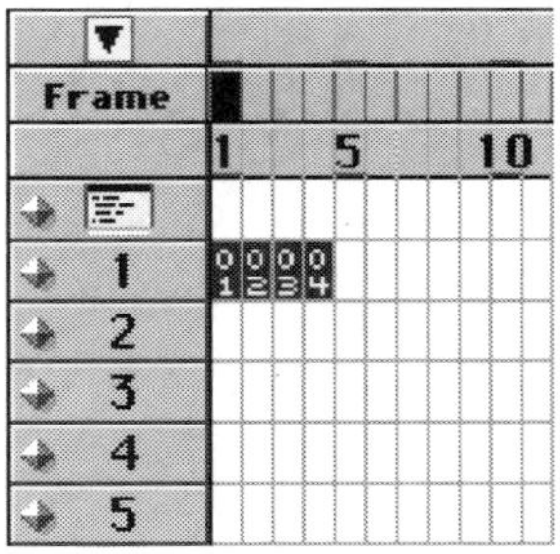

Figure 56. Transfer your film loop cast members into multiple frames using **Space to Time** from the **Score** menu.

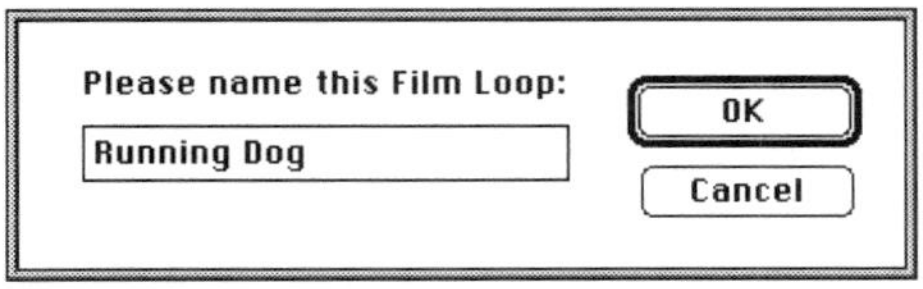

Figure 57. In the **Film Loop** dialog box, type a name for your film loop.

Please name this Film Loop:

Running Dog

OK

Cancel

Film Loops and Multichannel Film Loops

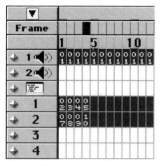

Figure 58. Select the cells that contain all the sequences that will be part of your multichannel film loop.

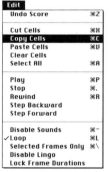

Figure 59. Choose **Copy Cells** from the **Edit** menu.

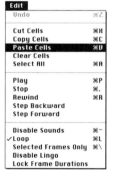

Figure 60. Choose **Paste Cells** from the **Edit** menu.

```
Please name this Film Loop:        [ OK ]
[ Film Loop              ]          [ Cancel ]
```

Figure 61. In the **Film Loop** dialog box, enter a name for your multichannel film loop.

ed element. For instance, while a conventional film loop could feature a single flying bird, a multichannel loop might consist of three birds flying in formation. Also, multichannel film loops can include sound effects from the sound channels.

1. In the Score, create an animation for the first channel that will be featured in your multichannel film loop, just as you would normally create animated sequences.

2. Create the animations for all the other channels that will be featured in your multichannel film loop, also placing any sound effects into the sound channels that you wish to include.

3. In the Score window, drag to select all the frames in all the channels you've just created, so they are highlighted **(Figure 58)**. Use Command-click to select nonadjacent cells.

4. Choose Copy Cells from the Edit menu **(Figure 59)**.

5. Open Director's Cast window, and select an empty cast member position.

6. Choose Paste Cells from the Edit menu **(Figure 60)**.

7. A dialog box appears asking you to name the multichannel film loop you're creating **(Figure 61)**. Type a name and click OK. The film loop is created in the cast member position you just selected.

To Real-time record with a film loop:

You can use Real-time recording to record a path for a film loop cast member to follow across the Stage (very similar to Real-time recording with a non-film loop cast member described earlier in this chapter). As your film loop cast member cycles through its frames during playback, it will also move across the Stage. This is

Multichannel Film Loops, Real-Time Record

a great technique to use to set up animations such as birds flapping their wings across the Stage.

1. In the Score window, click the desired frame in the desired channel to indicate where your Real-time film loop recording will begin. To record in a specific range of frames, select those frames and click the Selected Frames Only button in the Control Panel.

2. Select the film Loop cast member from the Cast window **(Figure 62)**.

3. Move the mouse pointer to the location on the Stage where you wish to begin your animation.

4. Hold down the Control key and the Spacebar, and drag to begin recording your animation path.

5. Release the mouse button to end your Real-time recording session. Director places this animation into the Score.

In-between with a film loop:

Making use of the In-between feature with a film loop cast member creates a powerful animation effect. For example, you could animate a film loop cast member of a racing dog, having it travel across the Stage in any variety of predetermined paths. This can be accomplished by simply setting up several key frames and using the In-between command with a film loop cast member. You can specify a straight, curved, or circular path for your film loop cast member to follow, just as you could with a regular bitmap cast member. Use the In-Between Linear or In-Between Special commands described on pages 164-170. Follow the same steps given there, but simply select a film loop cast member from the Cast window.

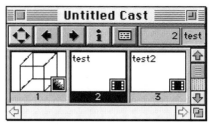

Figure 62. Select the film loop cast member in the Cast window with which you will be Real-time recording.

QuickTime Movies.

A QuickTime movie in Director is similar to a film loop in that it is a collection of frames, or a prerecorded animation sequence that can be manipulated as a single cast member. But QuickTime movies offer far greater flexibility in that they can incorporate virtually all aspects of an animation sequence, such as transitions, palette changes, and tempo settings. Unlike film loops, QuickTime movies can also be edited in Director, using the Digital Video window under the Window menu. QuickTime movies are essentially just that, digital video, and can be more elaborately edited in outside applications such as Premiere. QuickTime movies, such as live digitized video from a VCR tape, can also be imported into Director and played directly on the Stage. Working with QuickTime movies is beyond the scope of this book.

CREATING TEXT IN DIRECTOR

You can create and incorporate text into your Director movie as you would incorporate any other cast member. Director supports two kinds of text-types: first there is **bitmap** text that is created in Director's Paint window, but, like other painted graphics, cannot be changed once created (words cannot be rearranged, new fonts can't be applied, and so on); Second, there is **QuickDraw** text. Unlike the bitmap variety, QuickDraw text can be edited, and it also prints crisply and cleanly to laser printers, in case you plan to print portions of your Director movie to paper (perhaps as handouts in a business presentation). Bitmap text on the other hand animates more quickly in a Director movie, and has some other advantages discussed on the following page.

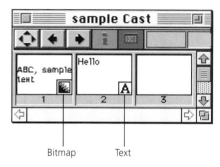

Bitmap   Text

Figure 1. The **Cast** window makes a distinction between bitmapped text and QuickDraw text as shown here.

✔ Tip

■ Any text that you create in Director automatically becomes a cast member in the Cast window. The Cast window makes a distinction between bitmap and QuickDraw text cast members, as you see in **(Figure 1)**. The cast member on the left is a bitmap (notice the bitmap icon in the lower-right corner, since the text is really just a painted graphic), while the cast member on the right is QuickDraw (notice the "A" text symbol).

BITMAP TEXT

Bitmap text is created in Director's Paint window. The most notable feature of bitmap text is that it cannot be edited once it's created. If you decide you want to change a word, a typeface, the text's coloring, and so on, you must erase the original text and start over again. On the other hand, like any other painted graphic, bitmap text can be selected and then modified with a variety of Director's Paint tools—for instance, it can be rotated, skewed, flipped, and so on *(see page 103 for more information about these features)*. It can also be easily incorporated into other painted artwork you might have.

When you create text in the Paint window, that text automatically becomes a cast member in the Cast window, where it can be dragged to the Stage and assigned to Director's Score like any other cast member.

To create bitmap text:

1. Choose Paint from the Window menu to open Director's Paint window **(Figure 2)**.

2. Click the Text tool icon in the Paint tool palette to select it **(Figure 3)**.

3. Click the mouse anywhere in the Paint window to select the location where your text will be placed. A text box containing a blinking insertion point appears at this spot.

4. Choose the desired font, size, and style for your text from Director's Text menu **(Figure 4)**.

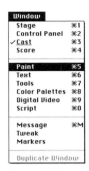

Figure 2. Choose **Paint** from the **Window** menu.

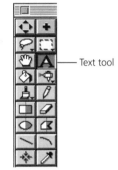

Figure 3. Select the Text tool icon in the **Paint** tool palette.

— Text tool

Figure 4. Choose the desired font, size, and style from the **Text** menu.

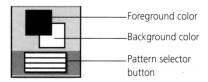

Figure 5. Select the text colors by clicking the **Foreground** and **Background** color chips. Apply a pattern to the text by clicking the **Pattern** selector button.

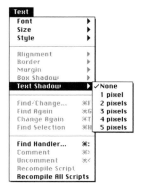

Figure 6. Add a drop shadow to the text by selecting **Text Shadow** from the **Text** menu, then selecting the desired pixel offset from the pop-up menu.

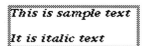

Figure 7. A text box with sample text.

Figure 8. The **Distort** effect from the **Effects** menu was used to alter this bitmap text.

5. Click the Foreground and Background color chips in the Paint tool palette to color the text. The Foreground chip sets the color of the text itself, while the Background chip sets the color of the box that surrounds the text. You can also apply a pattern to the text by clicking the Pattern selector button in the tool palette **(Figure 5)**.

6. To add a drop shadow to the text, select Text Shadow from the Text menu, and from the pop-up submenu choose the number of pixels that the shadow should offset the text by **(Figure 6)**.

7. Type in your text **(Figure 7)**. Press Return to start a new line.

8. To move the text to a new location on screen, drag the text box by its border.

✔ **Tips**

- Remember that bitmap text can be distorted with a variety of paint features listed under Director's Effects menu, from the Paint window. Director's Distort effect was used to make the text sample in **(Figure 8)** appear to have dimension.

- From the Cast window, you can double-click a bitmap text cast member and Director automatically opens the image in its Paint window.

Create Bitmap Text

QUICKDRAW TEXT

All the limitations of bitmap text—the fact that once you place the text, you can no longer edit it, and that such text prints poorly to laser printers—are overcome by QuickDraw text. Rather than being bitmap (built pixel-by-pixel), this text type is created by mathematical graphics routines that are built into your Macintosh. The benefit of QuickDraw text is that it can easily be edited, resized, and otherwise altered once it becomes a cast member in your movie, making it more flexible than the bitmap text created in the Paint window. Also, since QuickDraw text prints much more sharply to laser printers, you'll definitely want to use it if you plan to print portions of your movie on paper. On the downside, this variety of text can't be rotated or otherwise distorted for special effect, as bitmap text can. Also, Director animates QuickDraw text more slowly than bitmap text.

There are two ways to create QuickDraw text cast members in Director. The first is to create and position the text directly on the Stage, at the appropriate point in your movie's Score **(Figure 9)**. The second approach is to type your text into Director's **Text** window **(Figure 10)**, which in turn places the text in Director's Cast window (as a cast member), where it can be dragged to the Stage at a later time. The first approach is the quickest, most straightforward method of incorporating text into a movie, while the second is best if you'd like to create a number of text cast members at one time, and place them throughout your movie later on.

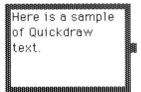

Figure 9. A QuickDraw text cast member positioned directly on the Stage.

Figure 10. The **Text** window.

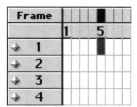

Figure 11. Select a cell in the desired animation channel where you wish to place QuickDraw text.

Figure 12. Choose **Tools** from the **Window** menu.

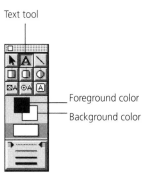

Text tool

Foreground color

Background color

Figure 13. Click the Text tool icon in the **Tools** window.

Figure 15. You can modify your text's font, size, style, and border, among other things from the **Text** menu.

Handle to adjust width

Figure 14. A QuickDraw text box on the Stage. Drag its handle on the right side to make it wider.

To create QuickDraw text directly on the Stage:

1. In Director's Score window, select the cell in the desired animation channel in which you wish to place QuickDraw text **(Figure 11)**.

2. Choose Tools from Director's Window menu to open the QuickDraw Tools window **(Figure 12)**.

3. In the Tools window, click the Text tool to select it **(Figure 13)**.

4. Position the crosshair pointer on the Stage, and click the mouse to place a text box there. If you want to make the box wider, drag the handle on its right side **(Figure 14)**.

5. You can choose the text's font, size, and style by making the appropriate selections from the Text menu. You can also use the Text menu to add a border or shadow, among other attributes, to the text box **(Figure 15)**.

6. In the Tools window, click the Foreground and Background color chips to assign color to your text. The Foreground color applies to the text itself, while the Background color applies to the text box **(Figure 13)**.

7. Type your text into the text box. Text wraps around to a new line automatically as you type.

8. When you've finished typing, click the pointer tool in the Tools window to make it final. The text is placed on the Stage and in Director's Cast window.

Create QuickDraw Text on the Stage

✓ **Tips**

■ When QuickDraw fonts are present in a Director movie, make sure that the Macintosh that the movie is playing on has those fonts installed in its System Folder. If the Macintosh does not have the proper fonts installed, it will try to play your movie with different fonts than it was designed for. Text that is created as bitmap graphics in the Paint window does not require any particular fonts to be installed.

■ You can apply Director's ink effects to QuickDraw text. In the Score window, select the cell or range of cells that contains the desired QuickDraw text and then click the Ink effects pop-up menu in the Score to make an ink selection **(Figure 16)**.

Ink effects
pop-up
menu

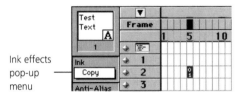

Figure 16. Select the desired cell or cells in the Score that contain QuickDraw text, then click the Ink effects pop-up menu to select an ink effect.

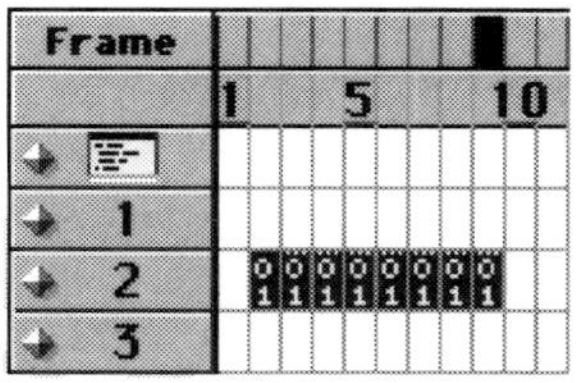

Figure 17. Select a frame or range of frames in the Score that contains the QuickDraw text you wish to edit.

Blah, Blah, sample text.

Figure 18. A text box on the Stage with all its text selected.

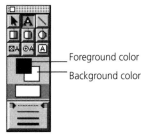

Figure 19. You can modify your text's font, size, style, color, and border, among other characteristics from the **Text** menu.

Foreground color
Background color

Figure 20. The **Tools** window.

To edit existing QuickDraw text on Director's Stage:

1. In the Score window, select the frame or range of frames **(Figure 17)** that contains the QuickDraw text you wish to edit. If you select a range of frames in which the text appears (as opposed to just one frame), the changes you make to the text apply to all the selected frames.

2. On Director's Stage, click the text box to select it. You can resize the box by dragging the handle on its right side.

3. Drag across the text you wish to edit so that it becomes highlighted. You can double-click to select a word at a time, or triple-click to select all the text in the box **(Figure 18)**.

4. With the text highlighted, you can change its font, size, style, and alignment, as well as add embellishments, such as a border or shadow, to the text box. To do so, make the appropriate selections from Director's Text menu **(Figure 19)**.

5. If you also wish to change the text's color, choose Tools from Director's Window menu, and use the Foreground and Background color chips to choose the desired colors **(Figure 20)**.

✔ Tip

■ To move text that has already been placed on the Stage, select the text box, then drag the box's border.

Edit QuickDraw Text on the Stage

To create QuickDraw text with the Text window:

1. Choose Text from Director's Window menu **(Figure 21)**.

2. With the Text window open **(Figure 22)**, you can choose your text's font, size, style, and alignment (left, centered, or right) by making the appropriate selections from the Text menu.

3. To add a drop shadow to either your text or the box that encloses the text, select Text Shadow or Box Shadow from the Text menu, and from the pop-up submenu choose the number of pixels that Director will offset the shadow by **(Figure 23)**.

4. To add a border around the box surrounding your text cast member, select Border from the Text menu, and from the pop-up submenu choose the pixel thickness of the border **(Figure 24).**

5. If you would like to add color to your text or the box surrounding it, choose Tools from the Window menu. In the Tools window, click the Foreground color chip to assign a color to the text itself, or click the Background color which applies to the text box **(Figure 25)**.

6. Type your text in the Text window. The text will automatically be formatted in the style that you specified, but borders and shadows will not appear until you actually place the text on the Stage. Text wraps around to a new line automatically as you type. You can also press Return to begin a new line.

The text that you type will automatically be entered as a cast member in Director's Cast window, where you can drag it to the Stage and assign it to the Score.

Figure 21. Choose **Text** from the **Window** menu.

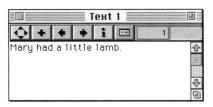

Figure 22. The **Text** window.

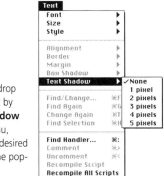

Figure 23. Add a drop shadow to the text by selecting **Text Shadow** from the **Text** menu, then selecting the desired pixel offset from the pop-up menu.

Figure 24. To add a border around your text cast member, select **Border** from the **Text** menu and choose the desired border pixel thickness from the pop-up menu.

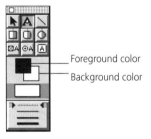

Foreground color
Background color

Figure 25. Click the Foreground chip to color the text, and the Background chip to color the text box.

The Plus button.

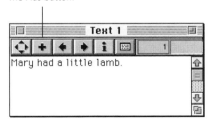

Figure 26. Click the plus button to create additional text cast members.

7. When you've finished typing, you can either close the Text window, or, if you would like to create more text cast members, click the Plus button at the top of the Text window. Director will clear the window, and create another cast member position in the Cast window to accommodate the new text **(Figure 26)**.

To edit QuickDraw text using the Text window:

Once a text cast member has been placed in your Score, it's often easiest to edit the text right from the Stage *(see page 183)*. To edit text using the Text window, however, simply open the Cast window and select the text cast member you wish to edit. Then choose Text from the Window menu to open the Text window for the selected cast member (you can also double-click the cast member to open the Text window).

Edit QuickDraw Text Using the Text Window

Adding musical scores, sound effects, and voice-overs to Director movies is easy. Simply import a preexisting sound cast member and then place it in the desired frames in Director's Score. If there's any trick to this, it's deciding in which frames the sound should play. For example, if you'd like Director to play the sound of footsteps as a character walks across the screen, you'd first animate the character and then note in which frames his feet touch the ground. You'd then place your footstep sound in these frames, and assign them to one of the Score's two sound channels **(Figure 1)**. Another movie might call for playing a musical score throughout an entire animation rather than timing it to specific events. In this case you would place the music into a sound channel through a range of frames.

It's important to note that Director's sound capabilities are not exactly robust. The biggest limitation is that Director supports only two sound channels (as opposed to 48 animation channels), which means that only two sounds can play simultaneously—for instance, a sound effect can be played over an ongoing musical score. This system is adequate in many cases, but it can also prove frustrating, especially if your project—an interactive video game, perhaps—calls for a rich soundtrack. If you're using a sound digitizer and editing package to create sounds from scratch *(see page 191 for more details)*, you may be able to cleverly combine custom sounds to make the most of Director's two-channel system.

Sound channels —

Figure 1. Sounds are placed in one of two **Sound** channels in the **Score**.

IMPORTING AND CREATING SOUND

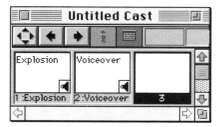

Figure 2. Select a cast member position in the Cast window into which you'll import a sound. Position 3 is selected here.

To import a sound into the Cast window:

1. In Director's Cast window, select the cast member position into which you'll import your sound. If you do not select a particular cast position, Director will place your sound in the first available slot **(Figure 2)**.

2. Choose Import from the File menu.

3. In the Import dialog box, choose Sound from the Type pop-up menu. This tells Director to display all Sounds in the file selector box **(Figures 3-4)**.

4. Choose the desired sound, and click Import. Director places your sound in its Cast window. Now it's ready to be assigned to the Score.

✔ Tips

■ Ordinarily when you import a sound, Director actually copies the contents of the selected sound file into your movie. This can significantly increase the disk size and memory requirements of the movie, since sound files can be so large. To avoid this, check the Link to File option in the Import dialog box before importing a sound file. This tells Director to merely refer to the original sound file when necessary, rather than copying its entire contents into your movie.

■ When you import a sound into Director, the sound can only be played *as is*. Director has no controls for editing the sound's various attributes, such as its pitch or modularity. You can't even use Director's Tempo channel to alter the sound's playback speed. Changes made to Director's tempo will affect the animation in your movie but not the sound.

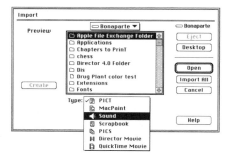

Figure 3. Choose **Sound** from the **Type** pop-up menu in the **Import** dialog box.

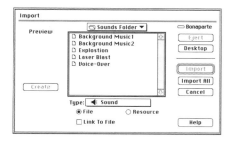

Figure 4. The **Import** dialog box with sound files displayed.

Importing Sound

About MIDI.

Besides playing digitized sound files, Director can also play sound effects and music by controlling a MIDI instrument such as a keyboard synthesizer, drum machine, or sequencer that has been attached to your Macintosh. Using these types of instruments allows your movie to play a very rich and intricate musical score; it is, however, a complex process. First, your Macintosh needs a special MIDI interface that allows it to work with MIDI equipment. Second, Director requires that you use a series of somewhat cryptic commands to control the instruments properly. This topic falls beyond the scope of this book. For more information consult your Director reference manual, which offers a full explanation of MIDI controls.

✔ Tips

■ An intricate soundtrack—especially one with long-lasting sounds such as voice overs and musical scores—can slow your entire movie down. This is a particularly important issue if you intend to play your movie on a wide variety of Macintosh models; while a top-of-the-line PowerPC may keep pace, a run-of-the-mill LC model might be overtaxed and slow your movie significantly. So try to think ahead about the types of Macintoshes likely to play your movie, and design your soundtrack accordingly.

■ Director accepts sounds saved either as SoundEdit, AIFF, AIFC, or 8-bit SND (Sound) Resources. These formats are standards supported by most, if not all, sound digitizers and editors for the Macintosh, as well as supported by a large library of prerecorded "clip-sounds."

MIDI

To record a sound in Director:

You can actually record (or "digitize") sounds within Director itself, using either the small, hand-held microphone that ships with most Macintosh models, or one from a third-party company. Although Director doesn't have sophisticated controls for top-notch sound production, it does offer a quick and easy way to engineer short sounds for your movies.

1. Make sure that you have a microphone attached to your Macintosh.

2. Choose Record Sound from the Cast menu **(Figure 5)**.

3. From the Record Sound dialog box, click the Record button to begin recording a sound via the attached microphone **(Figure 6)**.

4. Click the Pause button to pause a recording session, or the Stop button when you have finished recording a sound.

5. Preview your recorded sound by clicking the Play button.

6. Click the Save button to place the recorded sound into Director's Cast window, where it can easily be incorporated into your movie.

Figure 5. Choose **Record Sound** from the **Cast** menu.

Figure 6. Click the Record button to begin recording a sound.

Sound Production outside Director.

Director ships with a small library of prerecorded sounds that you can use in your own movies. These include video game sound effects such as explosions and gunshots, as well as short musical scores. A number of companies also sell sound libraries that you can draw material from. As useful as these resources can be, the process of making ambitious movies in Director will inevitably require custom sounds that you'll have to create from scratch.

The simplest way to create custom sounds is to use the small microphone included with all recent Macintosh models. In conjunction with Director's Record Sound feature, you can record (or "digitize") spoken sounds easily and save them in file formats that Director understands. Unfortunately the quality of such recordings is often too low for polished Director movies.

For serious sound production you'll want to use a third-party digitizer that can record sounds at high resolutions from a variety of sources such as microphones, tapedecks, and musical synthesizers. Digitizers also allow you to edit sounds, cutting out unwanted noise and adjusting pitch, volume, and other characteristics. One of the most popular digitizers available is Macromedia's SoundEdit Pro, which offers solid features for a reasonable price. Another excellent choice, if you see yourself heading heavily into sound production, is PassPort Design's SoundPro card, which provides a sophisticated set of software tools for tweaking and mixing sounds in almost every imaginable way.

Note: However you create your custom sounds, make sure that they are saved as SoundEdit, AIFF, AIFC, or 8-bit SND resource formats, since these are the only sound formats that Director accepts.

PLACING SOUND

To place sounds in the Score:

1. In the Score window, click the frame (or drag across a range of frames) in the desired sound channel to indicate where your sound should be placed **(Figure 7)**.

2. Choose Set Sound from the Score menu.

3. In the Set Sound dialog box, select the sound you'd like to place in the Score (A sound must have already been imported into Director's Cast window to appear in this list). With a sound selected, click the Play button to hear a preview, or click OK to place the sound in the Score **(Figure 8)**.

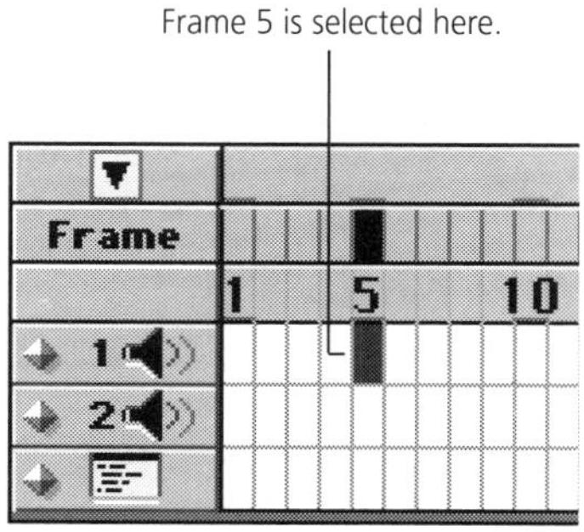

Frame 5 is selected here.

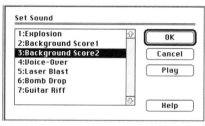

Figure 7. Select a frame or range of frames in a **Sound** channel in which your sound will be placed.

To extend sounds to play completely:

Most sounds are designed to play through multiple frames of Director's Score—a laser blast, for instance, might fill 20 frames, while a musical score could fill hundreds. If a sound is assigned to fewer frames than it is designed for, it will be cut off prematurely. For instance, if a sound is intended to last two seconds—the equivalent of 60 frames if movie tempo is set at 30 fps—but is only assigned to play in 45 frames of the Score, it will end without finishing in frame 45. If you find that your sound is

Figure 8. Select a sound to be placed in a **Sound** channel of the **Score**.

Place Sounds in the Score

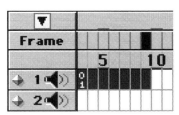

Figure 9. Select a range of frames through which you'll extend a sound.

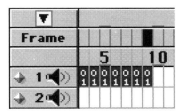

Figure 10. Choose **In-Between-Linear** from the **Score** menu to extend the sound through all the highlighted frames.

ending prematurely, you simply have to extend the sound to occupy additional frames in the Score.

1. In the Score window, click the last frame that your sound occupies, and drag to highlight the additional frames to which you will extend the sound **(Figure 9)**.

2. Choose In-Between Linear from the Score menu (Command-B) to extend the sound through all of the highlighted frames **(Figure 10)**.

3. Rewind and play the movie to confirm that your sound now plays completely. If it still cuts off, simply extend the sound into even more frames by repeating the steps above.

✔ **Tip**

■ To quickly determine the number of frames a sound requires, use the steps above to extend it into more frames than it can possibly require (for example, if you know that a laser blast sound effect will require roughly 20 frames, then extend it to 40 or 50). Then play back your movie while keeping the Score window open and visible. As the movie plays, Director will highlight each frame it moves through. Simply listen for your sound, and then note at which frame in the Score it finishes. Now you know how many frames the sound really requires, and can cut out any extra frames it occupies.

Extend Sound in Score to Play Completely

To repeat sounds in the same channel:

Often you'll want a particular sound to play repeatedly throughout your movie. In animating water dripping from a faucet, you might want a "drip" sound effect to play every five seconds or so. For an interactive storybook, you might want background music to loop over and over again. Setting up such repetitions is easy. Simply extend a sound through all the frames in the Score that you wish it to occupy, and then create at least one empty frame at each point prior to where the sound should repeat. It's this empty frame that allows a repetition to take place **(Figures 11-12)**.

1. Using the steps outlined in the section, *To extend sounds to play completely* on page 192, place your sound in the Score and extend it through as many frames as you wish it to play. When you extend the sound, you should also account for any repetitions desired. For instance, if a sound normally requires 10 frames, and you want it to repeat five times, then you should extend it through more than 50 frames in the Score to account for the empty frames between repetitions.

2. Decide at what points in the Score the sound should repeat itself (e.g., you might repeat the drip sound at frames 5, 10, 15, and 20).

3. For every frame in the Score that you've designated as a repeat point, click the preceding frame to highlight it (if a sound is to repeat at frame 20, for example, click frame 19).

4. Choose Clear Cells from the Edit menu, or press the Delete key. By doing this, you're creating the empty frame that triggers the sound to repeat.

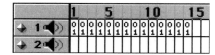

Figure 11. First extend the sound through all frames you wish it to occupy.

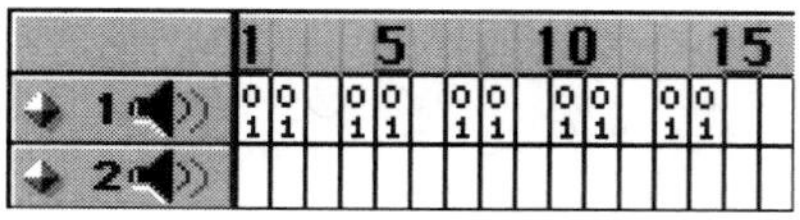

Figure 12. Create an empty frame to trigger a repeat in the sound.

✓ **Tips**

■ Remember that you can easily use Director's Copy Cells and Paste Cells commands (in the Edit menu) to place a sound at multiple points in your Score. Just be sure that there is at least one empty frame separating each instance of the sound.

■ You can use a sound editing program such as SoundEdit to make sounds loop automatically in particular spots. Suppose you've created some background music and have set a loop that makes the music's middle section repeat endlessly. You import the music into the Score and extend it through a few hundred frames. When your movie plays, Director plays the background music from the beginning and then continues to loop the middle section until it has reached the last frame that the music occupies in your Score. At this point, the looping section stops, but Director continues playing the last segment of the background music, even though it occupies no frames in the Score.

Sound Loops

SETTING SCENE TRANSITIONS

Window
Stage	⌘1
Control Panel	⌘2
Cast	⌘3
Score	⌘4
Paint	⌘5
Text	⌘6
Tools	⌘7
Color Palettes	⌘8
Digital Video	⌘9
Script	⌘0
Message	⌘M
Tweak	
Markers	
Duplicate Window	

Figure 1. Choose **Score** from the **Window** menu.

The Transition channel

Figure 2. Select a cell in the Transition channel where the transition should occur.

Score
Sprite Info...	⌘K
Delete Sprites	
Set Sprite Blend...	
Set Tempo...	
Set Palette...	
Set Transition...	
Set Sound...	
Insert Frame	⌘]
Delete Frame	⌘[
In-Between Linear	⌘B
In-Between Special...	
Space to Time...	
Paste Relative	
Reverse Sequence	
Switch Cast Members	⌘E
Auto Animate	▶
Score Window Options...	

Figure 3. Choose **Set Transition** from the **Score** menu.

Director offers more than 50 special effects **transitions** such as dissolves, wipes, and fades that you can use to smoothly move from one scene in a movie to another (a scene is a sequence of related action that takes place on Director's Stage). Without transitions, scenes simply cut abruptly from one to another, often creating a jarring effect for the viewer.

Transition's are placed into the Transition channel of Director's Score, at the particular frame where you wish the transition to occur.

To set a transition:

1. Choose Score from the Window menu to open Director's Score **(Figure 1)**.

2. In the Transition channel, select the cell at the particular frame in which the transition should occur **(Figure 2)**. The transition begins between the frame that you select, and the frame that precedes it. To transition between two scenes, you'd set the transition at the first frame of the second scene and not at the last frame of the first scene.

3. Choose Set Transition from Director's Score menu **(Figure 3)** or double-click the cell you've selected in the Transition channel.

Set a Transition

4. In the Set Transition dialog box, click the transition that you wish to apply **(Figure 4)**. Use the dialog box's scroll bars to move throughout all of the transition types. ***Note:*** Director features too many transition types to cover here. Fortunately, each type is identified with descriptive language. Experiment with the different transition types before selecting one for your scene.

5. Click the Stage Area radio button if the transition should apply to Director's entire Stage. Click the Changing Area button if the transition should apply only to areas of the Stage that are changing from one scene to the next (in other words, where sprites are present, but then are not, or vice versa).

6. Use the Duration and Chunk Size slider bars to give the transition a custom duration time and chunk size (chunk size refers to the size of pixel "chunks" used to dissolve one scene or introduce another).

7. Choose the Set button to apply the selected transition to your Score.

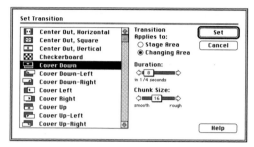

Figure 4. Select the transition you wish to apply in the **Set Transition** dialog box.

✔ **Tip**

■ You can create a few other transition types by changing the color palette that Director uses to display your movie at a given time. These transition effects, such as fade to black or a transition to a new color palette, are set in Director's Color Palette channel. *(See page 116 for more details)*

Set a Transition

Director plays your movie at a particular **tempo**, or speed, which you can easily adjust. The movie's tempo is measured in **frames-per-second** (fps), which means the higher the tempo rate (15 fps, 24 fps, 30 fps, etc.), the faster Director plays back animation. With a high tempo (say, 45 fps) you can make sprites zoom across the Stage, while you can use a low tempo (perhaps 7 fps) to create a slow-motion effect.

Your movie's tempo is set in the **Tempo channel** of Director's Score **(Figure 1)**. Although one tempo can apply to an entire movie, you can also vary your tempo on a frame-by-frame basis.

There are two important things to know about the effects that tempo settings have on your movie. First of all, while the tempo you set affects the speed at which cast member sprites are animated on Stage, it does not affect the playback of sounds or QuickTime movies.

More importantly, while you may set a high tempo in a movie, the Macintosh that Director is running on must be advanced enough to keep up with that pace. If a particular scene calls for the animation of a large number of sprites, or if it features special ink effects or anti-aliasing, or if cast members are painted at high color depths (such as 32-bit color), or if there are complex transitions or color palette manipulation at work, your Macintosh may simply not be able to manage all this without slowing the scene's tempo. If this is the case, you must either settle for this slow playback speed, buy a faster Macintosh, or redesign the movie's scene so that it is not so demanding.

Tempo channel

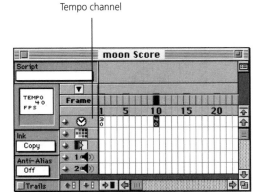

Figure 1. The tempo of your movie is set in the **Tempo** channel of the **Score**.

To set a new tempo in the Score:

When you set a new tempo in the Tempo channel, that tempo applies to all the following frames of your movie (until you set another tempo change).

1. Choose Score from the Window menu to open Director's Score **(Figure 2)**.

2. In the Tempo channel, select the cell where you would like a new tempo to occur. **(Figure 3)**.

3. Choose Set Tempo from the Score menu, or double-click the selected cell **(Figure 4)**.

4. In the Set Tempo dialog box, slide the Tempo scroll bar to set the movie's tempo in frames per second **(Figure 5)**.

5. Click OK to apply the tempo change to the Score. Director now uses this tempo setting to play the cell you selected in step 2, and all the cells to the right of it (until, that is, you set a new tempo).

✓ Tip

■ If your movie will be played on a variety of Macintosh models (for instance, if it's an educational game), try to set a tempo that even low-end Macintoshes will be able to keep up with. Otherwise, owners of low-end Macintoshes such as LC's may be disappointed with your movie's playback performance. The best way to determine how well a particular Macintosh will play your movie is to play it on that machine and compare the movie's set tempo to its actual playback speed by using the steps outlined on page 202.

Figure 2. Choose **Score** from the **Window** menu.

Figure 4. Choose **Set Tempo** from the **Score** menu.

Figure 3. Select a cell in the **Tempo** channel where you would like a new tempo to occur.

Tempo scroll bar

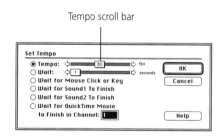

Figure 5. Use the **Set Tempo** dialog box to set the movie's tempo in frames per second.

Set a New Tempo in the Score

Figure 6. Choose **Set Tempo** from the **Score** menu.

Figure 7. Select one of five **Wait** options from the **Set Tempo** dialog box.

To set a pause in the movie's tempo:

Director's Set Tempo command allows you to create a pause in the playback of your movie. You can pause the action for a specified number of seconds, or create a pause that waits for a certain event to occur such as a mouse click or key stroke.

1. In the Tempo channel of the Score window, select the cell where you would like to set a pause.

2. Choose Set Tempo from the Score menu, or double-click the selected cell **(Figure 6)**.

3. In the Set Tempo dialog box, select the Wait option you wish to use by clicking the appropriate radio button **(Figure 7)**. If you are creating a timed pause, use the Wait scroll bar to specify the duration in seconds. If you want Director to wait for a QuickTime video clip to finish playing, be sure to specify which of the Score's animation channels contains the clip.

4. Click OK to apply the pause to the Score.

Note: If you create a pause that waits for a sound or QuickTime video clip to finish before resuming normal movie play, make sure that the sound or video clip begins playing before the frame where the pause takes place. In other words, a sound or QuickTime clip must already be in progress for this type of pause to work as expected.

Set a Pause in the Movie's Tempo

To compare actual playback speed versus the set tempo:

Director tries to play a movie at the particular tempo you've set. Unfortunately, the actual playback speed may fall short when complex animations are featured. This is very likely on a low-end Macintosh. Fortunately, Director makes it easy to compare this actual playback speed to the tempo you've set on a frame-by-frame basis.

1. Set the desired tempo for your movie as outlined on page 200.

2. Choose Control Panel from Director's Window menu to open the Control Panel **(Figure 8)**.

3. Click the Control Panel's Step forward button to step through your movie one frame at a time.

4. In each frame, compare the actual speed at which the frame is played to the tempo setting. Both of these values are displayed in the Control Panel **(Figure 9)**.

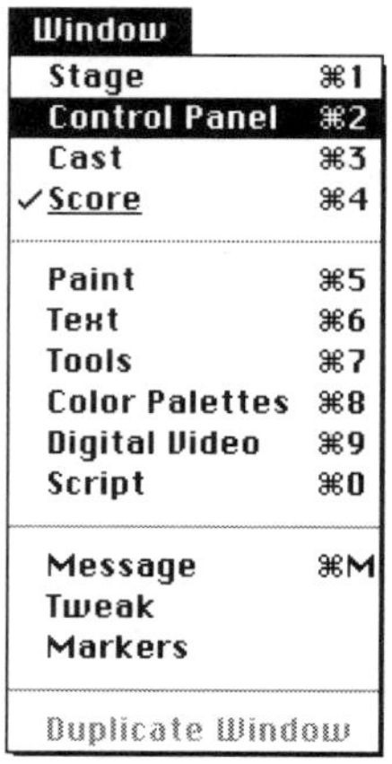

LOCKING PLAYBACK SPEED

When you've determined the proper tempo for your movie, you can then "lock" that speed so that it's used by whatever Macintosh your movie happens to play on. Doing so guards against your movie being played too fast on more advanced Macintoshes but does not prevent the movie from playing back *slower* when run on less sophisticated Macintoshes. If you're trying to set the movie's speed to play workably on even low-end Macintoshes, you should establish a speed that even those Macs can keep up with and then lock it in.

Figure 8. Choose **Control Panel** from the **Window** menu.

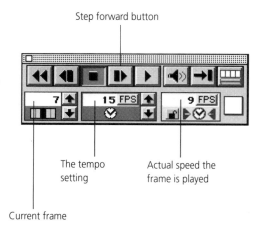

Step forward button

Current frame

The tempo setting

Actual speed the frame is played

Figure 9. The **Control Panel** shows the actual playback tempo of a single frame and the tempo setting for that frame.

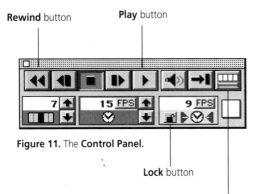

Window

Stage	⌘1
Control Panel	⌘2
Cast	⌘3
✓ Score	⌘4
Paint	⌘5
Text	⌘6
Tools	⌘7
Color Palettes	⌘8
Digital Video	⌘9
Script	⌘0
Message	⌘M
Tweak	
Markers	
Duplicate Window	

Figure 10. Choose **Control Panel** from the **Window** menu.

Rewind button   Play button

Figure 11. The **Control Panel.**

Lock button

Selected frames only button

Edit

Undo	⌘Z
Cut Cells	⌘X
Copy Cells	⌘C
Paste Bitmap	⌘V
Clear Cells	
Select All	⌘A
Play	⌘P
Stop	⌘.
Rewind	⌘R
Step Backward	
Step Forward	
Disable Sounds	⌘~
Loop	⌘L
Selected Frames Only	⌘\
Disable Lingo	
Lock Frame Durations	

Figure 12. Choose **Lock Frame Durations** from the **Edit** menu.

To lock your entire movie's playback speed:

1. Set the desired tempo for your movie as outlined on page 200.

2. Choose Control Panel from Director's Window menu to open the control panel **(Figure 10).**

3. Use Director's Control Panel to rewind and then play back your movie from beginning to end **(Figure 11)**. If the movie branches off into multiple segments (for instance, in an interactive presentation), make sure you play through all of these segments. In doing so, Director records the actual speed at which it plays each frame in the Control Panel.

4. Choose Lock Frame Durations from the Edit menu **(Figure 12)**, or click the Lock button in the Control Panel. Each frame is now locked to play at the actual speed that was recorded in step 3. To unlock the movie's playback speed, simply click the Lock button again.

To lock the playback speed of a sequence of frames:

1. Set the desired tempo for your movie as outlined on page 200.

2. While holding down the Option key, choose Lock Frame Durations from Director's Edit menu. This clears any previously recorded frame durations **(Figure 12)**.

3. In the Score window, select the sequence of frames that you wish to lock.

4. Click the Selected frames only button in the Control Panel **(Figure 11)**.

Lock Playback Speed, Selected Frames

5. Click the Control Panel's Play button to play the frames you've selected **(Figure 11).** Doing so allows Director to record the actual speed at which it plays each frame in the sequence.

6. Choose Lock Frame Durations from Director's Edit menu, or click the Lock button in the Control Panel **(Figure 12)**. Each selected frame is now locked to play at the actual speed that was recorded in step 5. To unlock the frames again, select them in the Score window, and click the Lock button again.

You can add interactive features to your movies by using **Lingo**—Director's scripting language. For instance, you can offer your users a great degree of control over the order in which the scenes of your movie are played. A common example involves a multimedia presentation that has a menu of choices, where users can select which scene of a movie they wish to view by clicking on an appropriate button **(Figure 1)**. Another example involves a movie that incorporates "previous" and "next" buttons, allowing users to pause in between scenes, and to go forward or backward through the movie at will.

In order for Director to know what to do in response to certain inputs from the user, you must write a **Lingo script**—a precise set of instructions that tells Director exactly what to do **(Figure 2)**. Suppose the mouse is clicked on a certain sprite, or a key is pressed during a certain frame. Lingo scripts tell Director how to respond to these inputs, and how the movie should be affected. Scripts can be written that allow user inputs to interact very elaborately with virtually every aspect of a movie, affecting sound volume, sprite attributes such as motion and color, the path the playback head follows through a movie, text output, and other aspects.

This chapter introduces the reader to the very basics of Lingo and script writing by focusing on a very simple and common application of Lingo scripts, adding interactive navigation controls to your movie. Also covered are creating buttons.

Figure 1. A menu of scene choices is shown here, composed of four interactive buttons.

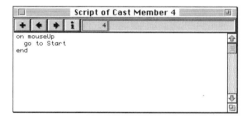

Figure 2. Lingo scripts are the instructions that tell Director how to process user inputs to affect a movie, but can be used more generally to control all aspects of your movie.

To Create a button:

In the Tools window, Director provides three tools that allow you to create three different types of buttons—these are the checkbox, radio, and standard button types **(Figures 3-4)**. You can create and place them anywhere on the Stage. Once placed on the Stage, buttons automatically become cast members, and are identified by the button icon as their cast member type in the Cast window **(Figure 5)**. For a button to cause anything to happen when clicked during a movie, a script must be attached to it. *(See "Scripts" below)*

1. Choose Tools from the Window menu **(Figure 6)**.

2. Select the tool for the appropriate button type you wish to create (your choices are checkbox, radio, or standard button types).

3. Drag the pointer to the left or right on the Stage until the box that appears is large enough to accommodate the text for this button.

4. Type the text that should appear next to or on this button **(Figure 7)**.

✔ **Tip**

■ To change the way your button text looks, select it, then choose the desired settings from the Text menu.

SCRIPTS

Scripts are instructions written in Lingo and are assigned to various objects in Director. Scripts tell Director exactly how a movie should be affected, if at all, in response to user inputs and to other events, such as the playback head entering a new frame.

There are five script types available in Director—Cast member scripts, Sprite scripts, Frame scripts, Movie Scripts, and Primary event handler scripts. The first

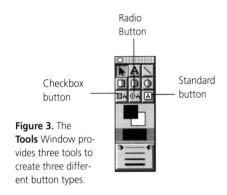

Figure 3. The **Tools** Window provides three tools to create three different button types.

Figure 4. The Standard, Checkbox, and Radio button types as shown on the Stage.

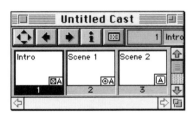

Figure 5. Button cast members are identified by the appropriate button cast member type in the Cast window.

Figure 7. Type in the button text.

Figure 6. Choose **Tools** under the **Window** menu.

Create a Button, Scripts

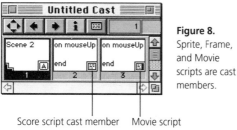

Figure 8.
Sprite, Frame, and Movie scripts are cast members.

Score script cast member
(is either a Sprite or
Frame script).

Movie script
cast member

Script button

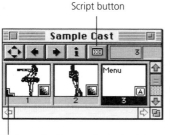

Figure 9. Select a cast member that you wish to attach a script to or edit its existing script.

Cast member has an attached script

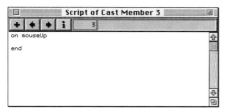

Figure 10. Click the script button in the Cast window to open the Script window.

The Script pop-up menu

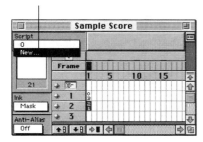

Figure 11. Choose **New** from the **Script** pop-up menu to open a new Script window.

three are the most common and examples of each are applied later in this chapter. Working with Movie and Primary event handler scripts is beyond the scope of this chapter.

Sprite, Frame, and Movie scripts are themselves cast members, and can be accessed from the Cast window **(Figure 8)**.

All scripts are edited in Script windows, that are accessed from several points in Director. The title bar at the top of a Script window indicates the script type being edited. These are either Cast member, Score, or Movie scripts. Sprite and Frame scripts are often called **Score scripts**, since they both appear in the Score.

To open a Cast member Script window:

1. Open the Cast window.

2. Select a cast member that you wish to attach a script to or edit its existing script **(Figure 9)**. These are limited to Bitmap, PICT, Shape, Text, or Button cast member types.

3. Click the script button in the Cast window to open the Script window **(Figures 9-10)**. A cast member that has a script already attached to it displays and L shape in its lower left corner in the Cast window.

✔ Tip

■ You can also open a Cast member Script window by clicking the Script button in the info dialog box for that cast member.

To open a new Score script window:

1. Open the Score window.

2. Choose New from the Script pop-up menu in the upper left side of the Score window **(Figure 11)**. A Score script window appears.

To edit an existing Score script:

1. Open the Cast window.

2. Select the desired Score script cast member you wish to edit **(Figure 12)**. Click the script button in the Cast window and the Score Script window appears.

✔ Tips

■ You can open and edit a Score script that is already assigned to a particular cell by selecting that cell in the Score, and clicking the large script button in the upper right side of the Score **(Figure 13)**.

■ You can also open an existing Score script by double-clicking it in the Cast window.

To assign scripts to sprites:

1. Open the Score window

2. Select the cell or cells that contain the sprites you wish to assign a script to.

3. In the Script pop-up menu, choose an existing script to assign to your selected sprite(s) **(Figure 14)**. Scripts attached to sprites are called **Sprite** scripts.

To assign scripts to frames:

1. Open the Score window.

2. Select the cell or cells in the script channel that you wish to attach a script to

3. In the Script pop-up menu, choose an existing script to assign to your selected cells in the script channel **(Figure 15)**. Scripts assigned to the script channel are called **Frame** scripts.

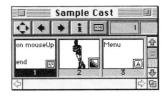

Figure 12. To edit a Score script, select its cast member in the Cast window and click the script button. A Score Script window appears.

Script button

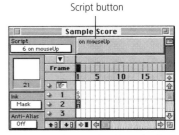

Figure 13. Select a cell in the Score that has a script assigned to it, and click the large script button to edit this script in a Script window.

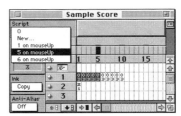

Figure 14. Choose a script from the **Script** pop-up menu to assign to your selected sprites in the Score.

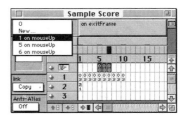

Figure 15. Choose an existing script from the **Script** pop-up menu to assign to your selected cells in the Script channel.

Assign Scripts to Sprites and Frames

Figure 16. Choose **Cast** from the **Window** menu.

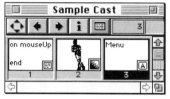

Figure 17. Select a cast member that appears in your movie.

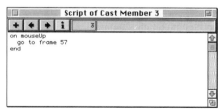

Figure 18. Type **go to frame number**, where number is the frame you want the playback head to jump to.

NAVIGATION

You can offer your movie viewers the choice of being able to jump to various segments of your movie while it is being played—they are not limited to watching from start to finish. This is accomplished by writing scripts that move the Playback head to different frames in a movie. These scripts are typically setup to respond to user input, such as clicking the mouse on a particular sprite (such as a button), or pressing a certain key. Below, steps for writing scripts for very common situations involving navigation are described. In the process, Cast member, Frame, and Sprite script types are introduced, as well as some of the basic language elements of Lingo.

To create an interactive cast member that moves the Playback head to a new frame when clicked:

1. Open the Cast window and select a cast member that appears in your movie **(Figures 16-17)**.

2. Click the script button at the top of the Cast window. A Script window appears. This example uses a Cast member script.

3. On the middle line of this script, type **go to frame number (Figure 18)**. In the number field, enter the actual frame number that you wish the playback head to jump to (e.g. go to frame 57).

4. Close the Script window or press Enter to enter the script. When you now playback your movie, clicking this sprite whenever it appears on the Stage causes Director to jump to a new segment of the movie.

Create an interactive Cast Member

In the previous example, you attached a script to a cast member. This script is called a Cast member script and it goes along with the cast member wherever it appears as a sprite in the frames of your movie. You can attach a Cast member script to any Bitmap, PICT, Shape, Button, or Text cast member **(Figure 19)**.

The first line of the script "on mouseup" instructs Director that whenever the mouse is pressed and released on this sprite, its cast member script should be executed. In this case, the result is that the "go to" command is executed and the Playback head jumps to a new frame. You can change the first line of the script to read "on mousedown" to activate the script as soon as the mouse button is pressed down on the sprite **(Figure 20)**.

FRAME SCRIPTS

The drawback with the previous example is that you must place the sprite in every frame where you want your viewer to have the chance to click it and access a new movie segment.

By creating a loop in Director's script channel, you can cause the Playback head to loop or effectively pause within a certain frame. You could then place your interactive sprite from the example on page 209 into this single frame and the movie would be paused until the user clicked the sprite or stopped the movie. You could even place multiple interactive sprites into this single frame, each having its own Cast member script, allowing the user to jump to a variety of movie segments, depending on which sprite was clicked. Such a loop can be created by assigning a script to the Script channel. Such a script is known as a **Frame** script **(Figure 21)**. A Frame script is associated with an entire frame in the Score instead of with a sprite or cast member.

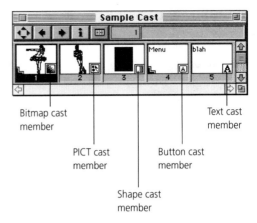

Bitmap cast member **Text cast member**

PICT cast member **Button cast member**

Shape cast member

Figure 19. Cast member scripts can be attached to Bitmap, PICT, Shape, Button, and Text cast member types.

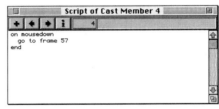

Figure 20. You can change the first line of the script to read "on mousedown" in order for the Cast member script to become activated as soon as the mouse button is pressed down on the sprite.

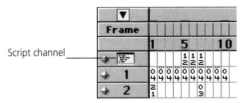

Script channel

Figure 21. Frame scripts are assigned to the Script channel in the Score.

Frame Scripts

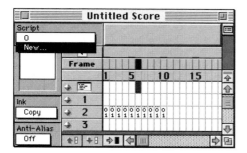

Figure 22. Select the frame in the Script channel where you wish your movie to pause. Choose **New** from the **Script** pop-up menu.

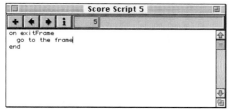

Figure 23. Type **go to the frame** on the middle line of the script.

To pause your movie in a certain frame using a Frame script:

1. Open the Score window and select the frame in the Script channel where you wish your movie to pause **(Figure 22)**.

2. Choose New from the Script pop-up menu at the top left side of the Score. A Script window appears with the text "on exitFrame" and "end" already in place.

3. Type **go to the frame** *(Figure 23)*.

4. Close the Script window. Now during playback, when Director reaches this frame, the Lingo statement "on exit-frame" tells Director to run the script when the Playback head is exiting the frame (the Lingo statement "on enter-frame" would cause the script to run at the start of the frame). In this case the command **go to the frame** is run which tells Director to jump to the beginning of the current frame. Your movie will effectively pause until you stop the movie, or another script becomes activated that moves the Playback head to a new frame.

✔ Tip

■ You can create a loop in your movie by entering **go to frame number** in step 3 above, where number refers to a frame number that precedes the current frame. During playback, when Director reaches the frame with this Frame script, your movie jumps back to the specified frame and will start looping within this movie segment.

SPRITE SCRIPTS

Sprite scripts are scripts that are assigned to sprites. Unlike a Cast member script, a Sprite script is assigned to a specific sprite at a particular cell location and is not automatically assigned to the same sprite in other parts of the Score. A Cast member script on the other hand goes along with the cast member wherever it appears as a sprite in the frames of your movie.

Note: Remember that a cast member is a template for a sprite, and a sprite is an image of the cast member that Director displays on the Stage. A sprite has information associated with it such as its position on the Stage that is not associated with its cast member counterpart. A sprite's information, including any Sprite scripts assigned to it are stored in the cells of the Score.

If a sprite has both a Cast member script and a Sprite script assigned to it, the Sprite script takes precedence. This is important to keep in mind when you are determining which type of script to use. If your sprite should always perform the same function throughout your movie, such as causing a jump to a certain movie segment, then use a Cast member script. On the other hand, if your sprite responds differently depending on its location in the movie, assign Sprite scripts to them.

By assigning different Sprite scripts to the same sprite throughout your movie, a single sprite such as a button can perform multiple functions depending on where in your movie it is clicked.

To create an interactive sprite that moves the Playback head to a new frame when clicked:

1. Open the Score window.

2. Select the sprite in the cell that you wish to assign this Score script to (remember a Sprite script is a type of Score script) **(Figure 24)**.

3. Choose New from the Script pop-up menu. The lines **on mouseup** and **end** automatically appear **(Figure 25)**.

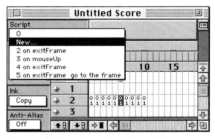

Figure 24. Select the sprite in the cell that you wish to assign a Score script to. Then choose **New** from the **Script** pop-up menu.

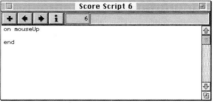

Figure 25. The lines **on mouseup** and **end** automatically appear in the Script window.

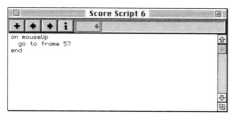

Figure 26. Type **go to frame number** on the middle line of this script, and insert your actual frame number in the number field.

Marker

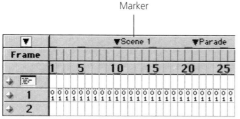

Figure 27. Markers are used to label different segments of your movie.

4. On the middle line of this script, type **go to frame number**. In the number field, enter the actual frame number that you wish the Playback head to jump to (e.g. go to frame 57). Don't change the rest of the script **(Figure 26)**.

5. Close the Script window or press Enter to enter the script (pressing Return produces a line feed in the Script window). To activate this script, click the sprite on the Stage during playback that's associated with the cell you assigned the script to.

✔ **Tip**

■ In this example, you will probably want to add a pause in the frame containing this sprite to ensure that the user has a chance to click it. *(See page 211 on pausing your movie using a Frame script)*

BROADER USE OF THE GO TO STATEMENT

The **go to** command in Lingo can be applied in many different ways in your scripts. For example, you can use the go to command to move the Playback head to a specific marker instead of to a frame number. Markers are used to label different segments of your movie **(Figure 27)**. *(See page 52 in the Score chapter for more information on creating markers)*

The advantage of using markers rather than frame numbers with the go to command is that frame numbers often change while you're editing the Score, whereas a marker name marks a specific movie segment independently of any frame number.

The Go To Statement

To write a script that moves the Playback head to a specific marker label:

A Cast member script is used in the following steps:

1. Open the Cast window and select a cast member that appears in your movie **(Figure 28)**.

2. Click the Script button at the top of the Cast window. A Script window appears.

3. Type **go to "marker"** on the middle line of this script **(Figure 29)**. In the marker field, enter the name of your marker.

4. Close the Script window. When you now playback your movie, clicking this sprite will cause Director to jump to the segment of the movie labeled by the marker.

To jump to a frame relative to the current frame:

You can write a script that jumps to a frame that is a certain number of frames before or after the current frame. To jump to a frame that lies before the current frame, type the phrase **go to frame -x** in your script **(Figure 30)**, where **x** is the number of frames before the current frame that you wish to jump to. Similarly, to jump to a frame somewhere after the current frame, use the phrase **go to frame x**.

To jump to a marker relative to the current frame:

Lingo allows you to refer to a marker in relation to how many markers it is ahead of or behind the current frame. To jump to the nth marker ahead of the current frame, include the phrase **go to marker(n)** in your script, such as **go to marker(2)** *(Figure 31)*. This tells Director to jump to the second marker after the current frame. Similarly, to jump to the nth

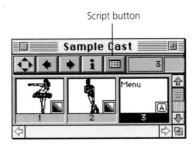

Script button

Figure 28. Select a cast member that appears in your movie and then click the Script button.

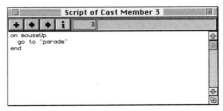

Figure 29. Type **go to "marker"** on the middle line of this script. Insert your actual marker name in the marker field.

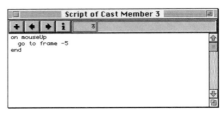

Figure 30. The middle line of this script causes a jump to the frame that is five frames before the current frame.

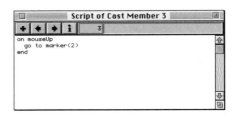

Figure 31. The middle line of this script causes a jump to the second marker that is ahead of the current frame.

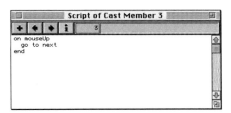

Figure 32. The **go to next** command jumps to the next marker after the current frame.

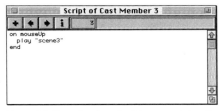

Figure 33. Type **play "marker"** in your script and insert your marker name in the marker field. This example uses a Cast member script.

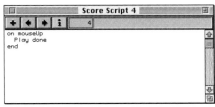

Figure 34. The **play done** command returns the Playback head to the frame from where the branch occurred.

marker before the current frame, include the same phrase, but make **n** a negative number. You can also jump to the next marker after the current frame by using the phrase **go to next** *(Figure 32)*. To jump to the marker immediately before the current frame, use **go to previous**. These commands are equivalent to **go to marker(1)**, and **go to marker(-1)**.

BRANCHING

In Director, **branching** is the process where the Playback head jumps to a certain movie segment, plays that segment, and then returns back to the original frame that caused the jump. Suppose your movie offers a tour of different restaurants. Let's say that this movie starts with a main menu of button sprites, each corresponding to a specific restaurant you can tour. When you click a button, Director jumps to a particular restaurant segment, plays that segment, and returns back to the main menu. This branching is best accomplished by using the Lingo branch command called "play" in your scripts.

To write a script that branches to a marker or frame:

1. Open a Script window for the script where a branch should take place.

2. Type **play "marker"**, and include the marker name you wish to branch to **(Figure 33)**. You can also type **play frame number** where number is the frame you wish to branch to.

3. At the end of the movie segment that is branched to in step 2, place the command **play done** in the appropriate script. This command returns the Playback head back to the original frame from where the branch occurred **(Figure 34)**.

A Sprite script that causes a branch might look as follows **(Figure 35)**:

On mouseUp

  play "explosion"

end

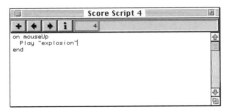

Figure 35. A branching script.

Somewhere in the explosion segment, a script will be included that returns the Playback head back to the original frame in which the branch was caused. A Sprite script that does this when its sprite is clicked might look as follows **(Figure 36)**:

on mouseUp

  play done

end

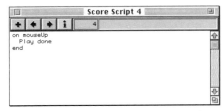

Figure 36. The **play done** command returns the Playback head to the frame from where the branch occurred.

To write a script that quits a movie:

The script that usually ends a movie is a Cast member script and it can look as follows **(Figure 37)**:

on mouseUp

  quit

end

The quit command exits Director and returns to the Finder.

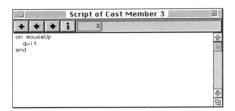

Figure 37. This script quits your Director movie when the cast member that it's assigned to is clicked.

Using the Lingo menu

When a Script window is made active, the Lingo menu becomes available in the menu bar **(Figure 38)**. An alphabetical listing of all Lingo commands can be viewed in this menu. Choose a particular command and it is directly inserted into your active Script window. You can get a description of each command by choosing the Help pointer from the Apple menu, and then choosing an item from the Lingo menu.

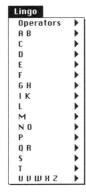

Figure 38. The **Lingo** menu contains an alphabetical listing of all Lingo commands.

Director allows you to create a play-only version of your movie called a **projector**. Projectors provide the best format to distribute your movies to the public since they cannot be opened or edited in Director. Anyone can watch your projector movie as long as they have a Macintosh that meets the minimum hardware requirements. It is not necessary to own a copy of Director to run a projector movie.

Figure 1. Choose **Create Projector** from the **File** menu.

To create a Projector:

1. Save and close any currently open movie.

2. Choose Create Projector from the File menu **(Figure 1)**.

3. From the left side of the Create Projector dialog box, select the movie that you wish to turn into a projector **(Figure 2)**.

4. Click the Add button. You can add as many movies as you wish to a single projector file by repeating steps 3-4 or clicking Add All to add all of the movies in the current directory. When you play the projector, its movies will play one after the other, in the order in which they appear in the Movie Play Order box (unless you uncheck the **Play Every Movie** option in the Projector Options dialog box. *(See page 218)*

5. Click the Options button to set projector options in the Options dialog box. *(See page 218)*

6. Click Create. The Save dialog box appears.

Add button   Options button

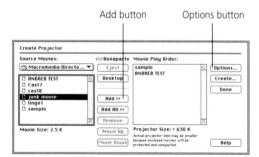

Figure 2. Select and add movies to your projector play list from the left side of the **Create Projector** dialog box.

Create a Projector

Chapter 16

7. Type the name of your projector and click Save.

8. Click Done.

9. To play a projector, double-click its icon from the Finder **(Figure 3)**.

Note: If any of the movies in your projector play list have links to external files, those files must be included on the disc along with the projector file for your users to be able to properly view the projector.

Figure 3. Double-click a projector icon to start the projector.

Projector Options

The Projector Options dialog box allows you to set some general settings that affect all the movies in your projector. Click Options from the Create Projector dialog box to open it **(Figure 4)**. These options take precedence over the settings in the Preferences dialog box set from the File menu.

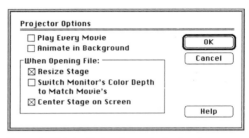

Figure 4. Click the Options button in the **Create Projector** dialog box to open the **Projector Options** box.

Play Every Movie

If checked, all the movies you add to the Movie Play Order list will be played in the order they are listed. If not checked, only the first movie on the list is played, unless other movies in the list are branched to from the first movie.

Animate in Background

If checked, your projector will continue playing even if you click outside on the desktop. If not checked, the projector stops playing if you click outside of it.

Resize Stage

If checked, the Stage size takes on the dimensions of any new movie in the projector play list that is opened. If not checked, the Stage size retains the dimensions of the current movie.

Projector Options

Switch Monitor's Color Depth to Match Movie's

If checked, you're monitor's color depth changes to match the color depth of each movie listed in the projector play list.

Center Stage on Screen

If checked, the Stage is automatically centered on the screen (this comes in handy when the Stage is smaller than the full screen dimensions). If not checked, the Stage retains the movie's original Stage position.

✔ **Tip**

■ You can include multiple interactive movies in a projector that branch between each other using Lingo commands such as "go to" and "play". Be sure that the **Play Every Movie** check box in the Projector Options dialog box is not selected. Also make sure that the first movie in the play order list has the necessary branching commands since Director in this case will only play the first movie listed.

Projector Options

Glossary

Anti-aliasing	Removes or reduces the rough and jagged edges around an image.
Bit depth	The number of bits each pixel can display. In Director, bit depth can be set to 1, 2, 4, 8, 16, 24, and 32-bit color.
Cast window	The storage area in Director that contains all your multimedia elements, such as graphics, sounds, color palettes, film loops, buttons, QuickTime movies, and scripts.
Control Panel	Provides VCR-type control over the playback of your movie, including Rewind, Play, and Step Forward buttons.
Cast member	An individual multimedia element that can be incorporated into your movie, such as a graphic, sound, film loop, color palette, or QuickTIme movie.
Cell	The small individual storage units that make up the Score. Each cell contains information about one cast member.
Channel	A row of cells in the Score window. Each channel holds a specific cast member type. There are 48 animations channels, 5 effects channels (Tempo, Palette, Transition, Sound 1 & 2) and a script channel.
Color cycling	A color effect whereby colors are rotated through a specified range in a color palette. Cast members that appear in these colors appear to pulsate and change color.
Color depth	The bit depth of a cast member, indicating how many colors it can display.
Common palette	A specially constructed palette that incorporates many of the colors shared by your entire cast. Its purpose is to replace the many cast member palettes your movie may be using with a single palette that can display your entire cast in approximately accurate colors.
Current frame	The frame that is currently displayed on the Stage. You can change the current frame by using the frame counter in the Control Panel, or the Playback head in the Score window.

Glossary

Current palette   The color palette used to display the colors of the cast members in the current frame on the Stage. You can change the current palette in the Palette channel of the Score.

Foreground   Sprites that appear to be in front of other sprites on the Stage are in the foreground. A sprite's foreground priority is determined by its placement in the animation channels. A sprite closer to the bottom animation channel (channel 48) is closer to the foreground.

Foreground color   The main color used to paint artwork in the Paint window, and to paint QuickDraw shapes and text in the Tools window. It is selected using the Foreground color chip.

Frame   A column of cells in the Score window that represents a segment of time in your movie. Each frame contains information about what your cast members are doing in that time segment.

Film loop   A cast member that is composed of a sequence of graphical cast members to form a looping animation.

In-Between   A command in Director that helps create an animation sequence by filling in the frames between two key frames that you specify.

Inks   Affect the quality and texture of the colors used to paint your artwork in the Paint window. Inks in the Score window determine how your sprites appear when they overlap on Director's Stage.

Mask   An image that allows you to control which parts of an artwork selection are transparent (you can see background artwork through these parts) and which parts are opaque. A mask could be used to make the windows in a house transparent, and the rest of the house opaque.

Movie   The term used to describe any multimedia animation created in Director.

Palette   A subset of colors used to display your cast members. Only one color palette can be active at a time.

Playback head   The position of the Playback head in the Score window indicates which frame is currently displayed on the Stage. You can drag the Playback head to display different frames on the Stage.

Projector   A play-only version of a Director movie. Projectors cannot be opened or edited in Director and are the best way to distribute your movies to the public. It is not necessary to own a copy of Director to run a projector movie.

Real-time recording   A feature in Director that allows you to record the path of mouse movements, and then substitute any graphical cast member to follow this path to form an animation.

Registration point   A reference point used to align the positions of cast members in an animation sequence.

Score   A frame-by-frame record of your movie, used to direct all the cast members that make up your animation. The Score is organized into 48 animations channels, 5 effects channels (Tempo, Palette, Transitions, Sound 1 & 2), and one script channel.

Stage   The background upon which your movie animations are played and viewed.

Step Recording   The most basic animation technique in Director, where you arrange and record each frame on an individual basis to create an animation sequence.

Tempo   Controls the speed at which the frames of your movie are played—measured in frames-per-second.

Glossary

Appendix B: List of Keyboard Shortcuts by Menu

Apple Menu
Help Pointer   Command ? or Shift Option click a menu command

File Menu
New   Command N
Open   Command O
Close Window   Command W
Close All Windows   Command Option W
Save   Command S
Save and Compact   Command Option S
Save As   Command Shift S
Import   Command J
Export   Command Shift E
Movie Info   Command U
Preferences   Command Option U
Print   Command Option P
Quit   Command Q

Edit Menu
Undo   Command Z
Cut   Command X
Copy   Command C
Paste   Command V
Clear   Delete
Select All   Command A
Play   Command P or Shift Enter to clear stage and play
Stop   Command Period or Enter or 2, 5
Rewind   Command R or keypad 0
Step Backward   Command Left Arrow or keypad 1 or 4
Step Forward   Command Right Arrow or keypad 3 or 6
Disable Sounds   Command ~ or Command ` or keypad 7
Loop   Command L or keypad 8
Selected Frames Only   Command \ or Command |

Window Menu

Stage	Command 1
Control Panel	Command 2
Cast	Command 3 or Command Up Arrow
Score	Command 4
Paint	Command 5
Text	Command 6
Tools	Command 7
Color Palettes	Command 8
Digital Video	Command 9
Script	Command 0
Message	Command M
Tweak	Command Shift T
Markers	Command Shift M

Cast Menu

Cast Member Info	Command l
Open Script	Command ´ (accent mark)
Edit Cast Member	Double-click cast member or Command Down Arrow
Launch External Editor	Command , (comma)
Reselect external editor and launch	Command Option , (comma)
Past as PICT	Command Shift Y
Duplicate Cast Member	Command D
Find Cast Members	Command ; (semicolon)

Score Menu

Sprite Info	Command K
Delete Sprites	Command Delete
Set Sprite Blend	Command Option B
Paste Relative	Command Shift V
Insert Frame	Command]
Delete Frame	Command [
In-Between Linear	Command B
In-Between Special	Command Shift B
Switch Cast Members	Command E

Text Menu

Find/Change	Command F
Find Again	Command G
Find Selection	Command H

Change Again	Command T
Find Handler	Command : (colon)
Comment	Command > (greater than)
Uncomment	Command < (less than)
Recompile Script	Command Shift R
Recompile All Scripts	Command Option R

Paint Menu

Show/Hide Paint Tools	Command Shift J
Show/Hide Rulers	Command Shift K
Zoom In	Command + and Command =
Zoom Out	Command - (minus) and Command _

Effects Menu

Repeat Effect	Command Y

A

Actual mode button, 67
Actual tempo display, 66-67, 202
Add ink effect in Score, 57
Add Pin ink effect in Score, 57
AIFC file format,
    import, 26
AIFF file format,
    import, 26
Air brush, 76
    adjust spray pattern, 101
    choose an air brush shape, 102
Air brushes command, 101
Animation, 19
Animation channels, 39
    foreground/background priority, 48
Anti-aliasing, 58
Apple menu, 4
    control panels, 88
Arc tool, 78
Auto Animation,
    banner, 140-141
    bar charts, 142-144
    bullet charts, 145-147
    credits, 148-149
    position on stage, 155
    preview, 154
    text effects, 152-154
    zoom text, 150-151
Auto Animate command, 139
Auto distort command, 106

B

Background color chip (Paint window), 85-86
Background color chip (in Tools window), 111-112
Background priority, 48
Background transparent ink effect in Score, 56
Banner, 140-141
    set speed, 141
    set text style, 140
Bar charts, 142-144
    set speed, 144
    set text style, 143
Bitmap graphics, (see Paint window)
Bitmap text, 177-179

Text tool (in Paint window), 76
Blend (see Set Sprite Blend command)
Blend Colors command, 123, 131-132
Blend ink effect in Paint window, 83
Blend ink effect in score, 56
Blend notation, 46
Border (in Text window), 184-185
Box Shadow, 184
Branching, 215-216
Brush Shapes command, 99
Bullet charts, 145-147
    set speed, 147
    set text styles, 146
Button tools, 110, 206

C

Cast members 2, 3, 17
    align registration points, 80
    color depth, 87
    copy, 30
    delete unused cast members, 31
    delete, 30
    duplicate, 30
    Find by color palette, 35
    Find by name, 34
    generate with Auto distort, 106
    how to create them, 18
    import, 23, 26
    name, 23, 25, 33
    number, 23, 25
    place into score, 21, 40, 41, 43
    positions in Cast window, 23
    purge value, 29
    remap to new color palette, 119-120
    reposition in Cast window, 32
    scripts, 206-207, 210
    set new registration point, 79
    sort, 36
    switch colors, 86-87
    types, 23-24
Cast Member Info command, 28-29
Cast Member Info dialog box, 29
Cast menu, 6
Cast notation, 45
Cast to Time command, 160-161
Cast window 2, 3, 17, 23
    cast member name, 25, 33
    cast member number, 25

info button, 25, 28
next arrow, 24
open, 17
place button, 24
previous arrow, 24
script button, 25, 207, 209
scroll bars, 25
window sizer, 25
Cast Window Options dialog box, 45
Cell color selector, 54
Cell notation, 45-47
Cells 2, 3, 20, 40
add color, 54
cut from score, 51
delete from score, 52
move within score, 49
shuffle backward button, 49-49
shuffle forward button, 48-49
Channels (see Score channels)
Clear Cast Members command, 30
Clear Cells, 52
Clipboard ink effect in Paint window, 84
Color cycling, 135-137
Color depth, 87
Color Palette 2, 3, 113
blend colors command, 123, 131-132
color picker, 128-129
copy colors command, 124, 129-130
duplicate Palette, 122
edit colors, 128-129
import, 28, 118
Invert Selection command, 123
optimal (or common) palette, 121-125
paste into palette command, 125, 130
reverse color order command, 133
select used colors command, 121
set a palette transition, 116-117
set default palette, 114
set palette dialog box, 115
sort colors command, 134
Color picker, 128-129
Control Panel 2, 3, 21, 63
actual mode button, 67
actual tempo display, 66
buttons, 63-64
frame counter, 65
lock playback speed (of movie), 67
stage background color chip, 68

tempo display, 65
Copy Colors command, 124, 129-130
Copy ink effect in score, 55
Not Copy ink effect, 56
Create Projector command, 217
Credits animation, 148-149
set speed, 149
set text styles, 149
Cycle ink effect in Paint window, 82

D

Darken command, 106
Darken ink effect in Paint window, 83
Darkest ink effect in Paint window, 83
Darkest ink effect in score, 56
Delete a cast member, 30
Delete unused cast members, 31
Digitize sound, 190-191
Disable sounds button, 64
Distort command, 104, 179
Duplicate Cast Member command, 30
Duplicate Palette command, 122

E

Easel, 70-71
Edit menu, 5
Editable checkbox (in Score), 61
Effects menu, 8, 69, 103-107
Auto distort, 106
Darken, 106
Distort, 104
Fill, 106
Flip horizontal, 104
Flip vertical, 104
Free rotate, 103
Invert colors, 105
Lighten, 106
Perspective, 104
Rotate left, 103
Rotate right, 103
Slant, 104
Smooth, 106
Switch colors, 87, 106
Trace edges, 105
Ellipse tool (in Paint tool palette), 77
Eraser tool, 77
Extended notation, 47
Eyedropper tool (in Color palette), 126

Eyedropper tool (in Paint tool palette), 80
    switch a cast member color, 86-87

F

File menu, 4
Fill command, 106
Film loops, 169, 173-176
    In-between with, 176
    multichannel film loops, 174-175
    Real-time record with, 175-176
Find Cast Members,
    by color palette, 35
    by name, 34
    command, 31
    dialog box, 31
Flip horizontal, 104
Flip vertical, 104
Fonts, (see Text menu)
Foreground color chip (in Paint window),
    85
Foreground color chip (in Tools window),
    111-112
Foreground priority, 48
Frames, 20, 38
    insert, 50
Frame counter (in Control Panel), 65
Frame scripts, 206-208, 210-211
Frames-per-second, 199
Free rotate command, 103

G

Ghost ink effect in Paint window, 82
Ghost ink effect in Score, 56
    Not Ghost ink effect, 56
Go To command, 209, 213-215
Gradient, 91
    create, 91
    cycles pop-up menu, 93
    direction pop-up menu, 92
    gradients dialog box, 92
    method pop-up menu, 93
    range pop-up menu, 94
    settings, 92-94
    spread pop-up menu, 94
Gradient destination color (in Paint win-
    dow), 85-86
Gradient ink effect in Paint window, 82

H

Hand tool, 75
Hardware requirements, 9
Help window, 12
Hide rulers command, 95
HSB color model, 127

I

Import,
    cast members, 23,26
    color palettes, 28, 118
    command, 26
    sound cast members, 187-188
Import dialog box, 26
In-Between animation, 19, 157, 164
    add acceleration, 166
    add deceleration, 166
    along circular path, 170
    along curved path, 168-169
    along straight path, 165-165
    In-Between Linear command, 165
    In-Between Special command, 167, 169
    In-Between Special dialog box, 166
    key frames, 19, 164, 168, 170
    preview path button, 169
    stretch or squeeze, 166-167
    with a film loop, 176
Ink effects in Paint window, 81-84
    Ink effects selector, 81
Ink effects in score, 54-58
    Ink pop-up menu, 55
Ink masks, 107-108
Ink notation, 46
Insert frames, 50
Interactivity (see Scripts)
Invert colors command, 105
Invert selection command, 123

J

Jump button, 51
Jump to Top button, 51

K

Key frames, 19, 164, 170
Keyboard shortcuts
    how to perform, 9
    list of, Appendix B, 225

Index

L

Launch Director, 10
Lasso tool, 72
    options pop-up menu, 75
Lighten command, 106
Lighten ink effect in Paint window, 83
Lightest ink effect in Paint window, 83
Lightest ink effect in score, 57
Line tool (in Paint window), 78
Line tool (in Tools window), 109
Line width selector (in Paint window), 84
Line width selector (in Tools window), 112
Lingo menu, 9, 216
Lingo script, 205-207
Lingo, (see Scripts)
Link to File,
    checkbox, 27
    range checkbox, 27
Lock button, 67, 203
Lock Frame Durations command, 203
Lock playback speed (of movie), 67, 202-
    204
Loop button, 64

M

Macpaint file format,
    import, 26
Marker well, 52
Marker window, 53
Markers, 52-53
Marquee, 73
Mask ink effect in Score, 56
    create an ink mask, 107-108
Matte ink effect in Score, 55
Menus,
    About them, 4
    Apple, 4
    Cast, 6
    Edit, 5
    Effects, 8
    File, 4
    Lingo, 9
    Paint, 8
    Palette, 7
    Score, 6
    Text, 7
    Window, 5

Menu bar 2,3
MIDI, 189
Motion notation, 46
Moveable checkbox (in Score), 60
Movie, 1
    a simple movie example, 22
Movie Info,
    allow outdated Lingo, 13
    anti-alias text and graphics, 13
    default palette, 14
    load cast, 14
    remap palettes when needed, 13, 120
    user info, 13
Movie scripts, 206-207

N

Navigation, 209
New movie,
    create, 10
    save, 11
Normal ink effect in Paint window, 81

O

Open a movie, 10

P

Paint brush, 76
    choose a brush shape, 98
    edit a brush shape, 99-100
    store shapes in Scrapbook, 100
Paint bucket tool, 76
Paint menu, 8
Paint tool palette, 72
    Air brush, 76, 101-102
    Arc tool, 78
    Ellipse tool, 77
    Eraser, 77
    Eyedropper tool, 80
    Hand tool, 75
    Lasso, 72, 74-75
    Line tool, 78
    Paint brush, 76, 98-100
    Paint bucket, 76
    Pencil, 76
    Polygon tool, 77
    Rectangle tool, 77
    Registration tool, 78-79
    Selection rectangle, 72-73

Text tool, 76
Paint window 2,3,18, 69
  add button, 70
  background color, 85-86
  easels, 70-71
  effects, 103-107
  foreground color, 85
  gradient destination color, 85-86
  gradients, 91-94
  ink effects, 81-84
  ink masks, 107-108
  line width selector, 84
  pattern selector, 88
  place button, 70
  rulers, 95
  tiles, 96-97
  zoom in, 95
Palette (see Color palette)
Palette channel, 39, 115
  set a transition, 116-117
Palette menu, 8
Paste into Palette command, 125
Paste Relative, 163
Patterns (in Paint window),
  copy to Scrapbook, 90
  create or edit, 89
  pattern edit box, 89
  pop-up pattern palette, 88
Pattern chip (in Tools window), 112
Pattern selector (in Paint window), 88
Pencil tool, 76
Performance (of movies)
  anti-aliasing, 59
  compare set tempo to actual tempo, 66,
    202
  ink effects in score, 58
  QuickDraw vs. bitmap graphics, 109
  sound, 189
Perspective command, 104
Photoshop, 18
PICS, 26
PICT,
  import, 26
Play (Lingo command), 215-216
Play button, 64
Playback head, 21, 38, 65
Polygon tool (in Paint tool palette), 77
Preferences, 15

Projector options, 218-219
Projector, 217
Purge Priority, 29
Purge value, 29

Q

QuickDraw graphics, 109
  set color, 111
QuickDraw text, 177, 180-185
  apply ink effects to, 182
  create on stage, 181
  edit in Text window, 185
  edit on stage, 183
  set color to, 111, 181
QuickTime movies, 26, 176, 199
  import, 26
Quit (Lingo command), 216

R

Real-time recording, 20, 157, 170-172
  adjust mouse sensitivity, 172
  Real-time record indicator, 171
  with a film loop, 175-176
Record Sound command, 190
Recording light, 158
Rectangle tool (in Paint tool palette), 77
Registration points, 78-80
  align cast member points, 80
  set a new point, 79
Registration tool, 78-79
Remap Colors, 28
Reveal ink effect in Paint window, 82
Reverse Color Order command, 133
Reverse ink effect in Paint window, 82
Reverse ink effect in score, 56
  Not Reverse ink effect, 56
Revert, 11
Rewind button, 63
RGB color model, 127
Rotate left command, 103
Rotate right command, 103
Rulers,
  hide, 95
  show, 95

S

Sample movie, 22

Save,
    a movie file, 11
Save and Compact, 11,31
Scene transitions, 197-198
Score 2,3,17,20,37
    anti-alias pop-up menu, 58
    assign Lingo scripts to, 44
    channels, 20
    channels, 39
    color cells, 54
    cut cells, 51
    delete cells, 52
    editable checkbox, 61
    foreground/background priority of
        sprites, 48
    frame counter, 51
    frames, 38
    insert frames, 50
    Jump button, 51
    Jump to Top button, 51
    markers, 52-53
    menu, 6
    move around in, 51
    move cells within, 49
    moveable box, 60
    notation, 45-47
    open, 37
    place cast members into, 21, 40, 41, 43
    playback head, 21,38
    set ink effects, 54-58
    shuffle backward button, 48-49
    shuffle forward button, 48-49
    trails, 59
Score scripts, 44, 207
    edit, 208
Scrapbook,
    store brush shapes, 100
    store custom patterns, 90
Scrapbook file format,
    import, 26
Scripts,
    branching, 215-216
    cast member scripts, 206-207, 210
    create cast member script, 209
    create frame script, 211
    create sprite script, 212-213
    frame scripts, 206, 208, 210
    go to command, 209, 213-215

movie scripts, 206-207
on mouseup command, 210
score scripts, 207-208
sprite scripts, 211-212
Script button (in Cast window), 207, 209
Script channel, 21,39
Script notation, 47
Script pop-up menu, 44, 207
Script window, 207
Select Used Colors command, 121
Selected Frames Only button, 64, 171, 203
Selection rectangle tool, 72-73
    options pop-up menu, 73-74
Set Color command, 128
Set Palette command, 115-117
Set Sound command, 192
Set Sprite Blend command, 46
Set Tempo command, 200
    set a pause, 201
Set Transition command, 197-198
Shape tools (in Tools window), 110
Show Rulers command, 95
Shuffle backward button, 48-49
Shuffle forward button, 48-49
Slant command, 104
Smear ink effect in Paint window, 83
Smooth command, 106
Smooth ink effect in Paint window, 83
Smudge ink effect in Paint window, 84
SND resource format,
    import, 26
Sort Cast Members command, 36
Sort Colors command, 134
Sound,
    create outside Director, 191
    import, 187-188
    loops, 195
    place in score, 192-193
    record sound command, 190
    repeat sounds, 194
    set sound command, 192
Sound channels, 21, 39, 187
Space to Time command, 162, 169
Spread ink effect in Paint window, 84
Sprite, 40
    apply anti-aliasing, 58
    apply trails, 59
    make moveable during playback, 60

make text sprites editable during play-back, 61
 set an ink effect, 54-58
 set color with Tools window, 112
 stretch or squeeze, 62
Sprite scripts, 206-208, 210-211
Squeeze sprites, 62
 using In-Between command, 166-167
Stage 2,3,17,19,37
 place cast members onto, 19,41-42
 set background color, 68
Start Director, 10
Step backward button, 63
Step forward button, 64
Step recording, 157-159
 step record indicator, 158
Stop button, 63
Stretch sprites, 62
 using In-Between command, 166-167
Subtract ink effect in score, 57
Subtract Pin ink effect in score, 58
Switch Colors command, 87, 106
Switch ink effect in Paint window, 82

T

Tempo, 38, 199
 compare actual tempo vs. set, 202
 Lock Frame Durations command, 203
 lock playback speed, 202-204
 set new tempo, 200
 set pause, 201
Tempo channel, 21, 39, 199
Tempo display (in Control Panel), 65
Text,
 bitmap type, 76, 177-179
 border, 184-185
 box shadow, 184
 menu, 7, 181
 QuickDraw type, 109, 177, 180-185
 set color in Text window, 112
 set color of bitmap text, 179
 set color of QuickDraw text, 111, 181, 184
 text shadow, 179, 184
 tool (in Paint tool palette), 76
 tool (in Tools window), 109, 181
 window 2,3, 180, 184-185
Text effects animation, 152-153

 set speed, 153
 set text style, 152
Text shadow, 179
Tiles, 96-97
Tools window 2,3, 69, 109
 background color chip, 111
 button tools, 110, 206
 foreground color chip, 111
 line tool, 109
 line width selector, 112
 pattern chip, 112
 shape tools, 110
 text tool, 109
Trace edges command, 105
Trails, 59, 172
Transform bitmap command, 87, 119
Transition channel, 21, 39, 197
Transparent ink effect in Paint window, 82
Transparent ink effect in Score, 56
 Not Transparent ink effect, 56

U

Undo, 5, 171

W

Window menu, 5

Z

Zoom in command, 95
Zoom out command, 96
Zoom text animation, 150-151
 set speed, 151
 set text style, 150